Archaic Latin Prose

AMERICAN PHILOLOGICAL ASSOCIATION
American Classical Studies

Series Editor

Harvey Yunis

Number 42

ARCHAIC LATIN PROSE

by
Edward Courtney

Edward Courtney

ARCHAIC LATIN PROSE

Scholars Press
Atlanta, Georgia

ARCHAIC LATIN PROSE

by
Edward Courtney

Library of Congress Cataloging in Publication Data

Courtney, E. (Edward), 1932–
    Archaic Latin prose / Edward Courtney.
      p.   cm. — (American classical studies ; no. 42)
    Includes bibliographical references and indexes.
    ISBN 0-7885-0544-0 (cloth : alk. paper). — ISBN 0-7885-0545-9
(paper)
    1. Latin language, Preclassical to ca. 100 B.C.—Texts. 2. Latin
language, Preclassical to ca. 100 B. C. —Style. 3. Rome—
Civilization—Sources. 4. Latin prose literature. I. Title.
II. Series.
PA2510.C68   1999
477—dc21   99-12849
                                       CIP

Printed in the United States of America
on acid-free paper

CONTENTS

PREFACE

Books which are designed to fulfil more purposes than one run the risk of not fully satisfying any of them. Nevertheless I have felt it worth while to take this risk. The central aim of this book is to show how certain prominent features of classical Latin prose became established because of factors which conditioned the formation of archaic prose style. The means chosen for this aim is to present texts ranging from about 450 B.C. to about 100 B.C. (with a few of later date but old-fashioned style) which will exemplify such features in their original setting and illustrate the linguistic and stylistic development of Latin prose. I also hope to promote a 'feel' for the essence of the Latin language and to impart a sense of some of the modes of thought which underly language in general. That will suggest the public which I have in mind, which may be roughly defined as advanced graduate students and beginning assistant professors; but I shall be pleased if more advanced scholars too pick up a few worthwhile details.

Style, my central concern, can hardly be exemplified except in passages of a certain length, and my selection has been dictated mainly by this (naturally the passages must also be in the original wording, so far as we can ensure that). That introduces the subordinate aim of the book. Probably the most widely-used collection of archaic Latin texts is that of Ernout, the focus of which is phonology and morphology. This book has a wider objective than Ernout's, and will, I hope, serve as a reader for early Latin in a way in which Ernout's could not; consequently I do not comment on word-forms unless they may cause difficulty to the reader or have some special importance. This wider objective extends to literary, cultural and political history, and my selection has been influenced by these considerations also. To take one example, I have felt it worthwhile to collect all the fragments, including the shortest (and, contrary to the principle just mentioned, some not quite in the original wording), of the *Euhemerus* of Ennius, so that now all the main works of Ennius have commentaries by Skutsch, Jocelyn and myself (here and in my *FLP*); conversely most early Roman laws in one way or another seemed unsuitable for my purpose, though I have in fact provided much information about legal usage. I have also felt that I ought to equip my selections with a full commentary not limited to stylistic issues, mainly for the reasons just suggested but also because of conviction that proper understanding of texts needs to be all-embracing.

From time to time reviewers of my books complain that I give too many references to secondary literature. I remain unrepentant because (a) many of these are in fact references to primary texts (e.g. 'Fraenkel on Aesch. *Ag.* x' implies that the passage of Aeschylus illustrates the phenomenon) (b) if the reader looks up my references, he will often gain instruction from the surrounding context beyond what the limited room of a note can provide (c) I have in mind that the reader's library may include one but not another of the works to which I refer, so that it is desirable to provide alternatives. I also feel that a good commentary should point the readers to material for their own investigation.

I hope that it will not offend if for the sake of brevity I refer to students of linguistics as 'linguists'.

My best thanks are due to Professor B. Vine for some corrections and helpful comments, to Daniel Holmes and the office for Information Technology and Computing, University of Virginia for technological help in producing camera-ready copy, and to the Department of Classics, University of Virginia for financial assistance.

E. Courtney

University of Virginia

BIBLIOGRAPHY

Texts

C. G. Bruns, *Fontes Iuris Romani Antiqui*, ed. 7 by O. Gradenwitz (1909)

R. S. Conway, *The Italic Dialects* (1897)

C(orpus) I(nscriptionum) L(atinarum)

M. H. Crawford and others, *Roman Statutes* (1996); for the sake of brevity, this is referred to simply as 'Crawford' without delimitation of the contributions of collaborators.

F(ontes) I(uris) R(omani) A(ntejustiniani) I Leges ed. S. Riccobono, *III Negotia* ed. V. Arangio-Ruiz (ed. 2, 1941-3)

P. E. Huschke, *Iurisprudentiae Anteiustinianae Quae Supersunt* (ed. 5, 1886; ed. 6 cur. E. Seckel - B. Kübler 1908)

I(nscriptiones) L(atinae) L(iberae) R(ei) P(ublicae) ed. A. Degrassi (1957-63)

I(nscriptiones) L(atinae) S(electae) ed. H. Dessau (1892-1916)

H. Malcovati, *Oratorum Romanorum Fragmenta* (ed. 4, 1976)

H. Meyer, *Oratorum Romanorum Fragmenta* (ed. 2, 1842)

H. Peter, *Historicorum Romanorum Fragmenta* (ed. maior, 1906-14; repr. 1967 with bibliographical additions by J. Kroymann)

J. W. Poultney, *The Bronze Tables of Iguvium* (1959)

E. Vetter, *Handbuch der italischen Dialekte* (1953)

E. H. Warmington, *Remains of Old Latin, III Lucilius and Laws of the XII Tables* (revised ed. 1967), *IV Archaic Inscriptions* (1940); Loeb Library

Fronto is referred to by page and line of the edition by van den Hout (Teubner 1988), Lucilius by the numeration of Marx, Festus by pages of Müller, Ennius by the numeration of Skutsch (Annals) and Jocelyn (Tragedies), Nonius by pages of Mercier. References to the sources of conjectures in Gellius can usually be found in the ed. maior by M. Hertz (1883-5).

Language and Grammar

O. Altenburg, *De Sermone pedestri Italorum uetustissimo* (Neue Jahrb. kl. Phil., suppl. 24, 1898-9, 485)

C. E. Bennett, *Syntax of Early Latin* (1910-14)

L. Callebat (ed.), *Latin vulgaire, Latin tardif IV* (1995)

H. Fankhänel, *Verb und Satz in der lat. Prosa* (1938)

S. A. Handford, *The Latin Subjunctive* (1947)

HS = J. B. Hofmann and A. Szantyr, *Lateinische Syntax und Stilistik* (1965)

W. Kroll, *Die wissenschaftliche Syntax* (ed. 4, 1962)

KS = R. Kühner and C. Stegmann, *Grammatik der lateinischen Sprache: Satzlehre*, ed. 3 by A. Thierfelder (1955)

M. Leumann, *Lateinische Laut- und Formenlehre* (1977)

E. Löfstedt, *Synt(actica)* I (ed. 2, 1942), II (1933)

      (Philologischer Kommentar zur) P(eregrinatio) A(etheriae) (1911)

C. de Meo, *Lingue techniche del Latino* (ed. 2, 1986)

NW = F. Neue and C. Wagener, *Formenlehre der lateinischen Sprache* (ed. 3, 1902)

O(xford) L(atin) D(ictionary), ed. P. G. W. Glare (1968-82)

G. Pascucci, *Aspetti del latino giuridico* (*SIFC* 40 (1968), 3)

H. J. Roby, *Latin Grammar* (1871-4)

A. Scherer, *Handbuch der lateinischen Syntax* (1975)

F. Sommer, *Handbuch der lateinischen Laut- und Formenlehre* (ed. 2-3, 1913);   SP = *Lautlehre* ed. 4 by R. Pfister (1977)

O. Szemerényi, *Scripta Minora 2, Latin* (1987)

T(hesaurus) L(inguae) L(atinae) (1900-)

H. Vairel-Carron, *Exclamation, Ordre et Défense* (1975)

J. Wackernagel, *Vorlesungen über Syntax* (ed. 2, 1926-8)

C. Watkins, *S(elected) W(ritings)* (1994)

      H(ow to) K(ill a) D(ragon) (1995)

E. Wölfflin, *Die Alliterierenden Verbindungen der lat. Sprache* in *Ausgewählte Schriften* (1933), 225

E. C. Woodcock, *A New Latin Syntax* (1959)

Other

ANRW = *Aufstieg und Niedergang der röm. Welt*, ed. H. Temporini - W. Haase (1972-)

M. von Albrecht, *Masters of Roman Prose* (1989)

G. Appel, *De Romanorum Precationibus* (1909)

E. Benveniste, *Indo-European Language and Society* (Eng. transl. 1969)

H. Blümner, *Die römischen Privataltertümer* (1911)

C(ambridge) A(ncient) H(istory) VII - IX ed. 2 (1989-94)

E. Courtney, *(The) F(ragmentary) L(atin) P(oets)* (1993)
        M(usa) L(apidaria) (1995)
D. Daube, *Forms of Roman Legislation* (1956)
K. J. Dover, *The Evolution of Greek Prose Style* (1997)
M. Ducos, *L'Influence grecque sur la loi des douze tables* (1978)
G. Dumézil, *Archaic Roman Religion* (Eng. tr. 1970)
E. Fraenkel, *E(lementi) P(lautini in) P(lauto)* (1960)
        K(leine) B(eiträge) (1964)
A. E. Gordon, *Illustrated Introduction to Latin Epigraphy* (1983)
F. Hache, *Quaestiones Archaicae* (1907)
H. Haffter, *Untersuchungen zur altlateinischen Dichtersprache* (1934)
F. V. Hickson, *Roman Prayer Language* (1993)
Der kleine Pauly (1979)
K. Latte, *Römische Religionsgeschichte* (1960)
H. Lausberg, *Handbook of Literary Rhetoric* (Eng. tr. 1998); referred to by section
numbers.
R. Lazzeroni, *Contributo allo studio della preistoria del carmen latino* (*ASNSP* 28
(1959), 119).
W. D. Lebek, *Verba Prisca* (1970)
A. D. Leeman, *Orationis Ratio* (1963)
F. Leo, *A(usgewählte) K(leine) S(chriften)* (1960)
        G(eschichte der) R(ömischen) L(itteratur), I (1913)
J. Marquardt, *Das Privatleben der Römer* (ed. 2 by A. Mau, 1886)
T. Mommsen, *Römisches Staatsrecht* (ed. 3, 1887-8)
E. Norden, *A(gnostos) T(heos)* (1912)
        A(us) A(ltrömischen) P(riesterbüchern) (1939)
E. Odelman, *Etudes sur quelques reflets du style administratif chez César* (1971)
RE = Realencyclopädie der klassischen Altertumswissenschaft, ed. A. Pauly - G.
Wissowa and others (1893-1974)
R(eallexicon für) A(ntike und) C(hristentum) (1950-)
E. de Ruggiero, *Dizionario epigrafico* (1895-)
R. Wachter, *Altlateinische Inschriften* (1987)
F. Wieacker (1988), *Röm. Rechtsgeschichte*
        (1967), in *Les Origines de la République romaine* (Fond. Hardt,
            Entr. 13)
        (1971), in *Studi in onore di E. Volterra*
J. Wills, *Repetition in Latin Poetry* (1996)
G. Wissowa, *Religion und Kultus der Römer* (ed. 2, 1912)

Unless otherwise specified, all references are to pages, not sections. Abbreviations
for periodicals are as in *L'Anneé Philologique* or more explicit.

INTRODUCTION

Take a sentence like Cicero, *In Cat.* 4.19 (this and others like it quoted by KS 2.629, HS 734): *atque haec non ut uos, qui mihi studio paene praecurritis, excitarem, locutus sum.* Short though this sentence is, the elaborate interlacing of clauses one inside another so that it ends in three successive verbs, which involves the presumption that the listener can hold all the beginning of the sentence in suspense in his mind until everything slots into its place with these verbs - this is obviously the product of a highly developed and sophisticated literary sensibility, directed to a correspondingly sophisticated audience. One may note that e.g. the composer of the SC de Bacanalibus 8-9 could have so arranged the clauses, *isque de senatuos sententiad, dum ne minus senatoribus C, quom ea res cosoleretur, adesent, iousisent*, but did not. The stages of development to the final result can be followed much more clearly in Latin than in Greek, for, though the earliest stages of Greek prose writing show much less stylistic maturity than the verse of Homer (see the discussion of Pherecydes of Syrus under Ennius), nevertheless Greek prose has a firm artistic base to build on and develops rapidly. Because this development was much slower in Latin than in Greek, features of its earliest stages become ingrained much more deeply, and appear still in classical prose more prominently. The central aim of this book is to illustrate such features in their original setting.

Several factors have to be identified in the analysis of this development; it will be understood that, while for clarity an effort has to be made to disentangle them, in practice they often interact with each other, and boundaries drawn between them will sometimes seem over-rigid.

I

First, there is the legacy of linguistic features derived from the ultimate Indo-European origins of the language. Such features are:

(i) The placing of enclitics and the like in or as near as possible to second position in the phrase ('Wackernagel's Law'),which may be illustrated from classical times e.g. by Cic. *De Leg.* 3.45 *praeter enim quam quod...praeterea*. See index, Enclitic Position and e.g. O. J. L. Szemerényi, *Introduction to Indo-European Linguistics* (1996), 82.

One should note that modern linguistic theory is in process of modifying this law in terms of the concept of Focus (see e.g. Adams, *Trans. Phil. Soc.* 92 (1994), 103 and cf. on Cato *De Agr.* 157.7). I have experimented with putting some of my notes on word order in this conceptual framework and terminology, but mostly I judged the result less satisfactory than retention of the term 'emphasis' (which, I observe, is still employed by H. Pinkster, *Latin Syntax and Semantics* (Eng. tr. 1990) 170, though on 168 he gives it quotation marks and talks of it as old-fashioned). To give examples, where on Cato *De Agr.* 5.4 I say that the separation of *eundem* from its noun gives it emphasis, modern linguistic theory would say that discontinuity marks it as having Focus function, and on Cato pr.2 my point about *bonum agricolam bonumque colonum* could be expressed thus, 'placement of the attribute before the Head marks it as having Focus function' (for both see Pinkster 185).

Here belongs too the misnamed tmesis; misnamed because, like many of our grammatical terms, it presumes a developed stage of language as a starting-point and looks back to an earlier stage as an aberration from that. In this case the presumption is that things which belong together have been sundered, whereas in fact these things were still separate. For instances of such 'tmesis' see XII Tables 8.13 *endoque plorato*, Cato *De Agr.* 157.9 *ferue bene facito* and in Cicero e.g. *De Or.* 1.205 *pergrata perque iucunda* (one might also count the above instance from the *De Leg.* here). Note that a distinction must be drawn between cases when the intervening item is of enclitic character (as in XII Tables l.c.) and those when it is not (as Cato l.c.); see Watkins *SW* 1.40.

(ii) The presumption that the prefix of a compound verb extends its force to repetitions of that verb; Eur. *Bacch.* 1064-5 κατῆγεν, ἦγεν, ἦγεν is a paradigmatic instance. See on XII Tables 8.12 and index, Verbs. Note that there are cases where the influence of the prefix extends backwards (see on Cato *De Agr.* 156.1).

(iii) The lack of specification of grammatical subject when the context is considered to make it plain who or what is intended; this has the corollary that unexpressed subjects often change abruptly. This is particularly common in legal and religious prescriptions (see on XII Tables 1.1 and Cato *De Agr.* 141.4), but Cato retains a general fondness for it (e.g. *De Agr.* 156.6 and with change of subject ibid. 5.2), and it is still strikingly common in the low stylistic level of the *Bellum Hispaniense*. For particular cases which persist in classical Latin see *KS* 1.5-7; e.g. *inquit* 'someone says' (HS 417), *uiderit* 'it is up to someone' (cf. my note on *ML* 126.10). See index, Subject.

(iv) The inherited copulative conjunction was *-que* (HS 473), which still has a monopoly in the Twelve Tables (in 8.15b the correct version is *lance licioque*, not *lance et licio*); it is also exclusively used in the *deuotio* of ch. 6 (with one exception), the *euocatio* (and in these, as Watkins *SW* 1.11 remarks, is used to connect sentences), the prayer in Cato *De Agr.* 141 and the temple law of Furfo. *et* is related to ἔτι (this is still visible in *etiam* = *eti-yam*) and develops its copulative sense from that of 'furthermore'; it is particularly suitable for enumeration (see on Cato *De Agr.* 5), but of course rapidly expands its field. *atque* is derived from *ad* (adverbial, 'in addition') and *-que*; it forcefully calls attention, and belongs to dramatic, elevated style. Accordingly it is not used by the author of the *Bellum Hispaniense*, and never established itself in colloquial Latin. For the usage of these conjunctions in individual authors see index, Copulative conjunctions.

(v) Under this heading one must also consider whether there is any inheritance from the particular branch of the Indo-European family tree to which Latin belongs. This concerns particularly the prominence of alliteration, which is a feature of western IE languages and seems to be linked to the system of accentuation developed by them. In Latin, as in Germanic, alliteration is most firmly established in correlative terms (e.g. *fuga formido* in the *deuotio* 10, *pretium et praemium* Gracchus 44; see in general Wölfflin and the collection of material from prayers in Appel 160), but that is true of other IE languages also, and this is a feature which is integral to the nature of language (cf. English 'plague and pestilence, fire and famine' etc.), not something which can be used as evidence of linguistic affinity. The *Carmen Aruale* (see my *ML* 1), where alliteration might have been expected, has a notable assonance *lue(m) rue(m)*, but no real alliteration, and, despite the small evidential basis, one might suspect that the prominence of alliteration in Latin post-dated this *carmen*; it would then be an independent development in Latin (perhaps one should rather say Italic, in view of the occurrences in the Iguvine Tables), and would properly belong under III below. Note that Cato in *De Agr.* 141.3 for reasons of literary style has introduced an alliteration into a formula which originally lacked it. The whole question is helpfully discussed by Lazzeroni 134 sqq.; see further on Cato *De Agr.* 141 (with Watkins *HKD* 23), HS 700 and index, Alliteration.

II

Secondly we may consider those features which characterise an early stage of thought and expression, one not yet habituated to the sophistication shown in the Ciceronian sentence which began this introduction.

(i) One such feature is the presentation of semantic units on the same grammatical level, with no distinctions made by syntactical means between less and more important. This is known as the paratactic or coordinated style as contrasted with the hypotactic or subordinated, and examples may be found in any language (e.g. 'Seek and ye shall find', which hypotactically would be 'If you seek, you will find'); in Latin the difference may be illustrated by Ter. *Eun.* 476 *tacent, satis laudant* as against Cic. *Div. Caec.* 21 *etiamsi taceant, satis dicunt*. This type of parataxis is found e.g. in Cato *De Agr.* 5.2 *opere bene exerceat, facilius malo et alieno prohibebit*, 157.10. Another, in this instance deliberately artless, type is in Ennius XI *sepulcrum eius est in Creta in oppido Cnosso, et dicitur Vesta hanc urbem creauisse*, where hypotactic style would replace *et hanc* with *quam*; and there are other good instances in Cato *De Agr.* 157.2, *Orig.* 83b. The origins of many types of subordinate clauses are to be found in this area; such syntactical consequences of the paratactic mode of expression are discussed in an appendix to this introduction.

(ii) Second is the presentation of a thought in a series of small, largely self-contained units, in such a way that, in contrast to the tightly-knit sentence from Cicero which headed this introduction, the grammatical tying together of the sentence at its end may not be fully foreseen at the beginning; this is what Eduard Fraenkel used to call the *guttatim* (see index s.v.) or drop-by-drop style. It is clear that e.g. *Ad Herenn.* 2.48 *secundus locus est, cum consideramus, illae res, de quibus criminamur, ad quos pertineant*, though syntactically unified, comes across as a succession of small units. A corollary of this is the tendency to place the salient point first (exemplified e.g. at Cato *De Agr.* pr.1, 1.7, 5.4, *Orig.* 83b) and if necessary worry later how it is to be given a grammatical function within the sentence; see e.g. Cato *De Agr.* 142 and index, Word-order. Sometimes indeed all attempt to give a grammatical function is abandoned, and the result is an anacoluthon (see index s.v.); Vergil finds this feature suitable for his narrative style at *Aen.* 11.552-5 *telum immane...huic natam...implicat*. Alternatively a resumptive pronoun may put the sentence back on track (see index, Pronouns); this method of expression proves suitable for adoption by classical writers as a conscious means of conferring emphasis (e.g. Cic. *De Opt. Gen. Or.* 13 *bene dicere, id sit Attice dicere*; see HS 187). Catullus 10. 29 cleverly uses it to convey stammering embarrassment, *meus sodalis, Cinna est Gaius, is sibi parauit* (not to be punctuated as by Housman on Manil. 5.451). The idiom of prolepsis (see Maraldi in G. Calboli (ed.), *Papers on Grammar* 2 (1986), 87 and index s.v.; the canonical instance is 'I know Thee who Thou art') enables two clauses to be taken one at a time, with the second functioning as an epexegesis of the first, whereas the fully subordinating form 'I know who you are' permits no mental pause after the main clause. Other types of epexegesis too belong in principle here (e.g. Cato *De Agr.* 156.1 *de brassica, quod concoquit*, 157.1), and so does the addition of extra items as if they were afterthoughts (ibid. 3.2, 157.7).

Comparable to this on a small scale is the presentation of a concept in general terms followed by a specification. This is found particularly, though not exclusively, with expressions of quantity (see index s.v., e.g. Cato *De Agr.* 109 *farinam facito, libras IIII*; cf. on 156.1) and of location (e.g. Ennius XI *in Creta in oppido Cnosso*); similar in principle are combinations like *uentus Auster* (see on

Gracchus 44d) and *ibi in eo monte* Ennius VI. Another form of this is the familiar 'whole and part' scheme, e.g. Plaut. *Men.* 858 *hunc senem...dedolabo...uiscera*, Verg. *Aen.* 12.273 *unum...transadigit costas* (see HS 44).

Another consequence of the tendency to think of a sentence as a series of semi-independent units is that sometimes at its end a grammatically unexpected finite verb or subject or the like is supplied so that the listener or reader does not have to fetch one from a previous unit; see e.g. Cato *De Agr.* 156.5 *postea salem addito...et pollinem polentae eodem addito* and on 2.2, 5.2, Twelve Tables 3.3. Or a word may derive its construction improperly (strictly speaking) from what is nearer, like the last *nemini* in Cato *De Agr.* 5.3. Or the sentence at its end may drift back into a finite verb not properly integrated with the construction of the rest, like *dixit* in Cato *De Agr.* 2.2 (*interesse* 4 in principle is similar), or *percussit* Quadrig. 10.58; again Vergil adopts this feature at *Aen.* 9.702-5 *tum sternit...Bitian...non iaculo...sed...phalarica uenit*.

Under this heading also belongs the so-called 'hysteron proteron' (see HS 698 and on Ennius V), another misnomer because it pedantically applies a criterion of temporal sequence (as Ennius himself was persuaded to do by Euripidean commentators in adjusting the beginning of the *Medea* of Euripides) where psychological factors are more important. When Vergil wrote *moriamur et in media arma ruamus*, he was not thinking which action preceded the other in time, but putting the vital point first and exercising his fondness for coordination instead of such subordination as would have been achieved by *moriamur ruendo*; this fondness for coordination appears on its smallest scale in his analogous fondness for 'hendiadys', as *pateris libamus et auro*, which could have been expressed as *pateris aureis*.

(iii) Word-order in early Latin tends to be standardised. In particular adjectives stand immediately after their nouns (so invariably in the Twelve Tables; cf. on Quadrigarius 10.33-4), and the Subject, Object, Verb order, or at least final placement of the verb, is normal, though not invariable, in utilitarian texts, such as the Twelve Tables, and simple narrative (see on Cato *Origines* 83, Piso, Quadrigarius 10). However Cato already understands the artistic potentialities of variation by e.g. initial placement of the verb (see on Speeches 58, 59, 173a). See index, Word-order.

(iv) Fourth comes the fact that, whereas Cicero and his generation largely standardised Latin usage in the same way as Addison and Steele did English usage, before that alternative forms and constructions, of which classical usage selected one as standard, co-existed, so that e.g. some nouns in *-us* could be declined either in the second or the fourth declension, verbs like *utor* could take either accusative or ablative; see on Cato *De Agr.* pr. 1 and index, Inconsistency. Likewise William Shakespeare is known to have spelt his own name in at least four different ways, none of them that which appears on the title-pages of his works and is generally used nowadays.

This is a convenient place to issue a reminder that, particularly in orthography, we may underestimate the extent of this variety because medieval scribes have often demonstrably modernised to what was familiar to them as classical usage or that of their own day. Accordingly we must always bear in mind that the spelling of e.g. the military oaths presented by the manuscripts of Gellius does not represent the original orthography. We could put most such texts back into an orthography normal for their date, as Bertini has done in his edition of the *Asinaria* of Plautus, but we would run up against the difficulty that we would be presuming consistency in the original orthography; it would be rather like trying to restore the digamma throughout in the text of Homer.

III

Thirdly there is a nucleus of forms of expression which are characteristic of the Latin language individually; alliteration, which seems to belong here, has been discussed under I (v).

(i) Most prominent among these is asyndeton (see index s.v. and HS 828, KS 2.148). Between three or more parallel words this remains common in classical Latin. In early Latin it is also common between paired words (*asyndeton bimembre*), particularly if these are synonyms (or in some way convey related concepts) or opposites; a considerable number of these combinations established themselves as fixed formulae which survived in classical Latin (many of them helped to survive by alliteration or assonance, cf. under I (v)), but otherwise this feature is comparatively restricted in classical writers (with exceptions like Sallust who cultivate an archaic patina), outside specific stylistic circumstances. Appel 160 collects instances in prayers.

On a larger scale, classical Latin develops a fondness for making the thought run smoothly by linking the sentences together with various forms of connection, though not quite to the same extent as Greek. Archaic Latin on the contrary tends to leave the listener or reader to work out for himself the relationship between one statement and the next; Cato is particularly sparse with logical linkage (see index, Connection).

However, there is one form of what may be called connection which is common in early Latin; though I discuss it here, it is not an individual characteristic of Latin, but is found in Greek also (see Dover 156), and is not confined to early Latin, but continues in use. That is chiasmus, so-called because when one finds two pairs of words in which the corresponding items are in reverse order, prints them one above the other and joins the corresponding items, the shape of the Greek letter chi is produced, e.g. (Cato *De Agr.* 4)

bubilia bona

bonas praesepis.

Not until very late is this regarded as a verbal ornament (Leeman 1.22); in origin it is simply a way of presenting a double series so that each item is linked to the preceding, thus, A - B (- C - D etc. - D - C) - B - A, whereas in the way which has become natural to us, A - B (- C - D etc.), A - B (- C - D etc.) there is a break at the end of each series. This latter method is based on thinking in columns, e.g.

```
A   B   C
|   |   |
A   B   C
|   |   |
A   B   C
```

so that the connecting lines run vertically and do not cross. The Homeric convention that when two questions are posed they are answered in reverse order, or boustrophedon writing (as on the Lapis Niger inscription), will show that the chiastic way of thinking can be considered equally natural. In Lucretius, who often has occasion to take up and elaborate a series of points, the two methods of arrangement are about equally common; e.g. for chiastic cf. 6.962 sqq. the sun dries up soil, but melts ice and snow; it melts wax too, as fire melts metals, though it hardens skin and flesh; water hardens iron, but softens skin and flesh; for columnar 5.753 sqq. (on eclipses) the moon may cut off the sun's light from the earth, some other body may be interposed, regions through which the sun passes may extinguish it: the earth may cut off the sun's light from the moon, some other body may be interposed, regions through which the moon passes may extinguish it.

It is convenient to add here a few remarks on some other forms of connection (see index s.v.) favoured in early Latin. The use of demonstratives is natural and common (in the Letter to the Tiburtines it is important enough to cause a long hyperbaton), but early Latin is willing to employ them in successive sentences in simple narrative (e.g. Gracchus 49; accompanied by -que Cato *Origines* 83, Piso 27; with the demonstrative adverb *ibi* Ennius III). By contrast connecting relatives are still rare (HS 569, KS 2.319). Another favoured method in simple narrative is simply to indicate temporal succession by *tum* etc. (Cato *De Agr.* 157.9 adopts this for the stages of a chemical process); this is often emphasised by pleonasm (see index s.v.) with temporal words. A technique which has much in common with the Greek 'strung together' style (consciously imitated, as it seems, by Ennius) is the repetition of a significant word from the previous sentence, a noun (e.g. Cato *De Agr.* 157.7 *ex cibo...ex multo cibo*, Quadrig. 57 *consul. ei consuli*; cf. Altenburg 492 and, with both archaic and classical examples, C. W. Mendell, *Latin Sentence Connection* (1917) 25-7) or verb (e.g. Cato *De Agr.* 157.9 *ferue bene facito. ubi feruerit*, 157.11 *fouere...fouebit*). The crudest method of connection is the 'this too' sometimes employed by Cato *De Agr.* (see on 142, 157.10).

(ii) Relative clauses seem sometimes to have no syntactical link with the main clause (e.g. Twelve Tables 10.8 *cui auro dentes iuncti esont, ast im cum illo sepeliet uretue, se fraude esto*; also Cato *De Agr.* 156.5, 157.9). These are generalising relative clauses which relate to the indefinite *quis*, not adjectival relative clauses which relate to the defining relative *qui* (HS 554-5).

(iii) Early Latin shows a particular fondness for etymological figure (see index s.v.), the association of two words from the same root. This is used in various ways, but in the prose texts here collected it is generally a means of adding weight and emphasis. See for details HS 790 and Haffter 10 sqq.

(iv) In the arrangement of clauses early Latin favours what is known as 'adjunct extraction', and this still sometimes appears in classical Latin. See for this on Cato *De Agr.* 1.7, Speeches 164, Quadrigarius 10.12.

IV

Some features belong less to linguistics than to cultural history.

(i) From the earliest days of Rome we have to reckon with Greek influence, however filtered and diluted; some of this will have come from the Greek colonies of south Italy, some indirectly through Etruria, some will be due to occasional Greek settlers in Rome (e.g. traders). This influence appears not only in the importation of some Greek words (see index s.v.) and occasional words (see index, Calques; e.g. *circumpotatio* Twelve Tables 10.6) or expressions modelled on Greek (there are some in medical technicalities in Cato *De Agr.* 156-7), but also in some of the formulations of the Twelve Tables (see the introduction there).

(ii) The social struggles of early Rome, much more protracted than e.g. in Athens, bestowed crucial importance on law, so that legal methods of expression became deeply ingrained in the Latin language. Since the Romans dealt with their gods in a very legalistic spirit and in formulae of legal type, religious and legal forms converge. The chief feature so produced is an insistence on clarity, which manifests itself in various ways. One obvious one is the tendency to repeat the antecedent of a relative pronoun within the relative clause, so that there can be no ambiguity about the reference of the pronoun; see on Piso 27, where a reference is given to a discussion which derives this feature from a linguistic rather than a social cause. Another is the accumulation of near-synonyms and exhaustive enumerations verging on pleonasm, so that no loophole is left unclosed; see SC de Bacanalibus 13-14 and the religious documents here collected (especially the notes on Cato *De Agr.* 141.2-3), with the parody in Plaut. *Amph.* 69-72. This feature is discussed by Appel 141, Haffter 81 and the chapter generally, D. Daube, *Collected Studies* 2 (1991), 1244. It seems to be at the origin of Latin's general fondness for coupling synonyms (see index s.v.) or near-synonyms, which however soon becomes a device for rhetorical emphasis (see on Cato Speeches 163 and *De Agr.* pr.3). A third is willingness to repeat the same word in circumstances in which classical writers would have been inclined to seek some elegant variation (sometimes even when a relative antecedent is repeated, e.g. Caes. *BC* 1.44.2 *quod fere fit, quibus quisque in LOCIS miles inueterauit, ut multum earum REGIONUM consuetudine moueatur*; see HS 563, KS 2.284) or simply to understand one occurrence from the other (e.g. Cato, Speeches 163 *aduorsae res...secundae res*); this latter is particularly common with demonstrative pronouns (e.g. Ennius III *concessit ei ut is regnaret*; see index, Pronouns). In general see index, Word-repetition.

V

Finally we have to recognise some features that derive simply from innate instincts of the human psyche. The most striking of these is the sense of rhythmical satisfaction given by an enumeration of three items, each, if possible, longer than the preceding; this is the famous 'Gesetz der wachsenden Glieder' (see HS 722, L. P. Wilkinson, *Golden Latin Artistry* (1963) 175) or rising tricolon, which may be exemplified by the English phrases 'Tom, Dick and Harry' or 'lock, stock and barrel'. The strength of this instinct may be gauged from instances in which a third item is added to a formulaic pair in order to achieve a triad (see on *deuotio* 10). For Cato's tendency to run counter to this tendency see p. 42; it should be noted that falling tricola are not absent even from Cicero (e.g. *De Rep.* 6.13 *conseruauerint adiuuerint auxerint*), but they constitute a small minority. See index, Tricolon and HS 725 (with interesting details on Cato).

The same tendency to prefer a weightier final item is found also in bicola (notably in the charm in Marcellus Empiricus) and in cases where a word on its second occurrence receives expansion (as Cato *De Agr.* pr. 1-3 *periculosum...periculosum et calamitosum*; see index, Word Repetition).

This introduction may suitably close with some remarks concerning what the Romans meant by the word *carmen*. Essentially this denoted a solemn formalised utterance in contexts such as ritual or law, as e.g. Cicero (*De Leg.* 2.59) says that he and his schoolfellows learned the Twelve Tables as a *carmen necessarium*. One obvious way of formalising utterance is to make it rhythmical or metrical, whence the later meaning of the word. In archaic Latin the formalisation appears rather in the clear marking out of short compositional units by devices such as alliteration and assonance, and by the pairing of words or their arrangement in tricola (all of this is an aid to memory in a predominantly oral culture); such features are helpfully discussed by Timpanaro, *RFIC* 116 (1988), 257-70, and can be seen clearly in the prayer in Cato *De Agr.* 141 as I have laid it out, and in the charm recorded by Marcellus Empiricus. Note that the prayer in Cato deliberately introduces a tricolon absent from the basic prose correspondent (see on 141.2).

APPENDIX: PARATAXIS AND SOME SYNTACTICAL CONSEQUENCES

The influence of the paratactic mode of thought on syntax is a large question; here I only pick out as illustrations a few constructions which because of this factor assume forms in early Latin different from those of classical Latin.

First, commands. In early Latin direct commands can be given by the subjunctive alone, but this subjunctive may be accompanied by the modal adverb *ut(i)*, which corresponds both to Greek πως 'somehow' and to πῶς 'how?', and indeed also to ὡς and ὅπως, though for present purposes this is irrelevant; the indefinite use survives in *neutiquam* 'not in any way'. Because in this indefinite function the word is enclitic, it originally was placed according to Wackernagel's Law (see I i above), as e.g. *CIL* 1.584.41 *id uti facere liceat* (this and other instances in *OLD*, *ut* 43, Kroll 86). Phrases like this could occur in combinations such as (Cato *De Agr.* 32.1) *arbores hoc modo putentur, rami uti diuaricentur*, which, however Cato thought of it, can comfortably be either two co-ordinate sentences, 'the trees should be pruned as follows; the branches should (somehow) be spread out', or as one complex sentence, 'the trees should be pruned in such a way that the branches are spread out'; thus a paratactic construction could give rise to a hypotactic (in this case a result clause). An indirect command can be similarly produced: *eadem uti curet faciatque moneo* (Cato *De Agr.* 142) can be understood either as 'let him see to these same things (somehow), that is my admonition' or as 'I admonish that he see to these same things'. Likewise final clauses. All this is most clearly explained by Kroll 85 and Bennett 1.164.

There are two corollaries. First, the presence of indefinite *ut(i)* not being imperatively required, constructions like *fac ualeas* can be created; the paratactic nature can be yet more clearly seen when the indicative appears in early Latin (e.g. Plaut. *Asin.* 131 *uestraque ibi nomina faxo erunt*). This is where constructions like Cato *De Agr.* 5.2 *consideret quae dominus imperauerit fiant* and Quadrigarius 10.8-9 *significare coepit utrisque quiescerent* fit; outside the strict category of commands note e.g. Cato *De Agr.* 69.2 *tepeat satis est*. Secondly, as awareness of the original indefinite modal sense of *ut* weakened, it began to assume initial instead of enclitic position, e.g. Cato *De Agr.* 1.4 *uti bene aedificatum siet*, and to be regarded as a subordinating conjunction in combinations like *impero ut ueniat*. One might draw a broad parallel between the urge to have such conjunctions where an earlier stage of language could dispense with them (even from later Latin one can quote instances like *dedisses huic animo par corpus, fecisset quod optabat* (Pliny *Ep.* 1.12.8), where the addition of a *si* would produce a subordinate conditional clause) and the urge to tie down by prepositions (which were in origin adverbs) senses which cases were once able to convey on their own, as still in classical Latin *toto litore* indicates place without need of a preposition.

On similar lines we have to think of indirect questions as once having existed as co-ordinate direct questions or exclamations, in that stage naturally for the most part with an indicative verb, e.g. Ter. *Hec.* 645-6 *nequeo satis / quam mihi uidetur factum praue proloqui*; the word-order here demonstrates that Terence did regard this as an indirect question, but this is a development from a stage in which one would have understood 'How wickedly I consider this to have been done! Words fail me'. There are however direct questions with subjunctive verbs, like Plaut. *Asin.* 407 *quid hoc sit negoti?*, which can readily give rise to e.g. id. *Men.* 384 *nimis miror quid hoc sit negoti.* Instances like this, together with the tendency to associate the SUBjunctive with an ever-increasing range of SUBordinate clauses, gave the impetus to the normal classical subjunctive in indirect questions. On all this see W. M. Lindsay, *Syntax of Plautus* (1907) 66, Kroll 73, Handford 172, Woodcock 134; for indicative indirect questions in particular see Bolkestein in *De Usu, études...M. Lavency* (1995) 59, with references to other modern discussions.

CHAPTER 1

THE TWELVE TABLES

According to Roman tradition, the codification of law into the Twelve Tables dates from mid-fifth century B.C. Some authors speak of an embassy to Athens to study the laws of Solon (almost certainly a fiction to account for perceived similarities), Dion. Hal. *AR* 10.51.5 of one to southern Italian Greek cities, which is in itself more plausible but again was probably invented to forge a connection with Charondas and Zaleucus. Whether the Tables, which (as their name implies) must originally have been inscribed on wood, were ever engraved on bronze, as the predominant tradition says, is uncertain (Wieacker (1988) 1.294); those who quote passages seem to know them from oral and written records, not from any inscribed source (hence the unhappy compromise proposed by Ogilvie on Livy 3.57.10, namely that they were originally written on wood and set up in bronze at the beginning of the first century B.C., must be rejected). One must therefore be wary of supposing that quotations are in all cases verbally exact; certainly the quotations which we have are not in the orthography of the fifth century but have been modernised in this respect. One might be tempted to link this modernisation with the restoration after the Gallic sack of Rome in 390 (Livy 6.1.10), but that is still too early for some features (perhaps even rhotacism [Leumann 178, SP 146], though this is subject to doubt); one should think rather of the need for practical convenience in citation in legal proceedings. Otherwise however the style and substance show indubitably primitive features which vouch for overall authenticity.

The stories about the embassies are based on the true proposition that close similarities can be detected to Greek laws. Similarities of substance need not imply direct derivation, but similarities of expression and syntactical framework in most cases must be due to this cause, though they do not necessarily imply embassies as the channel for knowledge of Greek law. The closest parallels are found in the following Greek codes of law:

Athens. For Solon see E. Ruschenbusch, *Solonos Nomoi* (*Historia* Einzelschr. 9, 1966).

Gortyn. See C. D. Buck, *The Greek Dialects* (1955), inscriptions no. 117; R. F. Willetts, *The Law Code of Gortyn* (1967).

Iulis in Ceos. See Buck 8; F. Sokolowski, *Lois sacrées des cités grecques* (1969) no. 97; R. Dareste and others, *Recueil des inscriptions juridiques grecques* (1891) no. 2.

Cyrene. See Buck 115, Sokolowski, *Lois...grecques, supplement* (1962) no. 115.

Delphi, law of the Labyadae. See Buck 52c, Sokolowski (1969) 77, Dareste etc., *Recueil...grecques, deuxiéme serie* (1898-1904) no. 28.

It is important to note that the code of the Tables is quite different stylistically from later individual enactments, which are concerned with precision and detail in covering all eventualities (see p. 8), whereas the Tables in a spare style show formulations of the essentials that are easy to remember (see Crawford 16); the composers must have been thinking in some degree of a largely oral culture, which fits the fact that in Cicero's youth the Tables were learned by heart as part of the school curriculum, a *necessarium carmen* (*De Leg.* 2.59 and 9). The formal articulation that determines the concept of *carmen* (see p. 9) is related to orality and is striking in the remains of the Tables. M. von Albrecht, *History of Roman Literature* (Eng. tr. 1997) 631 remarks how many legal words (e.g. *condictio*) imply oral procedure and how few (e.g. *circumscriptio*) written.

The assemblage and arrangement of the surviving fragments is the creation of modern scholarship and for the greater part is not based on ancient authority. The standard editions are by R. Schoell (1866), Bruns, Riccobono in *FIRA* 1. A text with English translation is provided by Warmington III and by Crawford etc.; see also D. Flach, *Die Gesetze der frühen röm. Republik* (1994) 109.

I 1-3

(1) SI IN IVS VOCAT, N<I> IT, ANTESTAMIN<O>, IGITVR EM CAPITO. (2) SI CALVITUR PEDEMVE STRVIT, MANVM ENDO IACITO. (3) SI MORBVS AEVITASVE [VITIVM] ESCIT, [QVI IN IVS VOCABIT] IVMENTUM DATO. SI NOLET, ARCERAM NE STERNITO.

1 Porph. ad Hor. *Serm.* 1.9.74-6
uocat ni it F. *Pithoeus*, uocationit *codd. Porph.*, uocat ito, ni it *Heindorf*
2 Festus 312
3 Gell. 20.1.25
uitium *del. Fraenkel, Hermes 60 (1925), 440 = KB 2.442*; uitium<ue> D. *Gothofredus (Godefroy)*
[qui...uocabit] *Schoell 74*

III 1-4

(1) AERIS CONFESSI REBVS[QVE] IVRE IVDICATIS XXX DIES IVSTI SVNTO. (2) POST DEINDE MANVS INIECTIO ESTO. IN IVS DVCITO. (3) NI IVDICATVM FACIT AVT QVIS ENDO EO IN IVRE VINDICIT, SECVM DVCITO, VINCITO AVT NERVO AVT COMPEDIBVS XV PONDO, NE MINORE, AVT SI VOLET MAIORE VINCITO. (4) SI VOLET SVO VIVITO. NI SVO VIVIT, [QVI EVM VINCTVM HABEBIT] LIBRAS FARRIS ENDO DIES DATO. SI VOLET, PLVS DATO.

Gell. 20.1.42-5, (1) etiam 15.13.11
1 [que] *Courtney*
iure *20.1.45, om. 15.13.11*
3 maiore...minore *cod. Cuiacii*
4 [qui...habebit] *Schoell 74*
farris *ed. 1513*, feri *codd.*

VIII 12-13 (= I 17-18 Crawford)

(12) SI NOX FURTUM FACSIT, SI IM OCCISIT, IVRE CAESVS ESTO. (13) LVCI...SI SE TELO DEFENDIT...ENDOQVE PLORATO.

12 Macrob. *Sat.* 1.4.19
facsit *Courtney praeeuntibus Cuiacio et Schoell 79*, factum sit *codd.*
13 Cic. *Pro Tull.* 47 legem de xii tabulis...quae permittit ut furem noctu liceat occidere et luci si se telo defendat; 50 furem...luce occidi uetant xii tabulae...'nisi se telo defendit' inquit...quod si repugnat, 'endoplorato', hoc est, conclamato, ut aliqui audiant et conueniant.
Festus 309 in legibus 'transque dato' 'endoque plorato'.
Paul. Fest. 77 endoplorato, implorato, quod est cum quaestione inclamare.

X 1-8

(1) HOMINEM MORTVVM IN VRBE NE SEPELITO NE<VE> VRITO. (2)...HOC PLVS NE FACITO: ROGVM ASCEA NE POLITO. (3)...TRIBVS RICINIIS ET TVNICVLA PVRPVREA ET DECEM TIBICINIBVS...(4) MVLIERES GENAS NE RADVNTO, NEVE LESSVM FVNERIS ERGO HABENTO. (5) HOMINI MORTVO NE OSSA LEGITO QVO POS FVNVS FACIAT...(6) seruilis unctura tollitur omnisque CIRCVMPOTATIO...ne sumptuosa respersio, NE LONGAE CORONAE, NE[C] ACERRAE...(7) QVI CORONAM PARIT IPSE PECVNIAVE EIVS

VIRTVTISVE ERGO †ARGVITVR† EI... (8)...NEVE AVRVM ADDITO.
[VT] CVI AVRO DENTES IVNCTI ESONT, AST IM CUM ILLO
SEPELIET VRETVE, SE FRAVDE ESTO.

1-6,8 Cic. *De Leg.* 2.58-64, 7 Plin. *NH* 21.7
3 uimcla *uel* uincla purpur(a)e *codd.*
5 *v.l.* quos
7 arguitur, diuiditur, du(u)itur *codd. Plin.*
8 [ut] *R. Stephanus (1554), Schoell 110, at Ascensius (1521)*
  iuncti *uel* uincti *codd.*
  esont *Courtney* (esunt *J. Raevardus (1563)*), essent *codd.*

I

'If <plaintiff> summons <defendant> to court, and <the latter> does not
go, <plaintiff> must call on witnesses, and then he should take hold of <defendant>.
If <defendant> attempts evasion or takes to flight (?), <plaintiff> should lay hands
on him. If illness or age is involved, <plaintiff> must provide an animal for
conveyance; he need not provide a covered carriage with cushions if he does not so
desire'.

The very beginning, as this seems to be, of the Tables provides a notable
exemplification of a primitive feature of both Greek and Latin, namely the lack of
an expressed subject; see on this p. 2, HS 412 and 733, KS 1.6-7, Pascucci 7, de Meo
36, Altenburg 521, Schoell 73, Keil on Cato 11.2, Calboli in Callebat 614. For this
feature in Greek law see e.g. Solon 23d, 49a, Cyrene § 6, 10-13 and often Gortyn;
cf. also for Italic ritual prescriptions Poultney 21. Failure to appreciate this archaic
feature has led Gellius or his source to interpolate a subject in 3 (wrongly taking *escit*
to be future) and in III 4.

Consequent on the absence of subject come frequent unsignalled changes
of subject where the context is free from ambiguity. Lucilius 552, referring to this
passage, makes a joke of this: *'si non it, capito' inquit 'eum, et si caluitur'. ergo /
fur dominum?* (sc. *capiat?*). The law does not say who is to do what; one might argue
that it means the thief (*fer* codd.; some other amazing emendations have been
offered) is to lay hands on the owner of the article. See HS 733 and in Greek law e.g.
Cyrene § 17, 19, Gortyn I 28, 41, in Roman probably (though the text is uncertain)
a 'Law of Numa' quoted by Festus 178. This happens when only plaintiff and
defendant are concerned; when a third party is involved, as in III 3, a subject (there
quis) is introduced.

Heindorf's reconstruction gets some support from a clause in the praetor's
edict (*FIRA* 1 p. 339 no. 11a, Bruns 213 *in ius uocati ut eant*) and *Ad Herenn.* 2.13.19

lege ius est id quod populi iussu sanctum est, quod genus, ut in ius eas cum uoceris,
and is widely accepted by those who think that textual criticism depends on adhesion
to the transmitted letters, but it is certainly wrong (rejected by Daube 28 and many
others); in fact such adhesion here is merely apparent, since the letters *io* represent
the erroneous restoration of letters omitted, as indicated (Crawford 585 dismisses
this as a 'text-critical argument', as if this were somehow an insult). The text as
presented above conforms to a formulation common in the Tables: (1) 'if' giving the
basic circumstances (2) 'and if' giving a subsidiary eventuality (3) 'then' giving the
resultant direction. For this frame cf. VIII 2 and 12, X 8, Cato *De Agr.* 4, 2.1 and
elsewhere, Gell. 10.15.10 (regulations for the flamen Dialis, quoted from Fabius
Pictor). See HS 734, KS 2.628; this is also common in Greek law (e.g. Solon 5a [the
inscription from which this comes, *IG* 1 (ed. 3), 104, is labelled πρῶτος ἄχσον =
prima tabula and reproduces some of the law of Drakon], 48b, 49a; Cyrene §16-17,
Gortyn I 12-14, 18-20). However it is not exclusive to Greek law; see *Exodus* 22.7.
Lists of contingencies with 'if' conform to the predominantly casuistic nature of
Roman law at this stage, though abstract principles can never be absent from law;
see F. Schulz, *Principles of Roman Law* (1936) ch. 4.

It is striking that the Tables, like the Law of Gortyn, start with what makes
the most immediate impact on the man in the street, procedure.

antestamino The plaintiff would call a bystander to witness with the words
licet antestari?, and on receipt of a positive answer would, as often in Roman legal
procedure, perform a symbolical act, that of touching the ear (regarded as the seat
of memory) of the witness: Horace l.c., Pliny *NH* 11.45, Plaut. *Persa* 747-8. See
Nachtergael in *Grec et Latin en 1982* (1982) 115. For this form of the second or third
person deponent imperative see Cato 141.2 *praefamino*, Leumann 572-3, NW
3.211, Sommer 520.

igitur This word began life as temporal 'then' (*TLL* s.v. 255.51, HS 513,
KS 2.135); it developed its later inferential meaning because of the logical fallacy
post hoc ergo propter hoc which caused many words in both Greek and Latin (e.g.
cum) to mean both 'when' and 'since'. In French and Italian too one may compare
puisque, poiché = postquam. Here it stresses 'then and only then', after all the
required preliminaries have been executed.

em The form *im* found in VIII 12, X 8 is older; Leumann 467, NW 2.380,
Sommer 418. Cf. on *endo* below.

caluitur is glossed *frustratur, decipit*; Gaius *Dig.* 50.16.233 *'si caluitur':*
ut (Schoell; *et* codd.) *moretur et frustretur*.

pedemue struit Festus 210 M explains this to mean *fugit* on the authority
of the jurist Servius Sulpicius ('to heap up footsteps' meaning 'to rush away'), but
id. 313 shows that there was much uncertainty about the sense (he quotes as rival
explanations *retrorsus ire* or *in aliam partem ire* or *fugere* or *gradum augere* or
gradum minuere; what follows is corrupt, but evidently gives another interpretation
'hangs back', i.e. sets his foot firm). Yet another possibility is 'equips his foot', i.e.

prepares to abscond (this would relate to a time when it was usual to go barefoot in the streets).

endo This form (III 3-4, VIII 13) and *in* (as in the first sentence here and e.g. III 3), developed from the inherited *en* (Leumann 45), coexist; consistency is not necessarily to be expected (cf. on Cato *De Agr.* pr. 1 and p. 5). *en* seems to be found on the Duenos-inscription (*CIL* 1 (ed. 2) 4 = *ILS* 8743 = Warmington IV 54) *en manom*; the *-do* seems to be the same deictic-local particle as in *quando* = *quamdo*. In classical Latin this would be *inicito* (cf. III 2 *iniectio*).

aeuitas i.e. *aetas*, 'advanced age' (*OLD* s.v. 4b).

escit This is a present form with the inceptive *-sco* suffix (Leumann 523, Sommer 531, Pascucci 24 n.2, de Meo 86 n.34, M. Keller *Rev. Ph.* 59 (1985), 38 and *Les Verbes latins à infectum en -sc-* (1992) 79); the comparison with the Greek imperfect ἔσκε is fallacious. It had developed a future sense by the second century B.C., but not in the Tables (V 4-5 and 7), in which, as Fraenkel l.c. 443 = *KB* 445 points out, it means 'exist' and is not used just as a copula. This bears on the establishment of the text (see next note, purposely postponed). Fraenkel also remarks (cf. Keller (1985) 41) that a regular form in the Tables is that an imperative in the main clause is accompanied by a present tense in a conditional clause, as in 1-2. The conditional clauses in the Tables are conveniently collected by Szemerényi 893; on this subject Coleman in H. Rosén (ed.), *Aspects of Latin* (1996) 403 is much too adventurous.

uitium The transmitted text has to mean 'if disease or age shall be impediment' (Warmington), but in law *uitium* (which Cuiacius again introduced by conjecture to mean 'impediment' into II 2) only means an obstacle to the validity of a legal provision; in religion too there must be reference to an act which the *uitium* invalidates (this covers Cic. *De Div.* 2.43, which Flach 115 quotes to the contrary). Accordingly Fraenkel suggested that the word was interpolated from Gellius' phrase (27) *uitium aliquod inbecillitatis atque inualentiae* explaining *morbus*. From this it follows that Gellius cannot have read the word as a predicate, nor can he have read it as Gothofredus intended, to mean 'disability' (it is so defined by Modestinus *Dig.* 50.16.101.2 in contrast to *morbus*; see also Gell. 4.2). Paschall *TAPA* 67 (1936), 227-9 dissents from Fraenkel, but without good ground.

iumentum Caecilius in Gellius 20.1.28 claims that this means 'vehicle', not (as in VII 7 and classical Latin) 'animal used for traction', but this is just an improvisation to suit his argument. The following clause suggests that a right to an *arcera* had been presumed, and that this presumption is now being struck down.

si nolet See on *si uolet* III 4.

arcera An archaic word for 'wagon'; it is defined by Gellius 29. Varro *Sat. Men.* 188 has this passage in mind: *cum arceram, si non uellet, non sterneret.* Bennett 1.364 remarks this as a rare negative permissive imperative.

III

'Concerning admitted debt, when matters have been formally judged thirty days shall be allowed by law. After that manual arrest <of debtor> is permitted. <The plaintiff> must bring him into court. If he does not satisfy the judgment, or no-one assumes protection in court over him, <the plaintiff> shall take <the defendant> with him and bind him either in stocks or in fetters, weighing not less than fifteen pounds, or if he wishes he shall bind him with a greater weight. If <the defendant> wishes, he shall live on his own means. If he does not live on his own means, <the plaintiff> shall give him one pound of wheat per day. He may give more if he so desires'.

Gellius explains that the debtor was granted 30 days to find money for discharging his debt, and that these days were called *iusti*. The Latin as it stands is unintelligible. Gellius' phrase *confessi aeris ac debiti iudicatis* implies that he took *iudicatis* to be masculine and the genitive to depend on it (cf. Livy 26.3.8-9), as genitives often do on judicial verbs; the *rebusque* which stands in his manuscripts in both places is ignored by him. This is no more than a fudged attempt to make sense of the text as he knew it. With the deletion of *que* the genitive will be what HS 74 call 'Gen. des Sachbetreffs', quoting in particular the Lex Osca Tabulae Bantinae 5 (*FIRA* 1.164, Bruns 52, Crawford 281), which in Latin translation runs *manum asserere earum rerum* (for this phrase see HS 75, 82*) and Livy 1.32.11 *quarum rerum litium causarum condixit*; these two examples both show the original limitation of the construction to expressions with *res*, and so would HS's quotation from Twelve Tables V 3 if the text there were certain. I notice that O. Behrends, *Die Zwölftafelprozess* (1974) 129 and 137 presents the text as I do, without *que*, apparently not intentionally but through a natural instinct that this is how to make sense of the sentence.

Provisions of the *Lex coloniae Genetivae Iuliae seu Ursonensis* c. 61 of 44 B.C. (*FIRA* 1.179, Bruns 123, Crawford 400) modelled on this (cf. Norden *AAP* 12 (-13) n.3) are relevant for comparison:

[cui quis ita ma]num inicere iussus erit, iudicati iure manus iniectio esto...ni uindicem dabit iudicatumue faciet, secum ducito. iure ciuili uinctum habeto.

This passage defends the *iure* transmitted in one of Gellius' quotations; so does the etymological figure introduced by the coupling with *iudicare*, for which Pascucci 38 and de Meo 121 quote parallels like *sanctione sancire*. E. G. Hardy, *Three Spanish Charters* (1912) 23 translates *iudicati iure* with 'on the legal ground of a judgment given', but *iudicati* is much more likely to mean 'arrest in the amount duly adjudged' (so Crawford 421), cf. an ancient inscription from Luceria (Bruns 283, *FIRA* 3.224, Warmington IV 154-7) *pro ioudicatod n(ummum) L manum iniectio estod*, Plaut. *Pers.* 71 *tantidem...iniciat manum, Truc.* 762 *te manum iniciam quadrupuli*, with a judicial genitive.

Compare also Gaius 4.21:

per manus iniectionem aeque de his rebus agebatur de quibus ut ita ageretur lege aliqua cautum est, ueluti iudicati [de Zulueta translates 'for a judgment debt', but Poste 'against a judgment debtor'] lege XII tabularum ...qui agebat sic dicebat: 'quod tu mihi iudicatus (siue damnatus) es sestertium x milia, quandoc non soluisti, ob eam rem ego tibi sestertium x milium iudicati manum inicio' ['I lay my hand on you for 10,000 sesterces of judgment debt' de Zulueta, but 'I arrest you as judgment debtor for 10,000 sesterces' Poste]...(iudicatus) uindicem dabat qui pro se causam agere solebat; qui uindicem non dabat, domum ducebatur ab actore et uinciebatur.

(*quandoc* is attested for the Twelve Tables by Festus 258; it is presumably *quandoqu(e)*).

Problems certainly remain: (1) Bruns objects *de confesso iudicium non fieri iure Romano* (2) what happens to those who deny the debt but are convicted anyway?

aeris sc. *alieni.*

confessi Gell. 15.13.11 comments on the passive sense of this, for which see NW 3.42, *OLD* s.v., *TLL* 4.232.19.

post deinde See Ennius III and Schoell 107, HS 525, *TLL* 10.2.163.33, KS 2.573, Hache 23, 54, E. Lindholm *Stilistische Studien* (1931) 30 (correcting some imprecisions) for this pleonasm.

manus iniectio esto This idea is so expressed also in the *Lex Ursonensis* (quoted above), a *senatus consultum* of the second half of the second century (Bruns 189, *FIRA* 1.273, Warmington IV 252-5) and with *manum iniectio* in the Luceria inscription; it contrasts with the verbal formulation *manum endo iacito* in 1.2. The nominal formulation has the nuance 'then the procedure of laying on of hands may take place'. Cf. on the *lex Furfensis* 14, which might be translated 'it is ordained that the duty of exaction of the fine belongs to the aedile'. In similar legal contexts cf. *actio nei esto* thrice in the Lex Acilia, and Ter. *Ph.* 292-3 *seruom hominem causam orare leges non sinunt / neque testimoni dictiost*. D. Daube, *Aspects of Roman Law* (1969) 45 remarks 'It is because the action noun implies institutionalization, solidity, durability, that it is favoured where a particularly impressive utterance is wanted' (with examples), but I find it hard to see 1.2 above as less impressive.

uindicit The conjugation reflects the etymology *uim dicit* (see *RE* suppl. 14.885 s.v. *uindex*; d'Avino, *Ricerche linguistiche* 5 (1962), 94); the verb later moved into the first conjugation. The series *uim dicere - uindex - uindicare* is formally paralleled by *ius dicere - iudex - iudicare*. The starting point was *uim illam ciuilem et festucariam quae uerbo diceretur* (Gell. 20.10.10) and the formula of claiming an object by laying a *festuca* on it and saying *ecce tibi uindictam inposui* (Gaius 4.16); *uindictam = uim dictam, uis* expressed in words. So *uimdictam* creates by hypostasis (see on Cato *De Agr.* 2.2) a noun *uindicta*, which then creates *uindicere* and hence *uindex*. A *uindex* (guarantor) either pays the debt or contests the justification of the *manus iniectio*; thereby he *manum depellit* (Gaius 4.21-4). *endo eo* means 'in his case' (cf. V 7); this is not the classical construction with *uindicare*, but is natural enough at a time when there was still a live sense of its etymology (Schoell 91-2). Szemerényi 1047 produces a far-fetched etymology for this group of words, but it is significant that *endo eo* causes him discomfort (1059 n.37).

   XV pondo With this *librarum* is understood; hence comes the later use of *pondo* (which is here still an ablative of respect) as indeclinable = 'pound'. See Kroll 41.

   minore...maiore At first sight the former seems surprising; evidently the state had an interest in seeing that the debtor should not escape. Many find that hard to swallow and adopt the transposition recorded in the apparatus. For comparable Greek formulations see Wieacker (1988) 1.298 n.68, (1967) 351, (1971) 778-80, Norden *AAP* 257. Cf. Livy 32.26.18 *captiui ne minus decem pondo compedibus uincti.*

   si uolet Cf.1.3; for comparable Greek formulations see again Wieacker ll.cc., Ducos 63 (Gortyn).

   uincito...uincito Like *dato...dato* below (where the lawgiver could have said *dato, aut si uolet plus*), the repetition serves to keep each member of the *carmen* self-contained, which is a help in a largely oral record (see above). Cf. p. 5.

   suo uiuito The debtor's person is distrained, but not his property. This is because land was originally inalienable from the family; Roman law does not recognise mortgage.

   [qui...habebit] Another interpolation to introduce a subject (see on 1.3); if it is genuine, *eum* has been modernised from *em.*

   libras farris endo dies Cf. Cato 54.1 *semodios singulis bubus in dies dari oportet,* 57 *heminas in dies...in dies sextarios...in dies heminas ternas.* Cf. generally Ter. *Ph.* 334 *dices 'ducent damnatum domum';/ alere nolunt hominem edacem* (a parasite).

VIII

   'If <A> commits theft by night, and <B> kills him, let it be considered justifiable homicide. By day...if he defends himself with a weapon...and let him call out'.

si...si A particularly clear case of the idiom discussed on I 1; note that here the unexpressed subject of the first clause is referred to by the demonstrative *im*.

nox For this adverbial use cf. Enn. *Ann.* 423 *si luci si nox* with Skutsch's note.

facsit...occisit The origin of these forms is open to much doubt; the best discussion is by Rix in *Mír Curad, Studies in Honor of Calvert Watkins* (1998) 619 (brought to my attention by Professor Brent Vine). To take *faxo* as an example, this has been regarded as (1) an aorist subjunctive: (2) a desiderative present indicative (so e.g. Benveniste, *Bull. Soc. Linguistique* 23.1 (1922) 32), to be associated with *uiso* and *quaeso*: (3) a special category which Rix calls 'Perfectivfutur'. The first view has to struggle with the fact that such forms appear in verbs which have no *s*-perfects. Except for *faxo*, all these forms are found only in subordinate clauses, mostly conditional as here; they function simply as futures. Cf. XII 2 *si seruus furtum faxit noxiamue +nocuit+ (noxit* Pithoeus); note the alliteration and etymological figure in this fragment. At VIII 4 *si iniuriam alteri faxsit* this spelling has best authority; *occisit* is found again in a 'Law of Numa' quoted by Festus 178 M. *occisus-caesus* exemplifies the ancient idiom of following a compound by a simple form; cf. p. 2, index 'Verbs', HS 789-80, Fraenkel *KB* 1.441, Pascucci 39, Wills 438 and other references in my note on *ML* 109.21.

luci is a locative form (Sommer 378, NW 2.644-5, *TLL* 7.2.1906.5).

endoque plorato i.e. *imploratoque*; see Leumann 271, 562, HS 217. Such 'tmesis' (see p. 2) is later used in dactylic verse as a literary artifice. The other example quoted by Festus (= *traditoque*) may also come from the Tables. The slayer must call out so that he may have witnesses that he is not a murderer trying to conceal his misdeed; so at least Cicero understood it (and Szemerényi 902 agrees), but it seems more likely that it related to the 'Volksjustiz' institution of calling for help.

This law is referred to also by Cic. *Pro Milone* 9, Gell. 11.18.7, 20.1.7 and many others; Macrobius probably drew on the now missing Gell. 8.1. Permission to kill a nocturnal thief was given by Solon (113; the same provision in Plato *Laws* 9.874b), and Hebrew law is similar (*Exodus* 22.2; cf. *Mosaicarum et Romanarum Legum Collatio* 7.1-3). Solon also ordained that killing of an armed robber who resisted was justifiable homicide (19b; νηποινεὶ τεθνάναι). For this law in general see Watkins *SW* 2.435.

X

'<One> must not bury or cremate a dead man within the city... <one> must not do more than this; <one> must not smooth the pyre with an axe...three shawls, one small purple tunic, ten oboe-players...Women must not tear their cheeks nor raise a lament because of a funeral. One must not gather the bones of a dead man in order to hold a funeral subsequently. (Anointing by slaves is abolished, and so are all) wakes...no expensive sprinkling, no long garlands, no incense-boxes...When a man wins a wreath, either personally or through a chattel, or as a mark of courage one (is given) to him...<one> must not add gold. But if <one> buries or cremates with gold a man with gold dental work, let that be without detriment'.

Cicero (though with modifying words *fere* 59, *prope* 64) stresses the similarity to Solon's laws, but could have spoken about Greek law generally; see e.g. Toher in K. A. Raaflaub, *Social Struggles in Archaic Rome* (1986) 306, 316 and *Georgika* (*BICS* suppl. 58, 1991) 159, S. C. Humphreys, *The Family, Women and Death* (1983) 85, R. Seaford, *Reciprocity and Ritual* (1994) 74. In Hebrew law too *Leviticus* 19.28 says 'You shall not gash yourselves in mourning for the dead' (New English Bible), cf. *Jeremiah* 16.6.

ne sepelito The negative future imperative is virtually confined to laws and Cato *De Agr.* (Bennett 1.363, KS 1.203, Vairel-Carron 244, 294). Cicero suggests fear of fire as the reason for this prohibition, but public health and particularly religion must have been the predominant factors. Cf. the *Lex Ursonensis* 72-3 *ne quis intra fines oppidi colon(iae)ue...hominem mortuum inferto neue ibi humato neue urito.* After this date cremation became usual.

hoc plus ne facito This corresponds to μὴ πλέον in Greek laws (Norden *AAP* 256). The preceding context will have explained *hoc*.

riciniis Festus 274 says that interpreters of the Tables declared this to mean *omne uestem quadratum.* Varro in his *De Vita Populi Romani* (quoted by Nonius 542 and 545; fr. 49 and 105 Riposati) declared that women wore it in times of adversity and grief, and more specifically *ut dum supra terram essent ricinis lugerent, funere ipso ut pullis pallis amictae* (nothing firm can be made out of the mention in his satire Ταφὴ Μενίππου fr. 538). But if this is the reference, here it will have to mean 'three women wearing *ricinia*', which is very odd. It is more probable that women are to be buried with three *ricinia* and men with a *tunicula purpurea* (so Wieacker (1971) 3.775). In that case Cicero's parallel with the τρία ἱμάτια which Solon allowed to be buried with the corpse is valid but not quite exact (72c; also in the law of Iulis). For the purple tunic, which is to be restricted in size (hence the diminutive), cf. Plut. *Lycurgus* 27.1 (where however it is the military uniform of the Spartiates). The law must have mentioned these items, but not necessarily in this form, since the ablatives seem to be required by the syntax of Cicero's sentence, even if that is somewhat obscure.

tibicinibus See Ovid *Fasti* 6.660-4 (which evidently means that the aediles enforced this restriction) and Blümner 491 n.12.

mulieres...radunto So also Solon 72c.

lessum This appears twice in the text of Cicero 59; on the second occurrence he reports that the grammarian Aelius Stilo took it to mean *lugubris eiulatio.* In 64 the tradition is divided between this and *flessum*, but the manuscripts which offer the latter precede it with *ney* or the like, so that *NEYFLESSUM* seems to be just an error for *NEVELESSUM*. In *Tusc.* 2.55 Cicero refers to the same word and gives the same explanation, but his mss. there offer *fletus* except for a variant *pessus* in V. In the light of all this S. Lundström's (*Vermeintliche Glosseme i. d. Tusculanen* (1964) 149) support of the form *flessus* has little basis. Information about the manuscript readings in the *De Legibus* was kindly provided to me by Professor Jonathan Powell in advance of his OCT.

quo here, as in Cato Speeches 173e, introduces a purpose clause even without a comparative (Bennett 1.261, HS 679, KS 2.233). The idea of this prohibition is to prevent inhumation after cremation, and Toher (1986) 324-5 suggests that this was intended to prevent diversion of economic resources from the construction of public sanctuaries (this seems somewhat far-fetched to me). After this quotation Cicero adds *excipit bellicam peregrinamque mortem*; those who died in these circumstances cannot be denied burial at home.

pos This form is commonest before *t* and *m*; before *f* apparently only *CIL* 4.6820 elsewhere.

The next two clauses bristle with difficulties. As transmitted the text of Cicero runs thus:

haec praeterea sunt in legibus de unctura qu(a)e seruilis...circumpotatio...ne sumptuosa respersio ne longae coronae nec acerrae praetereantur illa iam significatio est...

It would take us too far to analyse the problems here, so I shall just propose the following as a tentative solution:

haec praeterea sunt in legibus de unctura <iustis>que: seruilis...circumpotatio...; ne sumptuosa...ne acerrae <perhibeantur cauetur>. praetereantur illa; iam...

The upshot of this is that Cicero is paraphrasing the substance of the Tables, not quoting directly from them; all that we can confidently attribute to the Tables are the words *circumpotatio, longae coronae, acerrae* (possibly but not certainly *sumptuosa respersio* and *seruilis unctura*, which might well have been expressed verbally in the Tables), probably not in those grammatical forms since the Tables do not give orders in which things are the subject, nor orders in the passive, but always tell a person to do or not to do something (contrast *ne sumptuosa respersio* with the form of the 'Law of Numa' quoted below). The supposition that Cicero is quoting directly has compelled most editors to adopt the emendation *tollitor* (P. Manutius). This however cannot be right, since *-tor* imperatives exist only in deponent, not in passive, verbs. It follows too that Daube's (105) idea that the lack of copula in *ne sumptuosa...acerrae* accurately reproduces the form of the Tables, very improbable in itself anyway, must be rejected.

seruilis unctura Only relatives are allowed to do this (Enn. *Ann.* 147 etc.). For the anointing cf. Blümner 484.

circumpotatio Festus 158 belongs here: *murrata potione usos antiquos indicio est quod...xii tabulis cauetur ne mortuo indatur* [i.e. it must not be poured on a corpse], *ut ait Varro in Antiquitatum l. I* [I xii Mirsch]. The word must be calqued on περίδειπνον, which must originally have meant a meal consumed with the corpse placed in the middle (*RE* 19.723-4), as an Irish wake used to be (perhaps still is) conducted. Watkins *SW* 2.665 much less plausibly thinks of the Celtic custom of passing around the cup.

ne sumptuosa respersio... Pliny *NH* 14.88 quotes a 'Law of Numa' *uino rogum ne respargito* (see also Festus and Paulus 262-3); the law of Iulis restricts the amount of wine. *Coronae* (i.e. of flowers, not those of precious metal meant in the next section) and *respersio* are not forbidden (the 'Law of Numa' is stricter), only excess in them; see Blümner 485 n.7. Peruzzi *PP* 45 (1990), 116 thinks that *acerrae* here has the sense, attested by Paul. Fest. but not found elsewhere, of altars placed *ante mortuum* for burning scented herbs such as myrtle.

pecunia I take this to be nominative, with a slight anacoluthon, rather than (as HS 175) ablative with *eius* in place of *sua* (so also Thuillier in *Crise et transformation des sociétés archaiques* (1990) 364, but with a most improbable interpretation). Pliny explains that the reference is to wreaths won in circus contests, and that these might be won personally (as occasionally in Greece, e.g. by the Herodotus of Pindar *Isthm.* 1 or the Damonon of *IG* 5.1.213 = L. Moretti, *Inscr. Agonistiche Greche* 16; this became obsolete in historical times at Rome) or by slaves and horses owned by a man (*RE* suppl. 7.1636-7). This sense of the word is not found elsewhere. With *uirtutisue* the lawgiver turns to a different kind of wreath, that given as a civic or military mark of distinction. Cicero 60 gives the gist, but not the wording, of what followed: *coronam uirtute partam et ei qui peperisset et eius parenti sine fraude esse lex impositam iubet* (cf. Marquardt 348 n.1). It is worth remarking that *corona* is a Greek loan-word from κορώνη (Hesychius, Sophron 163 K); see E. Peruzzi, *Origini di Roma* (1970-3) 2.86 and *PP* 25 (1970), 402.

ei exemplifies the idiom whereby a second relative pronoun is replaced by a demonstrative (KS 2.324-5, HS 565-6, Altenburg 512). The corrupt verb must have meant 'is given'. For *uirtutis ergo* cf. Schoell 80, *TLL* 5.2.759.54-8; for the construction of the sentence see next note.

esont Whatever is restored here must match *sepeliet uretue* in mood and tense; this is achieved by the pre-rhotacism form of the future of *esse*. VI 9 (quoted by Festus) in this future perfect passive has been modernised to *dempta erunt*. Of course it may not be future perfect passive, but mean 'if a man has' (possessive not referential dative) 'teeth joined with gold'. In the Lapis Niger inscription (*FIRA* 1.20 = Bruns 14 = Warmington IV 242) *esed* may be a third person future. *escunt* is usually read here, but falls to the point made on I 3. For what looks like a relative without an antecedent see p. 8; here it in effect functions in a conditional sense. The preceding sentence too was probably like this.

Before this provision the mss. of Cicero present the interpolated phrase *praecipit altera lege*; the next word *ut* is probably part of this interpolation rather than a corruption of *at*, a word not found elsewhere in the Tables and contravening their usual asyndetic form. For archaeological finds of gold dental work see

Waarsenburg in *Stips Votiva, Papers presented to C. M. Stibbe* (1991) 241 and
Bliquez in *ANRW* 2.37.3.2640 with illustrations; the nature of the dental work
supports *iuncti* rather than *uincti*, though the latter gets support from Celsus 7.12.1.

   ast This is the original function of this word, to introduce the second half
of a conditional clause (which is what in effect this is, of the type discussed above
on I 1); HS 489, KS 2.88 (quoting a 'Law of Servius Tullius'), *TLL* 2.942.37,
Pascucci 29, de Meo 98, Skutsch on Enn. *Ann.* 93. Perhaps *ast* was so used also in
V 7.

   se fraude esto i.e. *sine* (HS 271-2); the same phrase in III 6 and modernised
in Cicero's continuation of the previous section here. It corresponds to ἄπατον
ἤμην (free from ἄτη) in the Law of Gortyn II 1, IV 17 (elsewhere in the form
ἄνατον).

CHAPTER II

ENNIUS, *EUHEMERUS*

The numeration of Vahlen is given in Roman numerals, that of M. Winiarczyk, *Euhemerus Messenius, Reliquiae* (Teubner 1991) in Arabic numerals; Winiarczyk also provides a general survey of the questions concerning this work of Ennius in *Rh. Mus.* 137 (1994), 274. All these fragments come from Book I of the *Diuinae Institutiones* of Lactantius (some of them reproduced in his *Epitome*); Winiarczyk (1994) 286, 289 discusses how Lactantius knew the work and the accuracy (clearly high, if not quite total) of his quotations. Most of the other fragments which are relevant to Ennius come from Diodorus Siculus 5-6. The most convenient and useful discussions of Euhemerus are by Jacoby, *RE* s.v. *Euemeros*, P. M. Frazer, *Ptolemaic Alexandria* (1972) 1.289 and Thraede, *RAC* s.v. Euhemerismus; see also Henrichs, *HSCP* 88 (1984), 148.

I = 51

Initio primus in terris imperium summum Caelus habuit; is id regnum una cum fratribus suis sibi instituit atque para<uit>.

II = 52

Caelo auo, quem dicit Euhemerus in Oceania mortuum et in oppido Aulacia sepultum.

III = 54

Exim Saturnus uxorem duxit Opem. Titan qui maior natu erat postulat ut ipse regnaret. ibi Vesta mater eorum et sorores Ceres atque Ops suadent Saturno uti de regno ne concedat fratri. ibi Titan, qui facie deterior esset quam Saturnus, idcirco et quod uidebat matrem atque sorores suas operam dare uti Saturnus regnaret, concessit ei ut is regnaret. itaque pactus est cum Saturno uti, si quid liberum uirile secus ei natum esset, ne quid educaret. id eius rei causa fecit uti ad suos gnatos regnum rediret. tum Saturno filius qui primus natus est, eum necauerunt. deinde

posterius nati sunt gemini, Iuppiter atque Iuno. tum Iunonem Saturno in conspectum
dedere atque Iouem clam abscondunt dantque eum Vestae educandum celantes
Saturnum. item Neptunum clam Saturno Ops parit eumque clanculum abscondit. ad
eundem modum tertio partu Ops parit geminos, Plutonem et Glaucam (Pluto Latine
est Dis pater, alii Orcum uocant). ibi filiam Glaucam Saturno ostendunt, at filium
Plutonem celant atque abscondunt. deinde Glauca parua emoritur. haec ut scripta
sunt Iouis fratrumque eius stirps atque cognatio; in hunc modum nobis ex sacra
scriptione traditum est.

ducit *Baehrens*
ne quid] ne id *Brandt*, ne *codd. aliquot*

IV = 54

      Deinde Titan postquam resciuit Saturno filios procreatos atque educatos
esse clam se, seducit secum filios suos qui Titani uocabantur, fratremque suum
Saturnum atque Opem conprehendit eosque muro circumegit et custodiam iis
apponit.

uocantur, muros *vv.ll.*

V = 56-8

      Iouem adultum, cum audisset patrem atque matrem custodiis circumsaeptos
atque in uincula coniectos, uenisse cum magna Cretensium multitudine Titanumque
ac filios eius pugna uicisse, parentes uinculis exemisse, patri regnum reddidisse
atque ita in Cretam remeasse.

      (etiam ante) Consedisse illi aquilam in capite atque ei regnum portendisse.

      Post haec deinde Saturno sortem datam ut caueret ne filius eum regno
expelleret; illum eleuandae sortis atque effugiendi periculi gratia insidiatum Ioui ut
eum necaret; Iouem cognitis insidiis regnum sibi denuo uindicasse ac fugasse
Saturnum, qui cum iactatus esset per omnes terras persequentibus armatis quos ad
eum conprehendendum uel necandum Iuppiter miserat, vix in Italia locum in quo
lateret inuenit.

VI = 62

      Deinde Pan eum deducit in montem, qui uocatur Caeli sella. postquam
ascendit, contemplatus est late terras, ibique in eo monte aram crea<ui>t Caelo,
primusque in ea ara Iuppiter sacrificauit. in eo loco suspexit in caelum quod nos
nunc nominamus, idque quod supra mundum erat, quod aether uocabatur, de sui aui
nomine caelo nomen indidit, idque Iuppiter [quod aether uoca(ba)tur] placans
primus caelum nominauit, eamque hostiam quam ibi sacrificauit totam adoleuit.

sella *Krahner*, stella *codd.*
<ei> (de sui) *repudiauit Vahlen*
v.l. caelum
[quod a. u.] *Courtney* (uocabatur *cod. unus*)

VII = 70

Ibi Iuppiter Neptuno imperium dat maris, ut insulis omnibus et quae secundum mare loca essent omnibus regnaret.

ut *edd.*, hoc est ut *uel* et *codd.*
in insulis *cod. unus*

VIII = 67

Ea tempestate Iuppiter in monte Olympo maximam partem uitae colebat et eo ad eum in ius ueniebant siquae res in controuersia erant. item siquis quid noui inuenerat quod ad uitam humanam utile esset, eo ueniebant atque Ioui ostendebant.

IX = 66

Saturnum et Opem ceterosque tunc homines humanam carnem solitos esitare; uerum primum Iouem leges hominibus moresque condentem edicto prohibuisse ne liceret eo cibo uesci.

XI = 69

Deinde Iuppiter, postquam quinquies terras circuiuit omnibusque amicis atque cognatis suis imperia diuisit reliquitque hominibus leges mores frumentaque parauit multaque alia bona fecit, immortali gloria memoriaque adfectus sempiterna monumenta sui[s] reliquit. aetate pessum acta in Creta uitam commutauit et ad deos abiit eumque Curetes filii sui curauerunt decoraueruntque eum; et sepulcrum eius est in Creta in oppido Cnosso, et dicitur Vesta hanc urbem creauisse; inque sepulcro eius est inscriptum antiquis litteris Graecis ZAN KPONOY, id est Latine Iuppiter Saturni.

sui *L. Mueller*

XII = 75

(Venus) prima artem meretriciam instituit auctorque mulieribus in Cypro fuit uti uulgo corpore quaestum facerent; quod idcirco imperauit ne sola praeter alias mulieres inpudica et uirorum adpetens uideretur.

I

initio = ἐν ἀρχῇ, a cosmological beginning, as *Genesis* 1.1 (cf. Gospel acc. to John 1.1). Protagoras wrote a work περὶ τῆς ἐν ἀρχῇ καταστάσεως.

Caelus Ennius coins the masculine to represent Οὐρανός. According to Euhemerus (49-50) Uranos became the first king of the οἰκουμένη and was the first to honour the οὐράνιοι θεοί with sacrifices, διὸ καὶ Οὐρανὸν προσαγορευθῆναι; he had two sons, Titan and Cronos (= Saturnus). As this stands it contradicts VI, but the latter cannot simply be attributed to an error of translation by Ennius (so Jacoby 957) because of (a) the strong emphasis given by Ennius and (b) Diodorus' earlier (3.56) account, that the first king of the Atlanteans was Uranus, that he was a careful observer of the stars, and that his name was then given to the sky. If we understand 'then' to mean 'much later by his grandson Zeus', it is not hard to emend Euhemerus 49 (quoted by Diodorus 6.1.8-9) to mean 'this is how the sky got its name οὐρανός' (see Winiarczyk's apparatus and T. Cole, *Democritus and the Sources of Greek Anthropology* (ed. 2, 1990) 205 n.6 referred to by Winiarczyk; one could think of other possibilities too). Bearing in mind that we do not have Diodorus' own words in Book 6 but only a summary in Eusebius, we might also suppose that Diodorus' meaning has been distorted in abbreviation. Of course this implies that Uranos was not represented by Euhemerus as thinking of the οὐράνιοι θεοί, by which he meant sky gods (see below), under that name. See K. S. Sacks, *Diodorus Siculus and the First Century* (1990) 70 n.78 and Cole 153-7. It must be added that all this is a subject of much controversy.

The ideas of this work are also in *Annales* 21 and 23-5:

> *Saturnia terra*
> *Saturno / quem Caelus genuit*
> *cum †suo† obsidio magnus Titanus premebat.*

Since the version of 25 is known only from Ennius IV (and the Sibylline Oracles, which draw on Euhemerus), O. Skutsch infers that Ennius wrote his *Euhemerus* before his Annals, which Skutsch sees as commenced about 184 B.C. In the prologue to his Annals Ennius briefly referred to doctrines which he had expounded in his philosophical works *Epicharmus* (see *FLP* 4) and *Euhemerus* (note the similar form of title).

fratribus Because of widely discrepant genealogies it is not clear who is meant by this. I think it likely that, as often, it means 'brother and sister', and that Ge and Oceanos are intended.

instituit atque parauit For this combination of near synonyms see on Cato, Speeches 163. It suggests that the beginning of the work, which is no doubt what we have here, sought a slightly higher stylistic level than the ensuing simple narrative (though note III *celant atque abscondunt* for weight at the end of a sentence, as here); similarly at the end of III *stirps atque cognatio* in an anaphoric sentence. Here unelided *atque* produces a hexameter clausula (though Ennius may well not yet have composed any hexameters), as in *Annals* 74 *atque secundam.*

II

> *auo* of Jupiter.
> *Oceania* An area of the mythical island Panchaea, like Oceanis (35), inhabited by Oceanitae (33-4); the island was described as situated in Oceanus (30, 61).
> *Aulacia* It has been suggested that this means 'Urn-city', an appropriate name for the site of a burial-urn. But there is much plausibility in *Huracia* (so Némethy), mentioned as a city of Panchaea in 35.

III

> *Opem* i.e. 'Ρέα (53), an equation found also in Plautus; *Vesta* is Hestia, the wife of Uranos (53); *Ceres* is of course Demeter. An individual *Titan* has only faint existence (Paus. 2.11.5; the brother of the sun). Empedocles 38 DK = 27 Wright = 39 Inwood as understood by Kingsley, *CQ* 45 (1995), 26 refers to the sun as Τιτάν, and in Roman poetry likewise the name is applied to the sun (first in Cicero, representing ἥέλιος in Aratus).
> *ibi...ibi* This is like the connection by successive occurrences of *is* remarked just below. For this temporal use in this work (cf. VII) and early Latin generally see Fraenkel (ref. p. 38) 50.
> *postulat...regnaret* Secondary sequence after historic present is common.
> *qui facie...idcirco* This is the style which thinks in small units; if he had so desired Ennius could have said *quod facie...esset* with no *idcirco.*
> *ei...is* Classical style would have regarded the second as superfluous, but early Latin is obsessed by clarity, and such repetition of *is* is common; see on Cato *Origines* 83 and Calpurnius Piso, and compare below *(dantque) eum, eumque,* IV *eosque,* XI *(decoraueruntque) eum.* For *isque* so used in classical prose see Cic. *Brut.* 106, *De Div.* 1.16, *De Off.* 2.82; for repeated *is* see *Bell. Afr.* 87.4, *Bell. Hisp.* 1.4, Livy 1.3.6-7, Plaut. *Poen.* 76-7, 903 etc. Despite this naive feature, this is the most syntactically complex sentence in these fragments.
> *liberum* gen. plur. For *si quid liberum* cf. HS 56; KS 1.430 quote Cic. *De Inv.* 2.122 *liberorum nihil.* The second *quid* does not suit the hypotactic way of thought, but is comprehensible if the two clauses are regarded in a more separable way.
> *suos* is so placed because of the contrast.
> *filius...eum* For this construction see on Cato *Origines* 83c.
> *necauerunt* This softens down the primitive story that Cronus devoured his children. The termination is like *curauerunt decoraueruntque* XI, but just below we have *dedere.*

deinde posterius For this pleonasm cf. V *post haec deinde* and on XII Tables 3.2.

in conspectum dedere Cf. *Ann.* 47 *nec sese dedit in conspectum.*

clam abscondunt...celantes...clam...clanculum abscondit...celant atque abscondunt Verbs of concealment tend to pleonasm (cf. Cic. *Pro Rab. Perd. Reo* 21 *inclusum atque abditum latere in occulto*, Juv. 6.237 *abditus interea latet et secretus*; Apul. *Met.* 8.5 and 16, Firm. Mat. *De Errore* 6.5 *latenter abscondere*), and for the same with *clam* see *TLL* 3.1248.10. But what we have here is deliberate reproduction of the simple style which does not shrink from verbal repetition; see on Cato *De Agr.* pr.2 and for the last item above on I. *Saturno* is probably dative depending on *parit*, since at this time the prepositional *clam* is followed by an accusative (KS 1.511, HS 282), as no doubt in *clam se* IV below. Of course one could argue that Lactantius has modernised.

partu...parit An etymological figure; see index s.v. and p. 8. For such 'cognate complements' see HS 124, KS 1.278-9, Rosén in *On Latin: Linguistic and Literary Studies in Honor of Harm Pinkster* (1996) 127 sqq., esp. 130. For Ennius' use of this figure see Jocelyn on *trag.* 6-7.

Glauce is really only the personification of the sea, ἡ γλαυκή (Hes. *Theog.* 440); it is a generic name for marine goddesses.

Pluto...uocant An explanatory addition by Ennius, cf. XI fin.; in a modern book it would be a footnote. This is comparable to *Ann.* 487 *<Graii> / Musas quas memorant, nosce<s> nos esse Camenas.*

haec...traditum est The question has been raised whether this is Ennius or Lactantius, but Laughton, *Eranos* 49 (1951), 48-9 points out that it appears in the *Epitome* (10 Winiarczyk) precisely as in the *Institutiones*, and therefore must belong to Ennius, who has added it to his original, emphasising it by the anaphora *haec...hunc*; for *stirps atque cognatio* see on I. In referring to the ἱερὰ ἀναγραφή of Euhemerus, he uses a close Latin equivalent *sacra scriptio* (taking up *scripta* in the first member), though he evidently gave his own work the title *Euhemerus, Sacra Historia* (so at least Lactantius' references suggest).

IV

This fragment shows both the Greek form *Titan* (as in III) and the Latin *Titanus* (as in IV and *Ann* 25, quoted under I; see Skutsch ad loc.).

deinde...postquam Cf. XI, Plaut. *MG* 124 quoted on p. 154, etc.

circumegit eos muro There is no good parallel to this construction until late Latin, but *circumduco* is so used.

V

56 and 58, which are consecutive in Lactantius, are introduced by him with *reliqua historia sic contexitur*, which indicates that we do not here have verbal quotation (as of course the accus. and infin. construction would anyway show); see

Laughton 46. 57 (quoted elsewhere) is introduced by *Sacra Historia...testatur*. The same applies to IX, introduced by *quamquam scriptum sit in Historia Sacra*. However, clear traces of Ennian style survive, e.g. the frequency of *atque*.

custodiis...coniectos in effect chiastically reverses the end of IV, so that it looks like what is unscientifically called a *hysteron proteron* (cf. p. 5).

atque ita HS 514 mean to quote Norden *AT* 376 n.2, who adduces parallels from the narratives of the annalists and also compares καὶ οὕτως twice in the myth in Plato's *Protagoras* 320c - 323a.

ante Before the war with the Titans; the word is part of Lactantius' summary of the events. Cf. Aglaosthenes 499 F 2 Jacoby.

post haec deinde An Ennian trace, cf. on III.

sortem 'oracular response'.

iactatus...terras Was Vergil thinking of this when he wrote *et terris iactatus* in *Aen.* 1.3 in reference to another civilising immigrant to Latium? Note also Ovid *Tristia* 3.2.15 *terris* (altered without warrant by Hall) *iactabar et undis*.

locum in quo lateret i.e. Latium; the legend of Saturn's reign there is widespread. The implied etymology of Latium must be an addition by Ennius (cf. Annals 21-4 quoted on I); Euhemerus himself must have interpreted the traditional legend of the casting of Cronos into Tartarus as flight to the West (55 specifies Sicily rather than Italy). See R. J. Müller, *Hermes* 121 (1993), 290. We therefore have here a nationalistic adjustment by Ennius.

VI

sella is the Οὐρανοῦ δίφρος of 50.

contemplatus...terras The Devil had precedent for the Temptation of Christ (Matthew 4.8 = Luke 4.5). The notion of looking down from a height on humanity is found in Plato *Soph.* 216c. It was much used in Cynic literature and was probably popularised by Menippus; see Varro *Sat. Men.* 117 and often in Lucian (*Piscator* 15 sqq., *Icaromenippus* 11 and 16, *Charon* 2 sqq.).

ibique in eo monte A type of pleonasm common in early Latin; see KS 2.574. In principle XI *in Creta in oppido Cnosso* is similar; cf. Hache 28, 56. Note also VIII *eo ad eum*. In general see Bannier, *Rh. Mus.* 69 (1914), 512, though his collection is somewhat indiscriminate.

aram crea<ui>t Caelo Cf. 61.

primusque...Iuppiter It is important to name the archegete at this point though the subject has not altered. This means that Jupiter performed the first sacrifice to be performed on this altar, not the first sacrifice ever, which would contradict 49 (see on I).

idque...indidit Brandt wished to alter to *eique*, but, though a scribe's eye could have wandered to the following *idque*, this is to impose the hypotactic style on Ennius. The construction is like that of *filius* in III; it is as if he originally had in mind to end the sentence with *caelum nominauit*. The addition of a demonstrative, as Vahlen tentatively suggested, would be usual in such cases, but is perhaps not inevitable. For the dative *caelo* in such situations see KS 1.421, HS 90-1; for *nomen indere* cf. Tragedies 99; for polyptoton in Ennius (*nomine...nomen* here) see Wills 207. In the following member the phrase which I have deleted seems intolerable, but the rest, though tautological in parts, does add something; *Iuppiter* is repeated for the same reason as above (in both cases with a *primus*). S. Mariotti, *Lezioni su Ennio* (ed. 2, 1991) 109 sees a case of author-variant here, an expedient generally to be regarded with suspicion and very unlikely in Ennius.

VII

    imperium dat maris This word-order is chosen to avoid placing a mono-syllable at the end of its clause.

    insulis The dative after *regno* seems to be found also at Cic. 2 *Verr.* 2.136, though there too Halm proposed to add *in*; one will understand it as due to the analogy of *impero*. The exact wording of this clause is uncertain, but the purport is clear. As it stands, *locis* is attracted into the relative clause to become *loca* and leaves *omnibus* behind; this is quite common with demonstratives, but rare with other adjectives (see my note on Juv. 11.85, Munro on Lucr. 1.14 and add Catull. 64.208-9, 68. 153-4, Livy 29.18.4).

VIII

    Olympo i.e. the mythical Τριφύλιος ῎Ολυμπος on Panchaea (34, 50), the *mons* of VI.

    (in ius) ueniebant sc. the local inhabitants. The notion of the fostering of inventions by a god and demonstration of them to him seems to have Egyptian roots (Isis and Osiris in Hecataeus of Abdera, 264 F 25, III A p. 215 Jacoby = Diod. Sic. 1.15.4; Thamus = Ammon and the inventor Theuth = Thot in Plato *Phaedr.* 274d). Many more of Euhemerus' ideas were derived from Egyptian lore (Jacoby 969, Frazer 1.290 and 293, 2.450 n.813); he himself wrote in Alexandria (Callim. fr. 191.10, on which see Frazer 1.292 and 2.453 n.824).

    siquis...inuenerat...ueniebant A quite natural change of number.

IX

    See on V. Again Ennian traces emerge; *soliti* is reminiscent of *Ann.* 214, *esitare* is found in Plautus, Cato (*De Agr.* 157.10), Varro *Sat. Men.* 250 (verse), and then not again until Pliny *NH*.

    For the allegation of primitive cannibalism see Festugière, *Harv. Theol. Rev.* 42 (1949), 216; its suppression is attributed also to Osiris, Uranos (Diod. 3.56.3) and Cronos (id. 5.66.4).

    ceterosque tunc homines The adverb approaches adjectival function, cf. Plaut. *Pers.* 385 *nunc hominum*; HS 171, KS 1.218.

humanam carnem The adjective is placed before its noun (contrast VIII *uitam humanam*) in order to underline the inhumanity by contrast with the preceding *homines*.

prohibuisse ne liceret For this type of pleonasm see HS 796, KS 2.569, Löfstedt *Synt* 2.182, Odelman 143, *TLL* 7.2. 1363.73.

(X = 64)

It has been firmly established by Leo *GRL* 203-4, Laughton 39, Fraenkel 56 that this fragment has been re-written by Lactantius and does not reproduce the words of Ennius (though the tricolon *diligeret augeret ornaret* looks Ennian, as Timpanaro, *RFIC* 116 (1988), 271 n.3 remarks); therefore a summary of the narrative suffices.

When Jupiter attained supremacy, he became so proud that he persuaded local rulers, whom he made his *hospites* as he traversed the earth, to set up temples to himself under the pretext that a record of this relationship could be preserved by consecrating the temples with an epithet derived from the name of each *hospes*, e.g. Jupiter Ataburius from Ataburus. Annual rituals and festivals were also so established.

XI

Wandering all over the earth and conferring of benefits is attributed by legend not only to Zeus (cf. Diod. 3.61.4) but also to Osiris (Diod. 1.20.6, Plut. *Is. et Os.* 13).

leges mores An Ennian asyndeton bimembre (on Cato *De Agr.* 2.2 and p.6). The word-order chosen in IX *leges hominibus moresque condentem*, for which see HS 693, requires a conjunction.

frumentaque parauit This is usually attributed to Demeter.

gloria memoriaque This pair is bound together by homoeoteleuton of -*ia*.

aetate pessum acta Cf. *mala* (*OLD* s.v. 1c) *aetas, aetate praecipitata* Matius in Cic. *Ad Fam.* 11.28.5.

uitam...abiit This represents the Greek term μετάστασις (e.g. Diod. Sic. 3.56.5, 61.6, 5.70.1, 72.1; for other similar terms in relation to Alexander etc. see L. R. Taylor, *The Divinity of the Roman Emperor* (1931) 25 n.61, C. Habicht, *Gottmenschentum und griech. Städte* (ed. 2, 1970) 177 n.54 and 200 n.36); *ad deos peruenisse* Cic. *De Nat. Deor.* 1.119 in relation to the doctrines of Euhemerus. This is further discussed below.

in Creta in oppido Cnosso See on VI and p. 4; Euhemerus probably wrote ἐν Κνωσσῷ τῆς Κρήτης.

Curetes...curauerunt An etymology which will only work in Latin; Ennius may have been aware of a Greek etymology from κουροτροφεῖν (Strabo 10.3.11.468 and 19.472), since the Curetes in another version were supposed to have reared the infant Zeus, but the narrative makes it very unlikely that this was in Euhemerus. It looks therefore as if Ennius introduced the etymology off his own bat. The god is the centre of attention, hence *sui* where strict grammar would call for *eius*.

    decorauerunt This verb is quite often applied to funeral honours (e.g. *CIL* 1.1837 = *CLE* 54.7); Ennius himself alludes to this in his epitaph (46 *FLP*) *nemo me lacrimis decoret*. κοσμεῖν is similarly applied (J. D. Mikalson, *Honor Thy Gods* (1991) 123). Classical style would regard the following *eum* as superfluous.

    sepulcrum eius est...inque sepulcro eius For this naive method of connection Norden *AT* 376 n.2 quotes parallels from the annalists, e.g. Quadrigarius 57 *consul. ei consuli*; one may compare also e.g. Plaut. *Merc.* 233-4 *simiae...ea simia.* Fankhänel 83 lists instances in Cato *De Agr.*, e.g. 1.4. Ennius is probably reproducing the λέξις εἰρομένη type of connection exemplified by τὸν γάμον...τῷ γάμῳ in Pherecydes (see below). For this 'strung-together' style see p. 7. For the tomb of Zeus cf. Callim. *Hymn to Zeus* 8 and fr. 202.16, Dionysius Scyt. 31 ap. Diod. 3.61.2 and many others subsequent to Ennius. Hypotactic style would have said *quam urbem* instead of *et...hanc urbem*, but one will note the abundance of *et* and *-que* linking clauses in this fragment.

    antiquis litteris A bogus attempt to shore up credibility; cf. Plut. *De Genio Socr.* 5.577f, 7.578f (a script resembling hieroglyphs at the tomb of Alcmena) and the *litterae Punicae* in which the narrative of Dictys is alleged (praef.) to have been written.

    ZAN The Doric form, reproduced by Callim. fr. 191.10 and taken from here by Schol. Bern. Lucan 8.872 (including the phrase *id est Iuppiter Saturni*, deleted by Usener in the scholiast; it is an addition by Ennius, cf. IV).

XII

    Though this is in direct speech, it is introduced by *ut in historia sacra continetur* and is probably not a verbal quotation (Laughton 46).

    sola praeter alias Pleonastic; cf. *TLL* 10.2.993.75. This is a distinctly unfavourable view of Venus.

    Euhemerus of Messene flourished around 300 B.C., and wrote a work Ἱερὰ Ἀναγραφή, which offered a curious blend of travel-novel, political Utopia, and theological tract with contemporary political relevance. It represented the author as travelling to the south-eastern end of the world and discovering in Ocean an island Panchaea. A temple inscription recorded the deeds of its first kings, Uranos Cronos and Zeus, who so impressed their subjects (and others) that they came to be regarded as gods. This should be considered not just as a rationalising treatise about the origins of religion, though his doctrines on a hasty reading were as liable to misrepresentation as those of Epicurus, and are condemned by many as 'godless'. It also possessed a topical point, in that the roaming of Zeus all over the earth, his creation of local cults of himself and recognition of his translation to the gods after his death all carried strong overtones of Alexander.

Because of the phrase *ad deos abiit* (XI) some clarification of the theology of Euhemerus must be attempted. Diodorus (25, 8) says that the ancients recognised two types of gods, the first consisting of the heavenly bodies, the winds etc. (these are presumably the οὐράνιοι θεοί (49, Diodorus just below) whom, according to Euhemerus, Uranos worshipped), the second of ἐπίγειοι θεοί, men who because of their services to humanity were recognised as gods after their death, such as Heracles (who, it should be remembered, was regarded as an ancestor of Alexander) and Dionysus (whose legendary journey to India was often assimilated to that of Alexander and with whom Alexander was linked in his Athenian cult). In 25 and 8 Diodorus alludes to Euhemerus, but not in such a way as to establish that any of the substance is due to him (we also have to note that we here have only the summary of Diodorus in Eusebius, not Diodorus' own words). It is likely that the terminology is Diodorus' own (in 1.13.1 he draws the distinction between οὐράνιοι and ἐπίγειοι θεοί calling it Egyptian, which in such contexts often means pseudo-Egyptian) and that Euhemerus did not use the term οὐράνιοι θεοί. Nevertheless in substance the ideas of Euhemerus cannot have been very different. Euhemerus apparently took these generally accepted conceptions farther and declared the same to be true of all the recognised gods, including Zeus himself. Diodorus 25 says only that such gods on their death won immortal honour and glory, but Ennius' phrase *ad deos abiit* (which in view of Cicero's corroboration, noted ad loc., it is hard to dismiss as just a piece of carelessness) seems to imply that Euhemerus did actually think of them as continuing an existence among the heavenly gods. It should be added that this is a much disputed point, but it must be remarked that those who dispute it all ignore the phrase of Ennius. If Euhemerus hinted this belief in a phrase as unobtrusive as that in Ennius, it could easily have been overlooked in the rush to revile him as ἄθεος (which does not mean the same as 'atheistic').

If we could better fix the exact publication date of Euhemerus, we might be able to discern whether his work had topical reference not only to Alexander but also to the first stirrings of ruler-cult among the Diadochi; Jacoby 963-4 remarks that the inscription recording the deeds of Zeus etc. is reminiscent of those set up by Hellenistic kings to commemorate their achievements. To Ennius too his respect for the elder Scipio may have attracted his interest to this work; he wrote an epigram concerning him (fr. 44 *FLP*, where see my notes), ending with Scipio's words

si fas endo plagas caelestum ascendere cuiquam est,
mi soli caeli maxima porta patet,

and may well have believed in the divine descent of Scipio (Livy 26.19.6-8, with comparison to Alexander; see further Winiarczyk (1994) 277).

The style of the *Euhemerus* of Ennius, which has enormous significance as the first work of literary prose produced at Rome, has received illuminating discussions from Norden *AT* 374 and Fraenkel, *Eranos* 49 (1951), 50 (referred to by this numeration) = *KB* 2.53. Evaluation would be easier if we knew anything about the style of Euhemerus himself, but only one fragment (27) of any length has a chance of preserving his wording, and Winiarczyk thinks that even this does not. As it stands that is a syntactically complex and well-organised period (with a poetical quotation), but it has to remain out of the reckoning.

Ennius' translation is written in a very simple narrative style, but it has touches which run counter to any suggestion that this was the only way Ennius knew how to write prose; the near-synonym pair at the end of I and Ennius' own palpable addition to Euhemerus at the end of III show an ability to elevate the style had Ennius so wished. It is therefore a reasonable hypothesis that Ennius was imitating the style adopted by Euhemerus himself, that of artless narrative which by its very lack of art suggests veracity (quite falsely, of course). The position which Ennius holds at Rome was held in Greece by Pherecydes of Syrus (7 Diels-Kranz), regarded as the first writer of literary prose; his subject-matter is comparable to that of Ennius, and it is worth quoting his longest fragment (2 DK = 68-9 Schibli) to illustrate some features of the style.

> col. 1 αὐ>τῷ ποιοῦσιν τὰ οἰκία πολλά τε καὶ μεγάλα. ἐπεὶ δὲ ταῦτα ἐξετέλεσαν πάντα καὶ χρήματα καὶ θεράποντας καὶ θεραπαίνας καὶ τἆλλα ὅσα δεῖ πάντα, ἐπεὶ δὴ πάντα ἕτοιμα γίγνεται, τὸν γάμον ποιεῦσιν. κἀπειδὴ τρίτη ἡμέρη γίγνεται τῷ γάμῳ, τότε Ζὰς ποιεῖ φᾶρος μέγα τε καὶ καλὸν καὶ ἐν αὐτῷ ποικίλλει Γῆν καὶ Ὠγηνὸν καὶ τὰ Ὠγηνοῦ δώματα...
>
> col. 2 βουλόμενος> γὰρ σέο τοὺς γάμους εἶναι τούτῳ σε τιμῶ. σὺ δέ μοι χαῖρέ τε καὶ σύνισθι. ταῦτά φασιν ἀνακαλυπτήρια πρῶτον γενέσθαι· ἐκ τούτου δὲ ὁ νόμος ἐγένετο καὶ θεοῖσι καὶ ἀνθρώποισιν. ἡ δέ μι<ν ἀμείβε>ται δεξαμ<ένη εὖ τὸ φᾶ>ρος...

(Note that this style makes comparatively little use of participles, and therefore <ἐγὼ μέν νυν, βούλομαι >, as E. Schulz suggested, would be a better supplement at the beginning of col. 2).

Here the sentences are made up of brief separate members; the short range of thought entails repetition and recapitulation. In the second sentence the writer feels obliged to resume and summarise the initial temporal clause, and πάντα is repeated to bind the thought together and placed in prominent positions. The connections are nearly all either by temporal conjunctions and adverbs or by personal or demonstrative pronouns. γὰρ is the only 'logical' connective, and that is necessitated by the parenthesis as restored by Schulz. However the author is capable of an anaphora ταῦτα... ἐκ τούτου, which in form resembles the last sentence of Ennius III. There is a fine discussion of this type of style in Dover 72-7.

The narrative of Ennius also is dominated by temporal sequence (cf. on Cato *De Agr.* 157.9 and p. 7), marked out by adverbs and conjunctions such as *postquam*, some of them pleonastic (III, V); *itaque* III too in effect can be similarly classified (apart from this, no 'logical' connective appears; cf. on Cato *De Agr.* pr. 1, 157.7). Fraenkel 50 draws particular attention to the occurrences of temporal *ibi*, a usage common in early Latin. For similar temporal connection in the verse of Ennius see G. Williams, *Tradition and Originality in Roman Poetry* (1968) 690. We also note connection by means of demonstrative pronouns, which is characteristic of this style and for long appears as a feature of the narrative technique of early Latin historians (so in Cato *Origines* 83b, Calpurnius Piso fr. 27, both compared by Laughton 37; see p. 7). Cic. *De Or.* 2.51-3 relates the style of early Roman historians (Cato and Piso) to that of the early Greek logographers, including Pherecydes. However, Ennius is clearly more complex syntactically than the specimen from Pherecydes (see on III).

CHAPTER III

M. PORCIUS CATO

General Bibliography
H. Jordan, *M. Catonis praeter librum de re rustica quae extant* (1860); R. Till, *Die Sprache Catos* (Philol. suppl. 28.2, 1935) = *La Lingua di Catone* (1968), translated with added notes by C. de Meo (page-references are given to both in the above order); A. E. Astin, *Cato the Censor* (1978).

    Cato was born in Tusculum in 234 and died in 149; his famous censorship was in 184. His family owned a moderate-sized estate on which, according to his own account, he himself performed manual work until the Hannibalic war propelled him into a military and then a political career, in which he provoked many animosities; he was prosecuted (and acquitted) 44 times. All this naturally required the composition of many speeches; fragments of about 80 survive, but Cicero knew 150 (*Brut.* 65). The earliest dates from 195. The total of direct quotation from earlier Roman oratory surviving to us consists of three words, and the only significant orator earlier than Cato's generation of whom any record was preserved was Appius Claudius Caecus, whose speech opposing peace with Pyrrhus in 280 was still read by Cicero (*Brut.* 61 etc.). Cato transcribed two of his own speeches into the *Origines*, one of them (106 Peter = VII.1 Chassignet = 196-9 Malcovati = 150-4 Sblendorio Cugusi) dating from the year of his death. This speech came in the seventh and final book; he seems to have been engaged on Book 2 or 3 in 168 (49 P = II.16 Ch).
    In the writing of history he was even more of a pioneer than in oratory; Fabius Pictor had set the precedent for writing in this genre in Greek, and all historians who may be earlier than Cato had followed his lead. It is a fact of enormous significance that Cato had enough faith in the Latin language to employ it in the composition of this recognised literary genre. The condition of his *De Agricultura* has aroused much controversy. I agree with those who think that it was composed over a long period of time; Cato seems to have made additions as they occurred to him, and there are doublets because he did not delete earlier versions

when he added later ones. The selection included in this book has been made in part so that a notion of the compositional problems can be gained. The preface, written in a literary style quite unlike the curt, factual presentation of most of the rest of the work, clearly shows an intention to publish, but Cato evidently had not revised and rearranged his compilation at his death (taken at face value Pliny *NH* 14.45 might imply that he was still working at it at the end of his life, but should not be pressed), so that some parts of it are little more than rough notes, and overall plan and structure are lacking. Despite this, the work has particular importance to us as the one continuous prose text surviving from the second century. His other prose works apart from those mentioned do not concern us here, since we know them only from brief fragments.

In analysing the style of Cato, the first step is to substitute the plural 'styles', since Cato clearly had an acute sense of generic distinctions; this is shown palpably in his use of copulative conjunctions and third person plural perfect indicative active terminations (see on *Origines* 83, Speeches 163 and Leo *GRL* 286). One may remark also the accumulation of synonyms or near synonyms in Speeches 163, *Origines* 83b and the rhetorically coloured preface to the *De Agr.* 2-3 (see the notes in those places and p. 8, also Haffter 77). Features which are a general characteristic of early Latin are discussed in the introduction; here we have to consider those which characterise Cato individually, and stylistic differences within his writings beyond those just mentioned.

Prominent among such features is that in his Speeches, instead of rising to a weighty closure, he may end the sentence with a shorter word (*augescere atque crescere* 163) or colon (*dum uiuent* 58); one particular manifestation of this tendency is his fondness for falling tricola (58, 59, 173d; though 58-9 also show rising tricola). This is what Gellius 6.3.53 means when, talking about the Pro Rodiensibus, he has to admit lack of rhythm (*numerus*). Cato's motive seems to have been partly to jolt the listener into attentiveness by his choppy rhythms, partly to project himself as a blunt, straightforward character interested only in substance, not smooth verbal artifice (following his own precept *rem tene, uerba sequentur*), and therefore as trustworthy. A similar effect is imparted by the general abruptness of the style; logical connectives are largely absent (see on Speeches 164 and index, Connection), and in the carefully written preface to the *De Agr.* putting the salient idea first is given precedence over connection (see on § 1). This image would be assisted by his tenacious, though not invariable (see on Speeches 163-4), avoidance of variation in vocabulary (see on *De Agr.* pr.2) or phraseology (*De Agr.* 2.1), even permitting change of meaning in the repeated words (see on *De Agr.* pr.1).

The Speeches in particular raise the question whether he was consciously availing himself of the resources of systematised Greek rhetorical doctrine or, as Leo (*GRL* 286) put it, was employing rhetorical devices in the same sense as this could be said of Homer. It is hard to find a way of answering this objectively, but it is not probable that Cato wrote on rhetoric without a degree of technical knowledge (Quintil 3.1.19 implies that this work was more than a tirade against rhetoric), and the clear sense of literary propriety remarked above in Cato also makes me favour the former answer. This sense was there illustrated generically, but it distinguishes not only one genre of Cato's writings from another, but also different parts within the *De Agr.* Some of this work consists merely of lists, and we also read such things as specimen contracts; here there is no stylistic discretion left to the author. But the notes will show how markedly the style becomes more elevated and rhetorical in such passages as the preface and the famous 'hymn to the cabbage' (157) than in the passages which merely give precepts, where anything like rhetoric is very rare (but see on 2.7). The same difference is apparent when *Origines* 83 passes from narrative to sententious reflection.

The above discussion has been as far as possible concentrated on those areas of Cato's writings where conscious stylization is at work; much of the pithy formulation of precepts in the *De Agr.* does not lend itself to such analysis, and features deserving comment in those parts are mostly remarked in the general introduction.

(a) *De Agricultura*

praef.

Est<o> interdum praestare mercaturis rem quaerere, nisi tam periculosum sit, et item fenerari, si tam honestum sit. maiores nostri sic habuerunt, et ita in legibus posiuerunt: furem dupli condemnari, feneratorem quadrupli. quanto peiorem ciuem existimarint feneratorem quam furem, hinc licet existimare. (2) et uirum bonum quom laudabant, ita laudabant, bonum agricolam bonumque colonum. (3) amplissime laudari existimabatur qui ita laudabatur. mercatorem autem strenuum studiosumque rei quaerendae existimo, uerum, ut supra dixi, periculosum et calamitosum. (4) at ex agricolis et uiri fortissimi et milites strenuissimi gignuntur, maximeque pius quaestus stabilissimusque consequitur minimeque inuidiosus, minimeque male cogitantes sunt qui in eo studio occupati sunt. nunc, ut ad rem redeam, quod promisi institutum, principium hoc erit.

1 est<o> *Birt (BPW 1915.923)*

1

praedium quom parare cogitabis, sic in animo habeto, uti ne cupide emas neue opera tua parcas uisere et ne satis habeas semel circumire. quotiens ibis, totiens magis placebit quod bonum erit. (2) uicini quo pacto niteant, id animum aduertito: in bona regione bene nitere oportebit. et uti eo introeas et circumspicias, uti inde exire possis; uti bonum caelum habeat, ne calamitosum siet; solo bono, sua uirtute ualeat.

(3) si poteris, sub radice montis siet, in meridiem spectet, loco salubri; operariorum copia siet bonumque aquarium; oppidum ualidum prope siet [si] aut mare aut amnis qua naues ambulant, aut uia bona celebrisque. (4) siet in iis agris qui non saepe dominos mutant: qui in iis agris praedia uendiderint, eos pigeat uendidisse. uti bene aedificatum siet. caueto alienam disciplinam temere contemnas. de domino bono colono bonoque aedificatore melius emetur. ad uillam cum uenies, uideto uasa torcula et dolia multane sient: (5) ubi non erunt, scito pro ratione fructum esse. [instrumenti ne magni siet, loco bono siet.] uideto quam minimi instrumenti sumptuosusque ager ne siet. (6) scito idem agrum quod hominem; quamuis quaestuosus siet, si sumptuosus erit, relinqui non multum. (7) praedium quod primum siet si me rogabis, sic dicam: de omnibus agris optimo <quo>que loco [iugera agri centum] uinea est prima, [uel] si uino <bono et> multo est; secundo loco hortus inriguus; tertio salictum; quarto oletum; quinto pratum; sexto campus frumentarius; septimo silua caedua; octauo arbustum; nono glandaria silua.

1 operae *laudat Plin. NH 18.26*
2 circumspicias et *Eussner (Philol. Anz. 14 (1884), 305)*
  solum *Plin. NH 18.28, unde* solum bonum *Merula (1472)*
3 [si] aut *Iucundus (1514)*, et *laudat Gell. 10.26.8*
4 eos *Gronovius ap. Schneider (1794)*, quos *codd.*
5 [instrumenti ne magni siet, loco bono siet] *Pontedera (1740)*
7 optimo <quo>que *Flach 185 tacite*, optimoque *codd.*
  [iugera agri centum] *Goujard 122 n.16 ut ex titulo capitis xi illatum*
  <bono et> *Pontedera ex Varr. RR 1.7.9*

2

pater familias, ubi ad uillam uenit, ubi larem familiarem salutauit, fundum eodem die, si potest, circumeat; si non eodem die, at postridie. ubi cognouit quo modo fundus cultus siet operaque quae facta infectaque sient, postridie eius diei uilicum uocet, roget quid operis siet factum, quid restet, satisne temperi opera sient confecta, possitne quae reliqua sient conficere, et quid factum uini frumenti aliarumque rerum omnium. (2) ubi ea cognouit, rationem inire oportet operarum, dierum. si ei opus non apparet, dicit uilicus sedolo se fecisse, seruos non ualuisse, tempestates malas fuisse, seruos aufugisse, opus publicum fecisse, ubi eas aliasque causas multas dixit, ad rationem operum operarumque uilicum reuoca; (3) cum tempestates pluuiae fuerint, quae opera per imbrem fieri potuerint: dolia lauari picari, uillam purgari, frumentum transferri, stercus foras efferri, stercilinum fieri, semen purgari, funes sarciri, nouos fieri, centones cuculiones familiam oportuisse sibi sarcire; (4) per ferias potuisse fossas ueteres tergeri, uiam publicam muniri, uepres recidi, hortum fodiri, pratum purgari, uirgas uinciri, spinas eruncari, expinsi far, munditias fieri; cum serui aegrotarint, cibaria tanta dari non oportuisse. (5) ubi <ea> cognita aequo animo sint, quae reliqua opera sint curare uti perficiantur; rationes putare argentariam, frumentariam, pabuli causa quae parata sunt; rationem uinariam, oleariam, quid uenierit, quid exactum siet, quid reliquum siet, quid siet quod ueneat; quae satis accipiunda sint, satis accipiantur; (6) reliqua quae sint uti compareant; siquid desit in annum uti paretur; quae supersint ut ueneant; quae opus sint locato locentur; quae opera fieri uelit et quae locari uelit uti imperet et ea scripta relinquat. pecus consideret. (7) auctionem uti faciat; uendat oleum si pretium habeat; uinum, frumentum quod supersit uendat; boues uetulos. armenta reicula, oues reiculas, lanam, pelles, plostrum uetus, ferramenta uetera, seruum senem, seruum morbosum, et siquid aliud supersit uendat. patrem familias uendacem, non emacem esse oportet.

1 si non eo die *v.l.*
    operaque quae *Iucundus*, opera quaeque *codd.*
4 runcari *v.l.*
5 <ea> *Keil*
    (animo) sunt *olim Keil*
7 re(i)icula...re(i)iculas *Merula*, delicula...deliculas *codd.*

3

Prima adulescentia patrem familiae agrum conserere studere oportet. aedificare diu cogitare oportet, conserere cogitare non oportet, sed facere oportet. ubi aetas accessit ad annos xxxui, tum aedificare oportet, si agrum consitum habeas. ita aedifices ne uilla fundum quaerat <neue fundus uillam>. (2) patrem familiae uillam rusticam bene aedificatam habere expedit, cellam oleariam uinariam, dolia multa, uti lubeat caritatem expectare; et rei et uirtuti et gloriae erit. torcularia bona habere oportet, ut opus bene effici possit. olea ubi lecta siet, oleum fiat continuo, ne corrumpatur. cogitato quotannis tempestates magnas uenire et oleam deicere solere. (3) si cito sustuleris et uasa parata erunt, damni nihil erit ex tempestate et oleum uiridius et melius fiet. (4) si in terra et tabulato olea nimium diu erit, putescet, oleum fetidum fiet; ex quauis olea oleum [uiridius et] bonum fieri potest si temperi facies...

1 <neue fundus uillam> *Iucundus ex Colum. 1.4.8 (ubi fructus codd. primarii; v. Kronasser, WS 79 (1966), 302);* ne<ue fundus uillam neue> uilla *H. Sauppe, Ausg. Schr. (1896) 820 ex Plin. NH 18.32.*
4 [uiridius et] *Keil*

4

bubilia bona, bonas praesepis faliscas clatratas, clatros interesse oportet pede; si ita feceris, pabulum boues non eicient. uillam urbanam pro copia aedificato. in bono praedio si bene aedificaueris, bene posiueris, ruri si recte habitaueris, libentius et saepius uenies, fundus melior erit, minus peccabitur, fructi plus capies: frons occipitio prior est. uicinis bonus esto, familiam ne siueris peccare. si te libenter uicinitas uidebit, facilius tua uendes, operas facilius locabis, operarios facilius conduces; si aedificabis, operis iumentis materie adiuuabunt; si quid (bona salute) usu uenerit, benigne defendent.

fundus melius *v.l., unde* fundo melius *Popma (1601)*
usu *Courtney,* usus *codd.*

5

haec erunt uilici officia. disciplina bona utatur. feriae seruentur. alieno manum abstineat, sua seruet diligenter. litibus familia supersedeat; si quis quid deliquerit, pro noxa bono modo uindicet. (2) familiae male ne sit, ne algeat, ne esuriat; opere bene exerceat, facilius malo et alieno prohibebit. uilicus si nolet male facere, non faciet. si passus erit, dominus impune ne sinat esse. pro beneficio gratiam referat, ut aliis recte facere libeat. uilicus ne sit ambulator, sobrius siet semper, ad cenam nequo eat. familiam exerceat; consideret quae dominus imperauerit fiant. ne plus censeat sapere se quam dominum. (3) amicos domini, eos habeat sibi amicos. cui iussus siet auscultet. rem diuinam nisi Compitalibus in compito aut in foco ne faciat iniussu domini. credat nemini; quod dominus crediderit exigat. satui semen, cibaria, far, uinum, oleum mutuum dederit nemini. duas aut tres familias habeat unde utenda roget et quibus det, praeterea nemini. rationem cum domino crebro putet. (4) operarium, mercenarium politorem diutius eundem ne habeat die. ne quid emisse uelit insciente domino, neu quid dominum celauisse uelit. parasitum ne quem habeat. haruspicem, augurem, hariolum, Chaldaeum ne quem consuluisse uelit. segetem ne defrudet, nam id infelix est. opus rusticum omne curet uti sciat facere, et id faciat saepe, dum ne lassus fiat; (5) si fecerit, scibit in mente familiae quid sit, et illi animo aequiore facient. si hoc faciet, minus libebit ambulare et ualebit rectius et dormibit libentius. primus cubitu surgat, postremus cubitum eat. prius uillam uideat clausa uti siet et uti suo quisque loco cubet et uti iumenta pabulum habeant...

1 familiae *v.l.*
2 [familiam exerceat] *Popma*
3 *post* domini *interpunxit Richter 101 coll. 143.1, post* faciat *ceteri*
4 defruget *codd. Plin. NH 18.200*

141

agrum lustrare sic oportet: impera suouitaurilia circumagi: 'cum diuis uolentibus quodque bene eueniat, mando tibi, Mani, uti [illace suouitaurilia] fundum agrum terramque meam, quota ex parte siue circumagi <uelis illaec suouitaurilia> siue circumagenda censeas, uti cures lustrare'. (2) Ianum Iouemque uino praefamino, sic dicito:
'Mars pater, te precor quaesoque
    uti sies uolens propitius

mihi domo familiaeque nostrae;
quoius rei ergo
    agrum terram fundumque meum
    suouitaurilia circumagi iussi;
uti tu morbos uisos inuisosque
    uiduertatem uastitudinemque calamitates intemperiasque
    prohibessis defendas auerruncesque;
utique tu fruges frumenta uineta uirgultaque
    grandire beneque euenire siris,
(3) pastores pecuaque salua seruassis
    duisque bonam salutem ualetudinemque
    mihi domo familiaeque nostrae.
harumce rerum ergo
    fundi terrae agrique mei
    lustrandi lustrique faciendi ergo,
    sicuti dixi,
macte hisce suouitaurilibus lactentibus immolandis esto.
Mars pater, eiusdem rei ergo
    macte hisce suouitaurilibus lactentibus esto'.
(4) item [esto item] cultro facito struem et fertum uti adsiet, inde obmoueto. ubi porcum immolabis, agnum uitulumque, sic oportet: 'eiusque rei ergo macte suouitaurilibus immolandis esto'. nominare uetat porcum neque agnum uitulumque. si minus in omnis litabit, sic uerba concipito: 'Mars pater, siquid tibi [in] illisce suouitaurilibus lactentibus neque satisfactum est, te hisce suouitaurilibus piaculo'. si <in> uno duobusue dubitabit, sic uerba concipito: 'Mars pater, quod tibi illoc porco neque satisfactum est, te hoc porco piaculo'.

1 *sic dubitanter constituit Courtney*
4 eius[que] *(cf. 139) uel* eiusdem *(cf. supra 3 fin., 134.3) Keil*
   (uetat) porcum *Gesner (1735)*, (uetat) Martem *codd.*
   omnibus *V. Pisani, Testi latini arcaici (1950) 54 dubitanter*
   [in] *Merula; infra* <in> *Keil*

142

uilici officia quae sunt, †quae domino praeceps†, ea omnia quae in fundo fieri oportet quaeque emi pararique oportet, quomodoque cibaria, uestimenta familiae dari oportet, eadem uti curet faciatque moneo dominoque dicto audiens sit. hoc amplius, quomodo uilicam uti oportet et quomodo eae imperari oportet, uti aduentu domini quae opus sunt parentur curenturque diligenter.

143

uilicae quae sunt officia curato faciat. si eam tibi dederit dominus uxorem, ea esto contentus. ea te metuat facito. ne nimium luxuriosa siet. uicinas aliasque mulieres quam minimum utatur neue domum neue ad sese recipiat. ad cenam nequo eat neue ambulatrix siet. rem diuinam ni faciat neue mandet qui pro ea faciat iniussu domini aut dominae; scito dominum pro tota familia rem diuinam facere. (2) munda siet; uillam conuersam mundeque habeat; focum purum circumuersum cotidie, prius quam cubitum eat, habeat. Kal. Idibus Nonis festus dies cum erit, coronam in focum indat, per eosdemque dies lari familiari pro copia supplicet. cibum tibi et familiae curet uti coctum habeat...

2 *v.l.* eos denique

156

de brassica, quod concoquit. brassica est quae omnibus holeribus antistat. eam esto uel coctam uel crudam. crudam si edes, in acetum intinguito: mirifice concoquit, aluum bonam facit, lotiumque ad omnes res salubre est. si uoles in conuiuio multum bibere cenareque libenter, ante cenam esto crudam quantum uoles ex aceto, et item, ubi cenaueris, comesto aliqua V folia: reddet te quasi nihil ederis, bibesque quantum uoles...(5) uerum quibus tormina molesta erunt, brassicam in aqua macerare oportet; ubi macerata erit, coicito in aquam calidam, coquito usque donec commadebit bene, aquam defundito. postea salem addito et cumini paululum et pollinem polentae eodem addito et oleum. (6) postea feruefacito, infundito in catinum uti frigescat; eo interito quod uolet cibi; postea edit; sed si poterit solam brassicam esse, edit. et si sine febre erit, dato uini atri duri aquatum bibat quam minimum; si febris erit, aquam. id facito cotidie mane; nolito multum dare, ne pertaedescat, uti porro possit libenter esse. ad eundem modum uiro et mulieri et puero dato...

157

De brassica Pythagorea, quid in ea boni sit salubritatisque. principium te cognoscere oportet quae genera brassicae sint et cuius modi naturam habeant. omnia ad salutem temperat commoetatque sese semper, cum calore <frigida>, arido simul umida et dulci [et] amara et acris, [sed] quae uoca<n>tur septem bona in commixturam; natura omnia haec habet brassica...(2)...et item est tertia, quae lenis uocatur, minutis caulibus, tenera, et acerrima omnium est istarum, tenui suco uehementissima. et primum scito, de omnibus brassicis nulla est illius modi medicamento. (3) ad omnia uulnera tumores eam contritam imponito. haec omnia ulcera purgabit sanaque faciet sine dolore. eadem tumida concoquit, eadem erumpit, eadem uulnera putida canceresque purgabit sanosque faciet, quod <aliud> medicamentum facere non potest...(7) et si bilis atra est et si lienes turgent et si cor dolet et si iecur aut pulmones aut praecordia, uno uerbo omnia sana faciet [et] intro quae dolitabunt (eodem silpium inradito, bonum est). nam uenae omnes ubi sufflatae sunt ex cibo, non possunt perspirare in toto corpore; inde aliqui morbus nascitur. ubi ex multo cibo aluus non it, pro portione brassica si uteris, id ut te moneo, nihil istorum usu ueniet [morbis]. uerum morbum articularium nulla res tam purgat quam brassica cruda, si edes concisam et rutam et coriandrum concisam siccam et sirpicium inrasum, et brassica ex aceto oxymeli et sale sparsa. (8) haec si uteris, omnis articulos poteris experiri. nullus sumptus est, et si sumptus esset, tamen ualetudinis causa †experirus†. hanc oportet mane ieiunum esse. <ins>omnis uel siquis est seniosus, hac eadem curatione sanum facies. uerum assam brassicam et unctam caldam, salis paulum dato homini ieiuno. quam plurimum edet, tam citissime sanus fiet ex morbo. (9) tormina quibus molesta erunt, sic facito. brassicam macerato bene, postea in aulam coicito, deferuefacito bene. ubi cocta erit bene, aquam defundito. eo addito oleum bene et salis paululum et cuminum et pollinem polentae. postea ferue bene facito. ubi feruerit, in catinum indito. dato edit, si poterit, sine pane; si non, dato panem purum ibidem madefaciat. et si febrim non habebit, dato uinum atrum bibat; cito sanus fiet. (10) et hoc: siquando usus uenerit, qui debilis erit, haec res sanum facere potest: brassicam edit ita uti s(upra) s(criptum) e(st). et hoc amplius: lotium conseruato eius qui brassicam essitarit, id calfacito, eo hominem demittito, cito sanum facies hac cura; expertum hoc est. item pueros pusillos si laues eo lotio, numquam debiles fient. et quibus oculi parum clari sunt, eo lotio inunguito, plus uidebunt. si caput aut ceruices dolent, eo lotio caldo lauito, desinent dolere. (11) et si mulier eo lotio locos fouebit, numquam miseri fient. et fouere sic oportet: ubi in scutra feruefeceris, sub sellam supponito pertusam. eo mulier adsidat, operito, circum uestimenta eam dato...

1 principio *Merula*
   <frigida>...[sed] *sic Courtney dubitanter*; amaro *codd.*
   commixtura *Keil*
3 <aliud> *edd. vett., cf. 5 infra*
7 id ut te] ita uti *Keil*
   [morbis] *Keil*
8 uterus *cod. uetustissimus*
   fort. experir<i meli>us
   <ins>omnis *Keil ; fort.* siquis est <ins>omnis uel
10 facies *Iucundus (cf. 157.8, 13),* -et *codd. (tum* haec *Keil)*
   item *ed. pr.,* idem *codd.*
   dolore *v.l.*
11 miseri] unseri *uel sim. codd. complures*; menses seri *Pianezzola (RFIC 103 (1975), 295)*

Commentary

Bibliography: H. Keil, *Commentarius in Catonis De Agri Cultura Librum* (1894); E. Brehaut, *Cato the Censor on Farming* (1933); S. Boscherini, *Lingua e scienza greca nel 'De agri cultura' di Catone* (1970); R. Goujard, *Caton, de l'Agriculture* (1975); W. Richter, *Gegenständliches Denken archaisches Ordnen* (1978); D. Flach, *Römische Agrargeschichte* (1990).

praef.

This preface is discussed by Leeman 22-3, von Albrecht 1, Kappelmacher, *WS* 43 (1922-3), 168. Leeman indicated that the mentions of merchant and money-lender are placed chiastically (see p. 6), but the arrangement is more complex than that: merchant (A), danger (a), money-lender and discredit (B) (b), farmer (C), merchant (A), danger (a), farmer (C). Leeman also draws attention to the categories of safety and honour (*honestum, pius*), which are used in deliberative oratory as criteria.

The preface has a strong Greek flavour. First, it resembles Xen. *Oec.* 5.1, where Socrates notes οἴκου αὔξησις and σωμάτων ἄσκησις as attractions of farming. Second, the comparison of βιοί is a traditional topic of Greek moralising and philosophy, though to Cato only varieties of the βίος χρηματιστικός are relevant.

1 For *esto* with accusative and infinitive see KS 1.691 (add Hor. *Serm.* 2.2.30 [probably], Lucr. 2.907); the sense is 'Let us grant that sometimes the acquisition of money by trade is preferable'. Attempts to defend *est* are made by HS 349, Lachmann on Lucr. 5.533, Löfstedt *PA* 122 and others, but the alleged parallels are few and weak (Plaut. *Capt.* 171, where both text and distribution of speakers are uncertain; *Trin.* 1035, where the construction of *fit* with infinitive is due to parallelism with the previous speaker's words; other passages which are quite irrelevant, e.g. Gell. 13.25.31 adduced by Wünsch, *Rh. Mus.* 69 (1914), 137). Ernout wished to understand 'to obtain money by trade is sometimes to show oneself superior', but *est* functioning merely as a copula would not be placed in the emphatic first position. If Birt's emendation is correct, the first word automatically brings with itself the figure *concessio* (Lausberg 856), for which cf. Speeches 169.

For Cato's opinion of money-lenders cf. his remark quoted by Cic. *De Off.* 2.89 and Astin 319; Livy 32.27.3 remarks that as governor of Sardinia he was *asperior in faenore coercendo*. But *rem quaerere* in itself is a respectable aspiration for a Roman (Cic. *De Off.* 2.87; Pliny *NH* 7.140 *pecuniam magnam bono modo inuenire*); in the case of Cato himself Plutarch (*Cato Maior* 21.5, 25.1) calls this πορισμός.

tam...tam Despite the apparent symmetry, the first means 'so dangerous', the second 'equally honorable'. Similarly *existimarint* means 'consider' (so *existimabatur* in 2, *existimo* in 3), *existimare* 'estimate'; in 1.7 *loco* means first 'situation', then 'rank'; in 157.8 *experiri* means first 'exert' and then 'try'; see too on *Origines* 83a, Scipio 17. Such things happen occasionally even in classical Latin, e.g. Cic. *Pro Marc.* 31 *arma ab aliis posita, ab aliis erepta sunt* and *ratio...ratio* at *De Div.* 1.125. For the verbal repetition here see on pr.2. For the form *existimarint* cf. *aegrotarint* 2.4, *essitarit* 157.10 and four examples within 144-150; otherwise Cato has a strong preference for forms in *-aueri(n)t* and the like.

    sit...sit This is the natural tense for Cato to use in an unreal present condition; in classical Latin the imperfect prevails, but does not entirely oust the present (HS 332 and 662, Handford 121, Woodcock 153). Likewise in Homeric Greek an unreal present condition is conveyed by an optative (W. W. Goodwin, *Syntax of the Moods and Tenses of the Greek Verb* (1897) 161), a construction used for remote future conditions in classical Greek. In their earliest stages Greek and Latin do not distinguish between the potential and the unreal.

    Both *sit* and *siet* (and similar forms) are transmitted in the *De Agr.* (beside each other e.g. at 5.2); so also *posiui* (below and ch. 4) and *posui* (cf. on Speeches 173c), *quom* (pr.2, 1.1 etc.) and *cum*, etc. In 2.6 one *ut* is transmitted in the middle of a series of *uti*. One might attribute all this to sporadic modernisation by scribes, but in the majority of cases it is more likely to reflect the instability of the language in Cato's day, before standardisation in the first century B.C. eliminated many options which had been previously available. See pp. 5-6 and on 2.4, 4 (*fructi*; cf. *icti* Quadrigarius 10.68); in relation to syntax 1.1 (*parco*), 142 (*utor*), Speeches 164.

    In a writer more concerned with smooth connection we might have found <*nam*> *maiores*, but *autem* 3 is the only such connective in the preface. In the next sentence too one might have had *hinc l. e. quanto...furem*, but Cato is more concerned to put the important point first (cf. p. 4) than to connect.

    in legibus See the Twelve Tables 8.16 and 18b (but nothing is known about any penalty for usury in them) and [Ascon.] on Cic. *Div. Caec.* 24 (p. 194.11 Stangl). The *RE* article *fenus* lists various legal restrictions imposed on usury. K. F. von Nägelsbach, *Lat. Stilistik* (ed. 9, 1905) §98 p. 423 remarks, quoting parallels, that the infinitive *condemnari* incorporates a notion of obligation.

    2 For the general purport of this section cf. Cato *Ad Filium* fr. 6 Jordan (quoted by Servius on *Georg.* 1.46) *uir bonus, Marce fili, colendi peritus, cuius ferramenta splendent.* Note the differentiation in order between *uir bonus, uirum bonum*, indicating membership of a class, and *bonum agricolam bonumque colonum*, which specifies a quality. One will observe the indifference to repetition of the verb *laudare*. Variation, even by use of the noun *laus*, in Cato's eyes would have shown a self-consciousness which would have distracted attention away from the more important words in the sentence (see von Albrecht 6). Cf. on pr.1, 1.1-4, 3.1, 5.4, 157.9, Speeches 163, 164, *Origines* 83b. We should probably not try to tie down *colonus* (elsewhere in Cato only 1.4, in the order *bono colono* as here) to anything very specific; the combination with *agricolam* indicates nothing more than em-

phatic praise (cf. next note). For *quom laudabant, ita laudabant* cf. Speeches 166 *quicumque...dicit, ita dicit.*

3 When he repeats *periculosum* Cato gives it some extra weight by adding a synonym *et calamitosum*, just as in Speeches 163 *consulendo* is taken up by *recte consulendo atque intellegendo*; such strengthening by synonyms is much developed in Cato's oratory, as Gell. 13.25.12 sqq. remarks (see on Speeches 163). Cf. also *Origines* 83b *fortem atque strenuam* and Till 84-5 = 140-1; *strenuus* is quite a favourite word of Cato, who was himself notably energetic. For Roman opinions about trading see J. H. D'Arms, *Commerce and Social Standing* (1981) 20.

4 Now the cola increase in length as Cato comes to a climax. His rhetoric overlooks the fact that the book is written for absentee owners (2.1, 4, 142) who presumably for the most part did not harden themselves by manual labour, though Cato himself did (Speeches 128; Plut. 4.1). The military virtues produced by farming are also noted by Xen. *Oec.* 5.4-5.

strenuissimi More usual in such adjectives would be *maxime strenui* (Leumann 498, NW 2.202 sqq.), but Cato has other such formations (Till 94-5 = 155-6, adding *industrior* Speeches 186). Note however that he here avoids the dubious *piissimus* (Leumann 499, NW 204-5), though the need to have a *maxime* to lead into *minime* is the decisive factor. The superlative *strenuissimi* contrasts with the trader in the previous sentence, who only earns a positive. There *STrenuum STudiosumque* produces an alliterative pair (see on 141).

male cogitantes sunt Cato probably felt the first two words as an adjective like *maledicens, maleuolens*; cf. *scientes esetis* in the SC de Bacanalibus 23. For *male cogitare* see *TLL* 3.1468.80; here it is probably in a political sense 'disaffected' (Xen. *Oec.* 6.10 makes the same point about farming). Note the fourfold *-que* in this sentence; cf. the prayer in 141.2-3. It is not however true, as HS 473 assert, that *-que* prevails over *et* in the *De Agr.*

redeam The force of the prefix is probably 'come, as I am under an obligation to do' (so Brehaut); so also Cic. *Ad Att.* 1.14.7 and other instances collected by Berry on *Pro Sulla* 35. It is highly improbable that, as Ruebel, *LCM* 5 (1980), 19, thinks, there is any play between *rem* 'point' and 'property' (as in *rem quaerere* pr.1).

quod...erit There are two reasonable (and several unreasonable) ways of interpreting this: (1) 'this will be the beginning of the project which I have promised', with *institutum* attracted into the relative clause and ellipse of *eius* (for this see SC de Bacanalibus 2 and HS 555-6, KS 2.281; the instances in Cato are collected by Keil on 16). *institutum* is often applied substantivally to a literary project (*TLL* 7.1.1993.84, which adopts one of what seem to me to be unreasonable interpretations of this passage); cf. *instituere* in Cic. *De Or.* 2.5. (2) 'this beginning of what I have promised will have been laid down', still with ellipse of *eius* and involving a pleonasm which is common with verbs of beginning (e.g. Ennius *Medea* 210-1 *neue inde nauis incohandi exordium / c(o)episset* [the last word is uncertain;

see Jocelyn's note for this and for parallels]; HS 793, 796, KS 2.569, C. F. W. Müller, *Syntax des Nominativs und Akkusativs* (1908) 44, Fordyce on Verg. *Aen.* 7.40). This pleonasm is not due to anything particular about beginnings, but has its roots in the striving for clarity and emphasis in early Latin. The 'promise' was not verbal, but implicit in the act of putting pen to paper to write about farming; the word is frequently applied to a literary prospectus (Hor. *Epode* 14.7, *Serm.* 2.3.6, *Epist.* 2.1.52, *AP* 45 and 138, Ovid *Fasti* 1.296 [where however the situation is complicated by a variant and authorial revision], Pliny *NH* 24.156).

1

1 *operae*, as quoted by Pliny, would be normal (Plaut. *MG* 1380, Cic. *Ad Fam.* 13.27.1; Plaut. *Most.* 104 has the accusative *operam*), but an ablative of separation, though not found elsewhere with this verb, is comprehensible.

et ne (for which cf. 32.2 and HS 536, *TLL* 5.2.905.12) is used instead of *neue* because Cato intends to structure his admonitions thus, A B(i) (ii). For *circumire* cf. 2.1.

bonum This word and its cognates occur ten times in 1.1-4; cf. on pr. 2.

2 *niteant* is properly applicable to animals, 'be sleek' (as Richter 19 n.3 points out) or to fields (*OLD* s.v. 4, *nitidus* 5); its use here is faintly humorous, as in Horace's (*Epist.* 1.4.15) *pinguem et nitidum bene curata cute*. Note Tib. 2.1.21 *nitidus...rusticus*.

id could be dispensed with, but this use of the resumptive pronoun helps Cato to put the important clause first; cf. for a similar use with nouns rather than clauses on 5.3.

As transmitted, we have in *uti eo introeas* an instance of the original, or close to original, use of *ut* as an indefinite modal adverb (see p. 10). With Eussner's emendation ('you must look around both how you can get in and how you can get out') *uti* is still modal (πῶς, 'how'), but no longer indefinite; this is in any case how *uti inde exire possis* has to be understood. However the text is constituted we have a jussive subjunctive in a main clause, but in Eussner's version without *ut(i)*, which is rare in Cato (see on 3.1).

The point of this injunction is not clear, and it has been understood in various ways. It seems simplest to refer it to the importation of materials and the export of products, but it is hard to grasp why ingress and egress should not be the same.

ne calamitosum siet and thus lose its superiority over the trader's life (praef. 3); for *calamitas* cf. 35.1, 141.2.

sua uirtute This word-order is because there is an implicit contrast with *aliena uirtus*, that imparted to soil by extraneous means such as fertilization or irrigation.

3 *oppidum ualidum* seems to be specified less for protection than as an outlet for produce. Gellius 10.26.8, quoting inexactly, substitutes the adjective

amplum, which is right for the sense.

aut amnis Cato could have made the thought plainer by *uel amnis*. In 1.1 he chose to achieve this by varying to *et ne*, but in Speeches 163 with *atque superbiam* he chose not to, at least partly for rhythmical reasons.

ambulant This is an extraordinary and unparalleled use. Cato probably made an etymological connection between *amb-* and the prefix *am* (Paul. Fest. p. 4 M; as in *anfractus* etc.) which was thought to be present in *amnis* (Paul. Fest. 16, Varro *LL* 5.28). Cato himself apparently used *an* as a preposition (*Origines* 124 P).

4 *in iis agris...in iis agris* Cf. p. 7 for this form of connection.

The reading *quos* can be defended by the interpretation *qui non saepe dominos mutant, quos pigeat (eos) uendidisse qui uendiderint*, with *agros* the antecedent of *quos* as well as of *qui*. However this is altogether too clumsy to be credible.

aedificatum (sc. *praedium*) 'equipped with buildings', cf. 3.2.

alienam disciplinam is vague; it may mean 'what you can learn from others', 'what others have learned' or 'the system adopted by others'. 5.1 favours the last. This sentence seems disruptive.

uasa...sient The postponement of *-ne* is a species of the *guttatim*-style (see on 5.3), in which the main point is put first and an epexegesis follows, of the 'I know Thee who Thou art' type (cf. 5.5, 141.4); HS 471, KS 2.579, Scherer 241, Calboli *ANRW* 2.29.1.138 and 154, Rosén in O. Panagl - T. Krisch (edd.), *Latein und Indogermanisch* (1992) 243. See index, Prolepsis.

5 *pro ratione* sc. *uasorum*:

uideto...siet This seems to mean 'see that the farm requires as little equipment as possible and does not involve expense', so that out of the *ne siet* of the second clause a positive *siet* is understood in the first. This however is very rare (KS 2.653-4, HS 825) and harsh here; perhaps we should read *minimi <uti>*. Speeches 200 *aduersus cognatos pro cliente testatur, testimonium aduersus clientem nemo dicit* is probably a case of an undefined subject (so E. Fraenkel, *Leseproben* (1968) 152; see on XII Tables 1.1) in the first clause, not involving the understanding of a positive subject from *nemo*.

Pontedera's deletion is probably correct, though Cato does not lack disorderly repetitions (cf. on 5.2); this would be a marginal note drawing attention to the next sentence and to *loco salubri* in 1.3.

6 Cato rounds off his discussion with a *sententia*; cf. 2.7.

erit At this date the subjunctive had not yet ousted the indicative from subordinate clauses in indirect speech; cf. Speeches 58, 164.

non multum Disappointment is underlined by holding this back to the end.

7 *praedium...rogabis* In early Latin it is common that one subordinate clause depending on another precedes that other; see HS 734, Scherer 240, with classical survivals noted by Housman on Manil. 5.338. Cf. 3.5 *si orbes contriti sient ut commutare possis*; 155.2, Speeches 164. Linguists call this 'adjunct extraction'

(see Hukari and Levine, *Journal of Linguistics* 31 (1995), 195 sqq., a reference which I owe to Sir Kenneth Dover). Here it is promoted by the *guttatim*-style of expression, which has as a central object that the main idea should be placed first.

de... 'Out of all farmland in the best situation in each case'. In what follows Cato does not seem to have clarified his mind whether he is rating different estates or different parts of one estate against each other (so Astin 346-8). The passage is still harder to interpret without the emendations adopted; the discussion by Ross, *CP* 74 (1979), 56 reaches an unsatisfactory conclusion. Stabile *RFIC* 49 (1921), 337 takes *iugera* to be accusative of extent, comparing 10.1, but that sentence is restored to the text of Cato from the chapter-heading and does not necessarily preserve Cato's exact words.

salictum see ch. 9. If Cato is using *arbustum* here as in 7.1, it is not plain how he is differentiating it from *silua caedua*; probably it here means 'orchard'. Note that in *silua caedua* the adjective has its ordinary position, but that when another type of *silua* is mentioned, *glandaria* has to come first because of the contrast.

2

1 *larem f. salutauit* as is proper on arrival (see on ch.4); see my note on Juv. 12.87. Note that *ubi...ubi* are not parallel; a later writer might have said *lare salutato*. There are similarly constructed sentences with *cum...cum* 98.2, *ubi...cum* 39.1. Cf. Hache 34, Scherer 241 and on XII Tables 1.1.

ubi cognouit...(2) *ubi ea cognouit* mark successive stages; again variety of expression is not important to Cato.

facta infectaque For this combination cf. 141.2 *uisos inuisosque* and Wills 453.

2 *operarum, dierum* Such asyndeton bimembre with words of associated import is deeply rooted in Latin (HS 828, KS 2.149, and see p. 6); many examples follow, and see also Speeches 173c. Cf. on 141.2, Keil on 83, Till 26 = 54, and see too Ennius XI, Lex Furfensis 11 and 16. For *operae* see below.

sedolo The adverb *sedulo* (so spelt twice elsewhere in the *De Agr.*, and a variant here) is derived from *se dolo*, 'without trickery' (Leumann 85; for *se* see on XII Tables 10.8), and by hypostasis (Leumann 386, 388; HS 72*-73*) creates the adjective *sedulus*. *seduloma* is written in the Lex Agraria 39 (Bruns 81, Warmington IV 304, Crawford 117, 132) for *se dolo ma(lo)*; in Festus' quotation of the Lex Silia *sedulum* appears to be a corruption of *se dolo m(alo)* (*FIRA* 1.79, Bruns 46, Crawford 737-8).

opus publicum Cf. 4 *uiam publicam muniri*; maintenance of the roads could be imposed on proprietors beside them (*RE* suppl. 13.1445). It would be easy to read *effecisse <se>*, but alteration of subject is no problem in early Latin (see on XII Tables 1.1 and cf. Speeches 58, 168), nor is omission of the subject-accusative (Altenburg 522; cf. the end of the *euocatio*, p. 110).

ubi...dixit Rather than saying simply *multas alias causas fuisse*, Cato prefers to remind the reader of the now distant *(si) dicit uilicus* with another finite verb; cf. 4 *(interesse)*, 5.2. For similar reasons he adds *uilicum* at the end of the sentence.

operarum 'man-power units', 'man-days'.

reuoca In ch. 1 Cato used 'future' imperative forms because he was giving instructions to a man who does not yet own a farm, whereas in this chapter his purchase is in the past. However Cato does not always seem to observe a distinction (HS 340; Vairel-Carron 288). Cato has 2nd person future imperatives 976 times, present only 31 in the *De Agr.* (Vairel-Carron 287-8). For the switch to the second person after *ei* cf. 117, 143.1. From this word 'remind him' or the like is extrapolated to provide a construction for the following.

3 Tasks for rainy weather are covered also in chs. 39, 155.

frumentum transferri If left undisturbed it might heat or be attacked by weevils.

4 Public religious holidays stopped work in the fields (cf. Cic. *De Leg.* 2.19 and 29), but permitted certain other specified tasks; see 138, Macrob. *Sat.* 1.15.21, *Moretum* 67, Mynors on Verg. *Georg.* 1.268 sqq., Murgatroyd on Tib. 2.1.5-8, Wissowa 441, Latte 198 n.4.

For the migration of *fodio* into the fourth conjugation see Leumann 545, 568, Sommer 540, 509, NW 3.243 (so also Colum. 11.2.35, *de arb.* 30.2); where the conjugation can be determined, Cato elsewhere (four times) sticks to the third. See on praef. 1.

The verb *runco* normally takes as object the area or crop to be weeded, not the weeds to be extracted (Pliny *NH* 19.157 is an exception), so *eruncari* is preferable here (so Goujard 127 n.12).

expinsi far I do not know why Cato chose to alter his otherwise invariable word-order in this one item, if he did so chose; a far-fetched explanation is given by Fankhänel (who for the list compares 23.1) 236-7, namely that the inversion signals the end of the list in the next item. I suggest that we should read *far expinsi*, supposing *far* to have dropped out after *-ari* and to have been restored in the wrong place.

munditias fieri probably refers to general tidying up around the farm, not just housework as in 143.2 and Plaut. *Stich.* 347.

5 Without Keil's addition, the subject of *cognita* will be *quae reliqua opera sint*, but then *aequo animo* is unmotivated; with the addition, this carries on nicely from *ubi ea cognouit* in 2.2. The subjunctive after *ubi* may be defended by 3.2, 151.4, where there is a jussive or *oportet* in the main clause, analogous to the imperatival function of *curare* here; yet 2.2 (just quoted) and 2.1 *ubi cognouit* strongly support emendation to *sunt*.

curare There is a general notion of obligation in the context, as if there were an *oportet* nearby, which motivates the infinitive in such cases; see HS 367 (with 851), Keil on 110. Daube 65 prefers to think that in general admonitions the mere indication of the verbal action is adequate.

rationes...rationem In cases like this either singular or plural is legitimate (KS 1.55); here the addition of a third adjective-equivalent (*pabuli...sunt*; understand *eorum* as antecedent to *quae*, cf. on pr. 4) to the first seems to have made Cato there prefer the plural (cf. on *harumce rerum* 141.3).

quid uenierit..(6)...conpareant 'what has been sold, what collected, balance due, and what is left that is to be sold; satisfactory guarantees of payment should be accepted; the balance remaining should be correct'. For *satis accipere* see *OLD, satis* 6a. The items *quae satis...accipiantur, quae opus...locentur* fit into the category of 'conditional instruction' defined by Wills 305, with an imperative or subjunctive verb in a main clause identical with a verb in a conditional or relative clause. The variation between enclitic placing of the relative *reliqua quae sint* here (cf. 157.7) and initial placing above (5 *quae reliqua opera sint*) seems to be quite arbitrary.

6 *quae opus sint locato* For this construction see Speeches 163, KS 1.765, Bennett 2.359, and compare in particular Ter. *Andr.* 523 *quod parato opus est para*; for work contracted out cf. 4.1, 144-6.

7 *uendat...uendat...uendat* The first is emphatically placed in initial position; then the repetition at the beginning and end of successive clauses constitutes the figure of *redditio* (Lausberg 625), at the end of successive clauses that of *epiphora* (ibid. 631; cf. Speeches 59, 163); finally the last is followed up by the creation of the extempore *uendax*, which unlike *emax* did not establish itself (for other such neologisms cf. Speeches 59, 163 and *trahax* Plaut. *Persa* 410). This last sentence forms a concluding *sententia*, as in 1.6. Cato here uses a rhetorical turn, which he rarely does in the *De Agr.*, for emphasis.

quod supersit clearly implies that self-sufficiency is a primary object.

uetulos...uetus The former is not actually a diminutive of the latter, and in old Latin is particularly applied to animals (Leumann 308).

reicula...reiculas The word *delicus* 'weaned' (from *lac*) is known from Varro *RR* 2.4.16 (*deliti* codd.) and glosses. However what we have here cannot be a diminutive of that because (1) why would Cato use a diminutive? (2) the sense requires something like 'blemished' (corresponding to *seruum morbosum* below, as *boues uetulos* to *seruum senem*). Some have tried to derive *deliculus* from *delinquere* (which does produce *delicuus* 'lacking', found at Plaut. *Cas.* 205), but it seems more likely that we should restore the word *reiculus* known from Varro 2.5.17 (*reiculae reiciundae*, with an etymological figure) and 2.1.24 (*epulae* codd.); it is also quoted by Nonius 168 from Varro's logistoricus *Catus de liberis educandis* (fr. xix Riese).

armentum means a herd of large beasts, as contrasted with *grex*, a flock of small beasts. It can also mean an individual large beast (*OLD* 2). Here it seems to apply to grazing cows, as opposed to oxen for traction (*boues*).

(uendat) seruum senem Plutarch 4-5 strongly criticises Cato for this advice. For the Polonius-like advice to be a seller, not a buyer, cf. *Ad Filium* 10 Jordan (Sen. *Ep.* 94.27, Plut. 4.4) and Cato quoted by Pliny *NH* 18.40.

siquid...uendat An emphatic concluding repetition of advice already twice given. For *et* ending the enumeration see KS 2.154.

3

1 The fivefold repetition of *oportet*, though each instance is at the end of its clause, gives less the impression of the rhetorical figure of epiphora (on 2.7) than of indifference to superficial elegance (on praef. 2).

The ancients tended to mark off life in hebdomads (see my note on Juv. 14.10), and the 36th year would be the beginning of the sixth hebdomad, the *floret* of a man (Leeman, *Helikon* 5 (1965), 534; Stok, *RCCM* 31 (1991), 29).

aedifices The 2nd person jussive subjunctive without *ut(i)* is very rare in Cato; see Vairel-Carron 290 and 291 n.1.

uilla...uillam This is the figure *commutatio* (Lausberg 800), case interchange (Wills 273 n.1).

2 *cellam oleariam...* are loosely attached.

et rei et uirtuti are unusual predicative datives, 'it will win both profit and respect'. At Fronto p. 104.11 *si quid rei esse uidebitur* (adduced by Roby 2 liii) it is not plain that *rei* is dative.

siet is subjunctive by attraction (this instance registered in Bennett 1.307).

4 For details about production of olive oil see 64-5.

4

bubilia bona, bonas praesepis is chiastically ordered, to Cato a natural order for enumeration (see p. 6). Cato intended these accusatives to be subjects of an *esse*, but when he comes to the end of the sentence he finds that he needs the compound *interesse* because he prefers to put the last item in coordination with a main verb instead of e.g. *clatratas clatris distantibus pede*; cf. on 2.2.

faliscas Cf. 14.1; the white Faliscan cattle were famous (Pliny *NH* 2.230 etc.). The accumulation of adjectives is noteworthy but natural enough, 'good Faliscan byres with rails'.

interesse = distare, as Ter. *Ad.* 76 and probably Lucil. 338.

uillam urbanam The dwelling-house, as opposed to the *uilla rustica* (3.2), the barns; see Varro *RR* 1.13.6-7, 3.2.10, Colum. 1.6.1.

in bono...habitaueris 'If you build substantially on a good farm and pick a good situation, and if you then live properly in the country'. For *si...si* cf. XII Tables 8.12. Others punctuate and interpret differently.

uenies implies that in Cato's rural economy the owner no longer lives on the farm; cf. 1.4, 2.1, 142.

fundus melius erit is perhaps correct; *bene est mihi* is usual, but *bene sum* exists; cf. Cic. *Ad Att.* 1.16.11 (with *melius*), Plaut. *Men.* 485, *Truc.* 741, Petron. 34.10 (probably) and in general HS 171.

fructi For nouns which waver between the second and fourth declension see *sumpti* 22.3 and perhaps 21.5, Leumann 442, 450, Sommer 403, NW 1.537. Cato uses the ablative *fructu* twice in 150. See on praef. 1.

frons...est This proverb is repeated from here by Pliny *NH* 18.31; its purport is that the owner should keep a sharp eye and not turn his back. It is the converse of *in occipitio oculos habere* (Plaut. *Aul.* 64).

Colum. 1.3.7 quotes Cato on the disadvantages of having a bad neighbour, Plut. 25.2 records his invitations of neighbours to dinner, probably drawing on Cic. *Cato* 46. As early as Hesiod *WD* 343 sqq. (see West's note) the importance of neighbours to the farmer is stressed; the scholia on 344 report from Plutarch (fr. 50 Sandbach) a dictum of 'Cato or Themistocles' to this effect (p. 108 no. 61 Jordan).

facilius...facilius...facilius Cato places these to avoid an anaphora too rhetorical for his taste. 18.4 *ibi foramen pedicinis duobus facito, ibi arbores pedicino in lapide statuito* looks like an anaphora, but is not; the first *ibi* means *in lapidibus* (just mentioned), the second *in foramine*, so that this is really more like *ubi...ubi* in 2.1, only spatial instead of temporal.

operas is defended by W. E. Heitland, *Agricola* (1921) 170 ('get employment for your own staff for a wage') and Flach 128 ('Arbeitskräfte vermieten'). *Locare* and *conducere* can be contrasted in two senses: (a) to lease out and to hire; (b) to put out for contract and to undertake a contract. With *operas* the contrast comes under sense (a); with Schneider's conjecture *opera* it is spoiled, coming first under (b) and then (a). Cf. Apul. *Apol.* 17 *mutuarias operas cum uicinis tuis cambies.*

operarii (cf. 1.3, 5.4 etc.) are here and usually free workmen (though see on 5.4).

bona salute (cf. 141.3) 'God forbid', an apotropaic expression, meant to avert the possibility that naming bad luck may cause it to occur. See *RE, Aberglaube* 90. In Cato *usus uenit* means 'a need becomes apparent' (102, 157.10), *usu uenit* means 'it happens' (157.7, Speeches 227); I do not understand the distinction drawn by *OLD, usus* 8. 'If anything happens' is a euphemism for 'if anything bad happens'; in extreme cases it refers to death (*TLL* 5.2.1013.46).

5

5.1-5 disrupt the connection; 5.6 would follow well on 4 fin. This chapter is particularly abrupt, with very short asyndetic sentences and only one logical connective (*nam* 4); it is the style of a list, hence the only copulative conjunction used is the enumerative *et*, 'and furthermore' (see p. 3).

1 *disciplina* 'management'; cf. on 1.4.

feriae seruentur comes in a disruptive and strangely prominent position, and the passive is oddly vague. In a finished version Cato might have smoothed things down.

alieno manum abstineat Cf. Xen. *Oec.* 14.2; but Cato did not need to read Xenophon in order to specify this. *alieno* presumably means 'belonging to the proprietor', but it is not clear why Cato is concerned that *sua seruet*, other than for the sake of an antithesis.

litibus familia supersedeat But Plut. 21.4 says that Cato stirred up quarrels among his slaves on the *diuide et impera* principle. However there is no contradiction if one adopts *familiae*, with *uilicus* as the subject. Nováková in *Studia Antiqua A. Salac* (1955) 90 suggests that Plutarch, whose Latin was shaky, misunderstood *supersedeat*, but the verb does not seem to invite such misunderstanding.

bono modo 'In due proportion'; see *TLL* 2.2096.6.

2 exerceat...prohibebit A paratactic condition. Though the subject here and in the next sentence is *uilicus*, Cato thinks it advisable there to remind the reader of this, and similarly below *uilicus ne sit ambulator.* Cf. 2.2, 156.5 and for abrupt change of unspecified subject on XII Tables 1.1, 3.3-4.

male facere sc. *familiam.*

impune is separated from *esse* (cf. Speeches 167) and brought forward to underline the menace.

beneficio good work by a slave. Reward for τὰ καλῶς τελούμενα is advised by Xen. *Oec.* 12.19.

semper is emphatically placed.

familiam exerceat repeats the beginning of this section and, as in 1.5, we might have a marginal heading; but this is much more comprehensible as a negligent repetition.

consideret...fiant Even in classical Latin subordination does not need to be signalled by an *ut* (cf. Keil on 73 and p. 10); for *considero ut* see KS 2.214, *TLL* s.v. 430.72.

ne...dominum Cf. Plaut. *Epid.* 257 *si aequom siet / me plus sapere quam uos* (said by the slave Epidicus), 262.

3 eos This use of the resumptive pronoun (HS 29, 187, 802; KS 1.625; Scherer 220; *OLD* s.v. *is* B6b; instances in Cato are collected by Keil on 128 and Altenburg 493) is extremely common in Cato; see p. 4. The Compitalia, since by now owners tended no longer to live on the farm (see on 4), had become largely a slave festival, and slaves then had special indulgences such as an extra ration of wine (57). Therefore it was felt that the festival should not be allowed to get out of hand, so Cato prescribes that its celebration be restricted to the chapels where the boundaries of the farms met. See Wissowa 167-8, Latte 90-1. The only other religious rite that the bailiff may perform is that of offerings to the Lar (cf. 143.2) and Penates at the hearth (Latte 90, Wissowa 162). At least part of the reason for this prohibition is that sacrifice is expensive.

satui semen For the final dative depending on another noun see HS 99, KS 1.346, Löfstedt *Synt* 1.209 (this passage 210, 213). This is an etymological figure (see index).

dederit nemini The perfect subjunctive in a 3rd person prohibition is rare (HS 336, Handford 49); this appears to be the only instance in early Latin, since *faxit* in Ennius fr. 46 *FLP* = *var.* 17-18 Vahlen is not a perfect subjunctive (on 141.2). This instance contrasts with *credat nemini* just above. For the emphatic placing of the negative pronoun at the end of the sentence see KS 2.592 and 602.

unde = *a quibus*; see on Calpurnius Piso and HS 208, KS 2.284, Pascucci 17, de Meo 93, *OLD* s.v. 6c and 8. Cato has the legal *unde petitur* in Speeches 206.

(praeterea) nemini owes its case to the nearer *det* rather than the more distant *habeat*. The position of the word emphasises it, cf. just above.

4 A *mercenarius politor* is implicitly contrasted (hence the adjective comes first) with a *politor* who is paid by a share of the produce (136, though there seems to be an omission in the text there). Others take *operarium mercenarium* together, in contrast to a slave *operarius* (like, apparently, those mentioned in 10-11) hired from another owner (cf. ch. 4 fin.). The occurrences of *polio* etc. in agricultural contexts are collected by Goujard, *RPh* 44 (1970), 84; see also Scheidel, *Maia* 45 (1993), 125. It is usually taken to refer to hoeing and weeding; Flach 132, quoting Pliny *NH* 3.60, supposes it to mean threshing to remove the chaff, but this cannot be the sense at Enn. *Ann.* 300-1.

For hiring by the day cf. Gospel acc. to Matthew 20.1-14 and Flach 129. The hyperbaton which separates *diutius* from the ablative of comparison and *eundem* from its nouns gives emphasis to those words; cf. on Speeches 58.

emisse...celauisse...consuluisse The perfect infinitive after *uolo* has its roots in administrative prohibitions in senate decrees (see on SC de Bacanalibus 3 and Gracchus 48) and edicts of magistrates, not in the language of laws, as HS 351-2 say. See Daube 37 sqq. (esp. 47) and in *ZRG* 78 (1961), 390 = *Collected Studies* 2 (1991) 1057 (cf. also ibid. 1109).

parasitum For this word outside comedy cf. Lucil. 717; its very Greekness conveys a sneer. C. Damon, *The Mask of the Parasite* (1997) 48 compares a scene in the *Persa* of Plautus in which one slave invites another to a meal at his absent owner's expense as if the latter were his parasite.

haruspicem...Chaldaeum For scepticism about forms of divination not integrated into official Roman cult see Latte 265-8 and especially Cato's sarcasm about *haruspices* reported by Cic. *De Div.* 2.51; *Chaldaei* were expelled from Rome in 139 B.C. (Latte 275). Cic. *De Div.* 1.132 contemptuously lists *eos qui quaestus causa hariolentur...Marsum augurem, uicanos haruspices, de circo astrologos*, cf. *De Nat. Deor.* 1.55. For private consultation of *haruspices* see my note on Juv. 6.392. The augurs meant are not of course members of the official Roman college (*augures publici*), but hedge-priests. Maróti, *Annales Univ. Scient. Budapest, sectio philol.* 1 (1957), 97 points out that Athenio, the leader of the Sicilian slave-revolt in 104 B.C., was both *uilicus* and astrologer.

  segetem The cornfield; it is 'cheated' if it is not given enough seed.

  facere...faciat...fecerit...facient...faciet Again no need for variation is felt; in Ter. *Ad.* 103-10 there are six forms of *facio* plus one of *fio*. Note how the main point *opus rusticum omne* is thrust into prominence, as *uilicae quae sunt officia* 143.1, *cibum* 143.2.

  5 *scibit...dormibit* For these forms of the future of the fourth conjugation see *inlargibo* Speeches 138, Leumann 578, NW 3.322, Sommer 526; they are not archaic, but innovated on the model of the first and second conjugations.

  minus libebit ambulare takes up *ambulator* 5.2.

  'Early to bed and early to rise' is advocated also by Aristotle *Oec.* 1.6.5, but of course Cato had not read Aristotle. *cubitu surgat, cubitum eat* show how classical uses of the supines develop from the accusative of motion towards and the ablative (here of separation) of a fourth-declension verbal noun; see HS 380-3, KS 1.721-4.

  uillam...clausa uti siet See on 1.4. Bennett 2.224 remarks that *uideo* quite commonly is accompanied by such an accusative prolepsis.

141

  1 *impero* quite often governs a passive infinitive (KS 2.231). A verb of saying is extrapolated from this.

  The prayer starts with formulae of good omen; for *quod bene eueniat* see Appel 172-3, for *cum diuis uolentibus* KS 1.789 and Skutsch on Enn. *Ann.* 190.

  Mani is used as a representative name, much as we speak of 'an ordinary Joe'. Conceivable parallels are Petron. 45.7 and Varro's satire *Manius*.

  It is impossible to believe in a feminine first declension *suouitaurilia*, especially as it is referred to by a neuter *circumferenda*. It is equally hard to believe in the combination *siue circumagi siue circumferenda*; instances in which a gerundive is followed by an infinitive (e.g. Varro *RR* 3.9.8) are quite different. I have tried to mend all problems (cf. on 157.8); the assumption behind my conjecture is that from *uelis* the scribe's eye leaped forward to the similar *siue* (of which four out of five letters are the same), causing the omission of three words, of which two were subsequently recovered and replaced in the wrong position. The point of *circumferenda* is that since these are sucking beasts (3-4) some of them might need to be carried rather than driven. It is more likely that *quota ex parte* refers to the number of the animals which might need to be carried than to the proportion of the estate that is to be purified, since the following prayer seems to be all-inclusive.

  uti...uti A common type of repetition for clarity (HS 808, KS 2.589).

2 For the form *praefamino* see on XII Tables 1.1; the words to be used are given in 134.2-3, but note that the form given there *mihi liberisque meis domo familiaeque meae* (slightly varied in 139) has been shortened here to produce a tricolon, which shows that the flat prose of 134 has here been raised to *carmen*. Cato himself is probably responsible for this; note Dumézil 234 n.44 'The formulas of Cato are definitely not traditional formulas, *ne uarietur*, but rather models which he is proposing, and on which he has set his mark'. Janus is regularly addressed at the beginning of prayers (see my note on Juv. 6.386, Oakley on Livy 8.9.5; Augustine *CD* 7.9); for Janus and Jupiter as recipients of a *praefatio* see Macrob. *Sat.* 1.16.25 and Latte 206 n.3 (the inscription which he mentions is dated much earlier by others). *sic dicito* also introduces a *praefatio*, this time to Mars, preliminary to the sacrifice.

For Mars in this context cf. 83 (where *Marti Siluano* appears to be an asyndeton) and the Carmen Arvale with my commentary, *ML* p. 202. It is not germane to this book to discuss the nature of Mars' ties with agriculture; see H. S. Versnel, *Inconsistencies in Greek and Roman Religion, II Transition and Reversal* (1993) 294, 300.

I have laid out the prayer, which is usefully discussed by Lazzeroni 122 and Watkins *HKD* 197, so that its structure and stylistic features are illuminated. The general framework is chiastic (see on ch.4): *Mars pater*...(A), *quoius rei ergo*...(B), *uti tu morbos*...(C), *utique tu fruges*...(C), *harumce rerum ergo*...(B), *macte*...*Mars pater*...(A). Within this large scheme the B phrase *agrum terram fundumque meum* is chiastically reversed to *fundi terrae agrique mei* (I do not know why in the introductory instructions in 1 it appears in yet a third form *fundum agrum terramque meam*). In addition to this and *mihi domo familiaeque nostrae* (also twice) there is a tricolon in *prohibessis defendas auerruncesque*, and a tricolon structure in *utique tu fruges*...*siris, pastores*...*seruassis, duisque*...*ualetudinemque*. The very word *suouitaurilia* is a tricolon; for such three-fold sacrifices see J. P. Mallory, *In Search of the Indo-Europeans* (1989) 133-5. The middle section is arranged so that a general negative section (*morbos*...*auerruncesque*) is followed by a specific positive section (*utique*...*ualetudinemque*). Within these two the items are paired, with all the pairs except one linked either by inflectional similarity (*uisos inuisosque, grandire*...*euenire*) or by alliteration; in the case of *uineta uirgulta* there is homoeoteleuton as well. *salua seruassis* (the verb being one of a series ending in -*is*) is not quite on the same plane as the other pairs, but is exactly the *saluo seritu* of the Iguvine Tablets VI a 3, where it has *uiro pequo = pastores pecuaque* for its object (cf. Wölfflin 273, Hickson 79; it is also on Appel's no. 34, from the Acta fratrum Arvalium). It has often been suggested that it had a parallel in an original *duisque duonam* (and also *dueneque*). However this idea was based on the belief that this was an ancient formula rather than one composed by Cato himself; it is of course clear that Cato was using archaic language in composing his *carmen*.

This is a fine example of what the Romans called *carmen*, a word which relates not to metrical form but to the clear marking out of compositional units by such formal devices as I have remarked (see p. 9); the means to this effect here is the enumeration of particulars instead of collective designations such as 'harm' or 'crops'. The legacy of this is clear in the number of alliterative combinations which remain as formulae in classical Latin (cf. pr.4, Speeches 163 twice); note too the five alliterative pairs in the curse in the Iguvine Tables VI b 60 and other instances adduced by Poultney 10. In its general structure the prayer has a close parallel in the invocation to Jupiter Grabovius in the Iguvine Tables VI a 22 sqq. (see Watkins *HKD* 214).

G. Calboli (*Papers from the Seventh International Conference on Historical Linguistics*, ed. A. G. Ramat and others (1987) 141 = G. C., *Über das Lateinische* (1997) 87) sees *quoius rei ergo* and *harumce rerum ergo* as relative pronoun and antecedent, with the relative clause preceding, as is usual in the earliest Latin legal and sacral texts. I disagree with this, and take the train of thought to be this: 'I beseech your grace, Mars; for this reason I have ordered the beating of my bounds' [here I have introduced the name of an analogous Anglican ritual]; 'you in your turn protect my property' [taking *uti* to be jussive, cf. on 1.2; the asyndeton suitably marks the reciprocity between man and god characteristic of Roman religion]; 'for these reasons' [now plural because of the preceding list of particulars; cf. on 2.5 and SC de Bac. 26] 'be honoured; for this same reason' [reverting to the all-inclusive singular] 'be honoured'. However I do not deny that *uti* could be final. I take it that *quoius rei ergo* employs the relative because of the close link with the preceding, whereas the demonstrative in *harumce rerum ergo* is used to mark off this part as a conclusion. It is however possible that we have stereotyped language no longer kept in strict relation to its context; similar problems arise in 139.

Note that in this prayer *-que* alone is used for 'and', including *benēque* in 3 (cf. on 156.1); the enumerative *et* (see on ch. 5 init.) does not appear.

precor quaesoque Cf. Appel 142 (adding his nos. 6, 29, 89 etc.), Hickson 49, *TLL* 10.2.1153.26 and on Macrob. *Sat.* 3.9.7 (p. 107). These formulae show the legalistic spirit in which the Romans approached their gods; essentially such coupling of near synonyms, like the exhaustive specification of aspects of one act in the prayer, is meant to close legal loopholes (see p. 8). Much the same applies to many combinations in the actual prayer and the lists *fundum agrum terramque meam* above (and in variations below), *mihi domo familiaeque nostrae*; cf. Appel no.6 (from the Secular Games of 17 B.C.) *fitote u[olente]s propitiae p. R. Quiritibus, XVuirum collegio mihi domo familiae* and the following instances. See Appel 144, who quotes parallels from the Iguvine Tablets but not the closest, VI a 5. Note that the land belongs to the proprietor alone (*meus*), whereas the household is shared (*nostrae*), just as Plautine slaves speak of *nostra domus*; nevertheless 134 and 139 use *meae*.

uolens propitius See Appel 122, Hickson 61 and for Greek examples Fraenkel on Aesch. *Ag.* 664, S. Pulleyn, *Prayer in Greek Religion* (1997) 144; cf. also *cum diuis uolentibus* above. For the asyndeton bimembre see on 2.2.

circumago naturally enough takes a double acusative, cf. on 157.11.

C. Zander, *Versus Italici Antiqui* (1890) 36 proposed *<mortem> morbos*, comparing the prayer in Festus quoted in the note on *prohibessis* etc. below (other instances of this alliterative pair in *TLL* 8.1479.44). This elegant suggestion certainly deserves consideration. If *mortem* fell out here, perhaps it was retrieved and wrongly replaced as *Martem* in 4.

uisos inuisosque Polar expression, whereby a totality is indicated by specification of its opposite extremes; see Watkins *HKD* 43, 208, with parallels from the Iguvine Tables. Note also 2.1 *facta infectaque* and the Carmen Saliare fr. 6 *pennatas impennatasque agnas* (ears of grain with and without the beard). Because of potential confusion with *inuisus* 'hated', *inuisus* 'unseen' in classical Latin is used only in combinations which make the sense clear (with *inauditus* Cic. *Har. Resp.* 57, with *incognitus* Caes. *BC* 2.4.4, with *inaccessus* Florus 2.30 = 4.12.27); cf. on *absque* in the *euocatio* (p. 109).

uiduertas 'barrenness' is formed on the analogy of *ubertas* and *paupertas*; elsewhere it is found only in Paul. Fest. 369. This and the following terms are illustrated by Norden *AAP* 128 n.3; Fraenkel *EPP* 342 remarks Ennius *trag.* 207 *uiduae et uastae uirgines*. For *calamitates* cf. 1.2 and figuratively Plaut. *Capt.* 911 *clades calamitasque, intemperies*.

prohibessis defendas auerruncesque Another legalistic list. For the forms *prohibessis* (Plaut. *Aul.* 611) and *seruassis* (3) see Leumann 622, Sommer 584-5; they lack all sense of tense and sit quite happily with present subjunctives. The same is true of *siris* (3); cf. Leumann 600, Sommer 581. *auerrunces* seems ultimately to derive from *uerro* and mean 'sweep away'; a god Auerruncus is mentioned by Varro *LL* 7.102. However the exact path of its formation is obscure; the sense 'turn out' of *uerrunco* (probably a back-formation) seems to be a secondary assimilation to *uerto*. See Walde-Hofmann, *Lateinisches Etymologisches Wörterbuch* 1.82. Perhaps the verb *runcare* has exerted some influence. *prohibessis* is probably in its original meaning 'keep away'(*OLD* 1c); *defendo* often means 'ward off'. See Norden *AAP* 126 n.3, who quotes another similar prayer (Festus 210) from the lustration of a farm, *auertas morbum mortem, labem nebulam impetiginem*, which looks later than Cato's prayer; note there *auertas* corresponding to *auerrunces* here. *prohibessis*, which became standardized in contexts like this (Leumann 622, 624), is one of the rare formations of this type outside the first conjugation, like *seruassis*. Attempts to link each verb with a specific object in the preceding list do not seem to me to work.

uirgulta 'plantations'; cf. Cic. *De Leg.* 2.21 *uineta uirgetaque*. For *fruges frumenta* cf. Cic. 2 *Verr.* 5.137, Ulpian *Dig.* 7.8.12.1.

grandire Verbs of this formation, including this one, are normally transitive (Leumann 556), hence Zander l.c. 37 proposed *grandirei*, cf. Pacuv. 142 *nec grandiri frugum fetum posse nec mitescere*; however the active assonates better with *euenire*, and Keil compares intransitive *lenire* at Plaut. *MG* 583.

 beneque euenire Cf. *quod bene eueniat* in 1 above and Hickson 70, also Wissowa 267 on the god Bonus Euentus in such contexts. For *siris* see on the formula of *deuotio* (p. 111).

 3 *pastores pecuaque salua seruassis* One of a large cluster of expressions denoting 'protect men and beasts' which are found in various languages and can be traced back to Indo-European (Watkins *HKD* 15, 42, 210, *SW* 1.650). In order to create *carmen*, Cato has introduced the alliterative *pastores* where the original form (as in Umbrian; see above) would have had *uiros*. Vedic has independently done the same.

 duisque, unlike the preceding verbs, takes initial position in order to indicate that the series is now at an end. Rounding off is also achieved by *ualetudinem* taking up *morbos* and *mihi...nostrae* taking up the first section.

 bonam salutem Cf. ch. 4 fin.

 lustrandi lustrique faciendi Again the god is to be in no doubt about the meaning (on 2 above); and *sicuti dixi* (see Appel 146) also impresses the point, as does the repetition of the last clause. Elsewhere *lustrum facere* is applied only to the activity of the censors.

 macte A god is 'increased, strengthened' by a sacrifice to him; Latte 45 and n.2, HS 79-80. Note the association of *macte* and *mactare* in 134.2-4; see Ogilvie on Livy 2.12.14.

 4 *cultro...adsiet* = *facito uti strues et fertum cultro adsiet*, with the construction remarked on 1.4. *strues* and *fertum* are kinds of sacrificial cakes (Wissowa 412 n.4, Latte 376, Vine *HSCP* 90 (1986), 111 sqq., esp. 123); in 134 the *strues* is given (again *obmouere*) to Janus, the *fertum* to Jupiter. Paul. Fest. 85 and 295 mentions functionaries called *strufer(c)tarii*. The *culter* is the knife for cutting the throat of the victims; perhaps the cakes were placed on it (like a modern pie-server) before being thrown into the fire, as the *mola salsa* was (see my note on Juv. 12.84).

 immolabis seems oddly placed, breaking up the list.

 uetat sc. the rubric of the ritual; Norden *AAP* 261 n.1 compares *inquit* Cic. *De Leg.* 2.59 and ἀγορεύει in a law quoted by Demosth. 23.28 (which are admittedly much easier since the contexts deal with laws); a more dubious case is Thuc. 1.144.2. See also *inquit* in Lucilius 552 quoted on XII Tables I; for unexpressed subject see ibid. *neque* carries on the implied negative in *uetat*; this is regular after *nolo* (Speeches 164), *nego* (Piso 27, Quadrigarius 41; see Madvig on Cic. *De Fin.* 1.30) etc. Cf. Wackernagel 2.309.

 As it stands, this sentence is nonsense; there can be absolutely no reason for not naming Mars. The point must be that in this private sacrifice the victims are not full-grown, but only sucking animals, not a *sus* but a *porcus* (piglet), not an *ouis* but an *agnus* (lamb), not a *taurus* but a *uitulus* (calf); these are acceptable offerings on the principle *in sacris simulata pro ueris accipi* (see my note on Juv. 6.527 sqq.), but the fiction must be maintained by not calling them by their proper names. It can still be maintained if all are unsatisfactory (see the next sentence), but cannot if only one or two are (the last sentence); then the unsatisfactory animal(s) must be specified. It follows (a) that Gesner's emendation must be adopted, as it is by Kronasser, *WS* 79 (1966), 307 and Petersmann, *Rh. Mus.* 116 (1973), 250, though I cannot accept their explanations: (b) that here *porcus* must apply to a young *sus* (see Benveniste 26), as at Cassius Hemina fr. 11 *sus parit porcos triginta*, Cic. *Cato* 56 *porco haedo* (kid, not goat) *agno*, Colum. 7.9.3, Varro *RR* 2.4.21. For a lustration of the whole Roman people Varro 2.1.10 specifies full-grown animals (*uerres aries taurus*). Cf. also Petron. 133.3.15 *fetus suis, hostia lactens*.

litabit, dubitabit sc. the officiant (Manius?); for unspecified subject see on *uetat* above.

uerba concipito This is the regular verb for framing a formula (*TLL* 55.6); common in the form *conceptis uerbis* (see on the 'Letter of Cornelia' (b) and Scipio 19).

neque This (normally in the form *nec*) was Latin's earliest word for 'not', and survives in classical Latin in compounds and some stereotyped formulae (cf. on the 'Letter of Cornelia' (d) and Norden *AAP* 92). *non* does not occur in the XII Tables. See Leumann 387, HS 448-51, KS 1.817, Pascucci 22, de Meo 91.

It is as hard to believe in a transitive verb *piaculo* as it is to accept a feminine *suouitaurilia*. Here we have an ellipse of something like *placo*, which is parallelled in the Iguvine Tables and in Vedic (HS 423, Petersmann l.c. 241, Watkins *HKD* 218 and 226, Berrettoni, *Studi e Saggi Linguistici* 7 (1967), 167, Porzio Gernia in *Lingue e Culturi in Contatto...* (Atti dell' viii Congresso internaz. di Linguisti (1993)) 479). *piaculo* is in apposition to the nouns, cf. 139, 'as an appeasement'.

porco...porco Or *agno* or *uitulo*, as the case may be; one example suffices.

142

Astin 344 suggests that the performance of part of the ceremonies of 141 by a deputy made Cato think of the *uilicus* and realise that he had said nothing about the *uilica*, so that he briefly recapped 5 in 142 and appended 143.

Parallelism with the preceding clauses dictates that the *quomodo* clause should have an indicative verb, which in any case Cato allows in an indirect question (see on Speeches 164). The whole construction of the first sentence is loose, though the list of the substantive items, put prominently first, is tied together by *eadem* at the end. The striking repetition of *oportet* underlines that these are *officia*. For rations and clothing for the slaves see 56-9. Down to *audiens sit* Cato seems to be summarising ch. 5, then with *hoc amplius* (see on 157.10) he adds an extra item to provide a transition to the *uilica*; this is the only attempt at sentence-connection in these chapters.

For the accusative after *utor* see KS 1.383, HS 123, Bennett 2.217 (with some adjustments in Löfstedt *Synt* 2.26). In the *De Agr.* Cato has an expressed object in the accusative 5 times (including 143.1, 157.8, where see Keil), in the ablative 8 times. For the form *eae* (found also 46.1) see Leumann 480, Sommer 445, NW 2.379-80, Keil on 14.3, Till 91 = 151.

143

This chapter is clearly modelled on 5.

1 The first three sentences, and *scito* below, *tibi* 2 fin., are addressed to the *uilicus*. For the switch to the second person cf. on 2.2, where the *dominus* is addressed; Cato has not made up his mind who is to be the addressee of the work. *uxorem* (rather than *contubernalem*) prima facie suggests that the bailiff is envisaged as free, or at least a freedman; but nearly all *uilici* were slaves, and ch. 5 seems to envisage a slave (esp. 5.2 *impune ne sinat esse*; for physical punishment of *uilici* see J. Carlsen, *Vilici and Roman Estate Managers* (1995) 75), so *uxor* is probably used loosely. In these circumstances Colum. 1.8.5 specifies a *contubernalis*. In the *Casina* of Plautus Lysidamus seeks to bestow his slave Casina as *uxor* on his slave *uilicus* Olympio, and a wedding (albeit in Greek form) is celebrated. A slave *uilicus* has an *uxor* on *CIL* 5.8650, another has a *coniunx* on *CIL* 9.820. Carlsen in *De Agricultura, in memoriam P. W. de Neeve* (1993) 198 quotes two other inscriptions on which a *uilicus* has an *uxor*, and there are others too with mention of a *coniunx*.

ad cenam...rem diuinam facere Cf. 5.2-3. The archaic form *ni = ne* (see my note on *ML* 19.4) is also transmitted at 20.1; *niue* (HS 671) is not recorded in Cato. Strict grammar might prefer *pro se*; understand *neue <cui eam> mandet*. For *iniussu domini* cf. 139.

2 *conuersam* is from *uerro* 'sweep'; for the combination with an adverb by -*que* see HS 172, 817.

Kalendis...supplicet For the offering on the Kalends cf. Prop. 4.3.53. For garlands for the Lar(es) see my notes on Juv. 9.138 and 12.87.

cibum For the position of this see on 5.4. Cf. Plaut. *Merc.* 398 *quae habeat cotidianum familiae coctum cibum.*

156-7

These extracts give an adequate impression of the famous chapters on the medicinal virtues of the cabbage. Cato's low opinion of Greek doctors is recorded and discussed by Pliny *NH* 29.14 sqq and Plutarch 23.3-4 (= *Ad Filium* 1-2 pp. 77-8 Jordan); both report that he kept a *commentarius* from which he treated his son and household. Despite his professed aversion, he clearly drew on Greek medical writings. He calls the cabbage *Pythagorea*, doubtless taking the allusion from his source and therefore not indicating any personal interest in Pythagoreanism (see my

FLP 31). Pliny 20.78 states that Pythagoras and Cato lauded the cabbage; the mention of Pythagoras is probably drawn from Cato and not from independent knowledge, but at 25.13 Pliny does mention a book of 'Pythagoras' *de effectu herbarum* (his citation at 24.158 probably comes from this book too). Epicharmus fr. 61-2 DK (= Pliny *NH* 20. 89 and 94) also shows interest in the medicinal effects of cabbage. More importantly, an extract from a medical writer called Mnesitheus of Cyzicus (of unknown date) quoted by Oribasius (*Corpus Medicorum Graecorum* 6.1.1. p.100; translated by Brehaut 139 n.10) is clearly the source of 156.5-6 and 157.6-9. That leads on to an interesting question about the compilation of this treatise, because in the passages about colic (156.5-6, 157.9) the former is considerably closer to Mnesitheus; 157 omits the concluding advice to repeat the dosage every morning and to observe restraint. Richter 121 shows that 157 abbreviates 156, in some respects unfortunately; he deduces (which however seems a questionable deduction) that Cato cannot have spoiled his own work by abbreviation, and that 157 must have been interpolated (in the first century B.C., he claims on the basis of verbal usage; this is quite incredible).

In these extracts 156.1, 157.1-8 refer to self-treatment, 156.5-6, 157.9-10 to treatment of others; no doubt the latter often had to be practised by the owner or *uilicus* of a farm. For Cato's writings and remarks on medicine generally see Boscherini, *ANRW* 2.37.1.730.

156

1 *de...concoquit* 'On the cabbage, its digestive properties', a species of the *guttatim*-style; in principle 157.1 *de brassica...ea* is similar (cf. HS 29 and on 5.3). This heading applies only to the first section of this chapter. *De* is likewise often used by Varro *RR* to introduce a rubric. For *concoquit* see *TLL* 4.82.50.

est quae 'It is the cabbage that surpasses' is a method of emphasising (or conferring Focus function) which is commoner in English than in Latin; see B. Löfstedt, *Indog. Forsch.* 71 (1966), 253.

uel coctam uel crudam These alternatives are taken up chiastically, *crudam* in the next sentence, *coctam* in the next section (not reproduced here).

lotium...est This is hardly intelligible without 157.10; accordingly Richter 128 n.30 sees it as a secondary addition to this chapter.

cenareque Classical prose shows a certain restraint in adding -*que* to -ĕ(cf. *beneque* 141.3; *saepeque, Origines* 83b); KS 2.14 (there are about 40 cases in Cicero). This passage reminds us that *narratur et prisci Catonis / saepe mero caluisse uirtus* (Hor. *Odes* 3.21.11); see also Sen. *Tranq. An.* 17.4, Pliny *Ep.* 3.12. For suppression of drunkenness by cabbage see Goujard's note here and Arnott on Alexis 15.7.

crudam quantum uoles For this type of *guttatim*-style in expressions of quantity see HS 44, 57, KS 1.250-1 and especially J. Svennung, *Untersuchungen zu Palladius* (1935) 200, Keil on 69, Bennett 2.7, Altenburg 501-2, where examples from Cato are collected; in fully coordinated style we might have *crudae*. For the usage in Apicius see the edition of J. Gómez Pallarès (1990) 20, modifying Milham, *Helikon* 7 (1967), 201.

ex aceto This is the 'recipe' use of *ex* (*OLD* 19b), cf. 157.7; it indicates the vehicle in which a substance is prepared.

esto...comesto It is commoner to find the compound taken up by the simple; see however HS 789-90, Pascucci 40 n.2, Dressel *Zeitschr. Vergl. Sprachforsch.* 85 (1971), 21, Wills 443. For *aliquis* with numerical approximations see KS 1.637, HS 211.

5 *tormina* is colic.

quibus For the loosely-attached relative cf. 157.9 and p. 8.

eodem addito A superfluous addition made for the sake of clarity; see p. 5.

6 *uolet* This and the following third persons refer to the patient; *quibus* at the beginning of 5 is dropped (the same happens in 157.9). For the unspecified subject see on XII Tables 1.1 and Keil on 11.2.

The repetition of *edit* at the end of successive clauses is not to be taken as anything so self-conscious as the rhetorical figure of *epiphora*.

dato...bibat Cf. 73, 157.9, Plaut. *Stich.* 757 and for the paratactic construction in general KS 2.227-8, *TLL* 5.1.1691.10, p. 10.

uini atri 157.9, Plaut. *Men.* 915, Apicius 1.6; *nigri*, as in 126.1, would be commoner (Fitton Brown, *CR* 12 (1962), 192 sqq., esp. 194 n.5). For *duri* cf. *TLL* 5.2305.41; it is contrasted with *suaue*, so it means the same as *austerum* (cf. 126.1 *uini nigri austeri*).

aquatum 'diluted'; ὑδρομιγές in the Greek medical writers. Since the verb *aquor* means 'to fetch water', not 'to add water', this is a calque.

quam minimum is postponed to the end for emphasis; note *nolito multum dare* in the next sentence.

libenter esse No doubt from *edo*, though this is a common combination with *sum* (HS 171).

157

1 *principium* seems to be accusative on the analogy of *primum*.

commoetat i.e. *commutat* (Leumann 65, SP 66); cf. *oeti* in the Lex Furfensis 6-8. The Sicilian word μοῖτος ('thanks, favour'), for which see Varro *LL* 5.179, is probably taken from the pre-Latin *moi-to-* that underlies *mutuus* and *mutare*.

<frigida>...[sed] When the text is so established, the *septem bona*, otherwise inexplicable, are the seven qualities just mentioned; these are regarded as the qualities needed for a good bodily κρᾶσις or *temperamentum* (whence 'temperament'; cf. *temperat* above). The cabbage unites the four humors, hot and cold, wet and dry, and also incorporates another antithesis, sweet)(bitter and pungent.

arido simul umida = ὑγρὰ ξὺν τῷ ξηρῷ; *arido* and *dulci* are nouns, like *uiride* 54.5, and are governed by *cum*. Pacuv. 97 consists of the tantalising phrase *aesti forte ex arido*, and Plautus four times couples *dulce* and *amarum*. The same result might be achieved by other means, e.g. *cum calore <et frigore> arida simul <et> umida et dulci<s> et amara* (this adapts emendations made by early editors). The most helpful discussion of the passage is by Boscherini 64-7, though I differ from him in detail. He refers to Hippocrates, *De Prisca Medicina* 14, where we find τὸ γλυκύ, τὸ πικρόν, τὸ ὀξύ associated as δυνάμεις with the four humors. The passage, especially in my preferred restoration, gives the impression of being a close adaptation of a Greek original.

My punctuation in what follows enables us to avoid the difficulty re-marked by Boscherini 70, that elsewhere in the *De Agr.* the resumptive pronoun after a relative is *is*, not *hic*; one may however remark at 143.3 a resumptive *haec omnia*, though not directly after a relative. *sed* is probably just a dittography (*s'*). *omnia* rams home the universal efficacy of the cabbage by repeating the first word of the sentence.

commixturam The accusative seems defensible, 'the seven good ingredi-ents for an amalgam'.

brassica is so placed for maximum emphasis.

2 *tertia* The third variety specified by Cato; modern botanical identifica-tions cannot be made.

lenis Perhaps so called by antiphrasis (Goujard 312 n.4; see Lausberg 466, HS 777, my note on Juv. 8.30), since in fact it is *acerrima*, 'most pungent' (cf. *acris* above).

scito is followed by a paratactic construction instead of accusative and infinitive, cf. HS 528, KS 2.161 and on *Origines* 83a.

nulla...medicamento 'No <other> has a medicinal effect comparable to it'. *medicamento* is predicative dative (rather than ablative of quality, as Bennett 2.323 and HS 118 take it), and *illius modi* substitutes for an adjective of quantity (= *tanto*) which may accompany such a dative (Roby 2 xxix).

3 *purgabit sanaque faciet* (plus four more occurrences of *san(um) facere* and one of *sanus fieri* in my extracts from this chapter) Boscherini in *Mille: i debatti del circolo linguistico Fiorentino 1945-70* (1972) 27 points out that ὑγίεα ποιεῖν is much commoner in Hippocrates than ἰᾶσθαι; Cato does not use *sanare*.

eadem...eadem...eadem 'It brings swellings to a head and makes them burst...'; for *concoquit* see *OLD* 3b and cf. Dioscorides 2.86 συμπεπτικὴ τῶν οἰδημάτων (barley), for *erumpit* see *TLL* 5.2.843.32. The style becomes excited, almost hymnodic (cf. 7); in a hymn this would be part of the recital of the ἀρεταὶ τοῦ θεοῦ with the usual 'Du-Prädikation', involving anaphora of the second-person pronoun, here tranferred into the third person. The reference to the unique power of the cabbage also recalls the use of *solus* in such invocations (Norden *AT* 350 n.1); cf. 12 below *nulla res tam bene purgabit*.

7 *uno uerbo* See *OLD, uerbum* 3b.

intro quae dolitabunt For enclitic placing of the relative pronoun cf. 2.6 etc. and HS 399, Kroll *Glotta* 3 (1912), 10-11, who from Cato quotes 14.4, 23.1; Leo *AKS* 2.227 adduces this feature from the Cippus Abellanus (Vetter no. 1 p. 8, Conway no. 95 p. 92), and one may compare e.g. *CIL* 1 (ed. 2) 698 = *ILS* 5317 = Warmington IV 276.30-32 *paries qui est...ostium intro itu in area quod nunc est.* In terms of modern linguistics, this position gives Focus function to *intro.* Cato's iterative verbs fall into three classes: first, those which have ceased to be felt as iterative or have a special sense, e.g. *specto, habito*; second, true iteratives, like *essito* (157.10, 'eat habitually'), *dato* Speeches 173e; thirdly, those used in a colloquial fashion (HS 297) with no real difference in sense from the root verbs, like *obiecto* Speeches 169. *dolitabunt* (not found elsewhere) here must be intended to reinforce the idea of recurrent occasions present in *omnia.* Paul. Fest. 89, 121, 379 comments on some remarkable iterative verbs in Cato.

uenae...nascitur This is based on the Greek medical theory that the flow of *pneuma* through ueins and arteries is impeded by residues of food. This view is most clearly expounded by *Anonymus Londiniensis*, ed. W. H. S. Jones (1947) pp. 35-9 (where 'Aristotle' means Menon; ibid. p.2); it is also put forward in the pseudo-Hippocratic *De Flatibus* 7 (2.234-7 in the Loeb edition). This is the only passage in the *De Agr.* in which Cato gives a theoretical basis, and he is here parading his medical knowledge; at this point Mnesitheus says only 'it purges the veins'.

ubi ex multo cibo Cato was forced into a connection with *nam* (almost as lonely here as in 5.4) in the previous sentence, but here *ex multo cibo* seems to him to provide an adequate logical link with that sentence (cf. on Speeches 163 *laetitia*). No word meaning 'therefore' appears in the *De Agr.; nam* is the only logical connective at all common in Cato.

aluus non it Cf. 156.4 and 7.

id ut te moneo A reference back to 157.6. *id ut* seems to cross *ita ut* with *id quod*; some rather distant parallels in HS 557.

et rutam Again the paratactic habit, as in 157.6; the hypotactic would say *cum ruta.*

sirpicium is not found elsewhere, though *sirpe* is (Plaut. *Rud.* 630 [commenting on this Priscian *GLK* 2.329 produces the form *sirpis*], Solinus 27.48); it is the same thing as *silpium* just above, the plant from which *laserpicium* (116; = *lac sirpicum*, cf. Solinus 27.49) is obtained.

oxymeli A mixture of honey and vinegar. The declension of this word is confused because it has been influenced by both μέλι and *mel*; for this ablative see NW 1.361 and *TLL* s.v. 1210.11. *Oenomeli* and *hydromeli* are affected in the same way.

8 *haec si uteris* For the accusative see on 142. It is possible that Cato used the form *uterus*, for which see Leumann 517, Sommer 494, NW 3.201; most

inscriptional instances of this are from non-urban areas, and Cato came from Tusculum.

Pliny *NH* 20.82 and others (Goujard 314 n.20) note cabbage as a cure for insomnia, which corroborates Keil's correction. The manuscript order of words gives an ἀπο κοινοῦ construction (HS 834-5) in which (despite Leo *AKS* 1.84), it is hard to believe in Cato. My suggested rearrangement, as at 141.1, is intended to localise the corruption, if there is corruption; *siquis est ins* will have been obliterated, and then *siquis est* re-deciphered and restored in the wrong place.

seniosus = 'lethargic'.

assam brassicam et unctam caldam This looks as if it means 'broiled cabbage with oil on it served warm', implying that the oil is to be added after the broiling. The problem is that cabbage is usually boiled because it needs moisture for cooking, but it has some natural moisture and can be cooked dry (*experto credite*) in a covered earthenware pot, though that seems a strange procedure.

quam plurimum...tam citissime For this construction see Keil on 34.1, HS 590, KS 2.458.

9 *addito oleum bene* For *bene* = 'generously' cf. 156.7, Plaut. *Men.* 121. The word occurs five times in this vicinity (only once in 156.5; there and here remarkably in most cases at the end of a colon); cf. 1.2-4. For *ferue bene facito* see Leumann 566, Wackernagel 2.175, Löfstedt *PA* 186 and add Cic. 2 *Verr.* 5.38; it contrasts with *deferuefacito bene* above. This is linked to the next sentence by *ubi feruerit* on the same lines as *macerare oportet...ubi macerata erit* 156.5 (for this type of polyptoton in recipes see Wills 312); for the mechanical link to the preceding by *postea* (following *postea in aulam coicito* above) cf. 156.6 *postea feruefacito*, preceded by *postea salem addito* (and in 156.2-4 connection is made by *postea* six times; cf. *deinde* in Speeches 173). *Ad Herenn.* 4.11.16 in an instance of the *genus exile* offers three occurrences of *post(ea)* in four lines. See on Ennius *Euhemerus* (p. 39) and Norden *AT* 377 n.1.

dato edit See on 156.6; *purum* = plain, with no relish on it.

si non...si..non For the first, *si minus* would be usual in classical Latin (HS 667, KS 2.418). In the second case, the sense is *si febre carebit* (*si sine febre erit* 156.6), hence the *non* goes closely with *habebit* and *nisi* is not required. Here the alternative *si febris erit* expressed in 156.6 is omitted.

10 *et hoc* 'moreover'; cf. *hoc amplius* 142 and *et hoc amplius* below and elsewhere (*TLL* 5.1.902.8, 6.3.2732.52). Henceforward items are strung on to each other mechanically; *item, et quibus, et si, et*, though the last two are better linked with *fouebit, fouere*.

essitarit See on praef. 1 and 157.7.

eo hominem demittito Bathe him in it (*TLL* 5.1.489.29).

cura Apart from here, *curatio* (as in 157.8) is invariable in this sense until Augustan times (Richter's (127) alleged Ciceronian instance (*Ad Fam.* 5.16.5) is invalid).

inunguito...uidebunt is a paratactic condition, like the following sentence and *conseruato...facies* above, which is followed by a hypotactic condition.

11 *locos* For this euphemism see *OLD* 2b, *TLL* 1578.44 s.v., J. N. Adams, *Latin Sexual Vocabulary* (1982) 94.

miseri 'painful'; so Plaut. *Truc.* 520 and other instances in *OLD* 3a, *TLL* 1103.63. But *menses seri* is strongly supported by the parallels adduced by Boscherini 78.

circum uestimenta eam dato It is an unreal question whether (a) *circum* is a preposition separated, as dissyllabic prepositions often are, from its noun: (b) it is a verbal prefix in 'tmesis', implying the construction of *circumdare* with double accusative, as in 114.1 (where see Keil). Cf. with (a) Varro *LL* 5.154 *circum aedificatus est Flaminium Campum*, with (b) Verg. *Aen.* 1.175-6 *arida circum / nutrimenta dedit*.

(b) *Origines* and Speeches

Origines 83 Peter = IV.7 Chassignet (Budé) = Gell. 3.7.19

(a) di immortales tribuno militum fortunam ex uirtute eius dedere. nam ita euenit: cum saucius multifariam ibi factus esset, tamen uulnus capitale nullum euenit, eumque inter mortuos, defetigatum uulneribus atque quod sanguen eius defluxerat, cognouere. **(b)** eum sustulere, isque conualuit, saepeque postilla operam rei p. fortem atque strenuam praehibuit, illoque facto, quod illos milites subduxit, exercitum ceterum seruauit. sed idem beneficium quo in loco ponas nimium interest. **(c)** Leonides Laco qui simile apud Thermopylas fecit, propter eius uirtutes omnis Graecia gloriam atque gratiam praecipuam claritudinis inclitissimae decorauere monumentis, signis statuis elogiis historiis aliisque rebus gratissimum id eius factum habuere; at tribuno militum parua laus pro factis relicta, qui idem fecerat atque rem seruauerat.

(a) capitale *Mommsen*, capiti *codd.*
(b) praehibuit *Quicherat*, per- *codd.*
(c) (Laco) quia *Madvig (Adv. crit. 2.592)*

For ease of reference I have subdivided this long section. The passage is discussed by von Albrecht 23.

This is the only substantial passage of the *Origines* in which Cato's actual words are preserved. It recounts an episode in the First Punic War when the Roman army in Sicily was caught in a trap. A tribunus militum volunteered to head a body of 400 men who would attempt to occupy a hillock, thus distracting the Carthaginians and allowing the rest of the Roman army to escape at the cost of their own seemingly inevitable death. It is not clear whether Cato named the tribune. Though Nepos *Cato* 3.4 could be interpreted to mean that Cato's principle of suppressing the names of commanders was applied only after the Punic wars, Pliny *NH* 8.11 mentions it in a context referring to the Punic wars, and it seems to be applied in fr. 87 (even to the Carthaginians in fr. 86; see Leo *GRL* 296). Gellius calls the tribune Q. Caedicius, and Frontinus *Strat.* 1.5.15 = 4.5.10 offers this name as an option, so that one might think that it came from Cato, but other sources give him other names, and Florus 1.18 (= 2.2). 13-14, who has the comparison with Leonidas (accentuated by the adjustment of the number of Roman soldiers from the 400 in Gellius to 300) which might suggest derivation from Cato, has one of these (Calpurnius Flamma). Moreover *tribuno militum* in (c) strongly suggests that he was not named. Unlike Leonidas, this tribune survived.

Gellius 6 also gives the interesting information that Cato represented the tribune as calling the hillock *uerruca*; Quintil. 8.3.48 and 8.6.14, quoting the phrase *saxea est uerruca in summo montis uertice* (usually but without reason taken to be a quotation from tragedy), describes this as a *humilis translatio* (Calboli, *Maia* 48 (1996), 17, who discusses the whole fragment at length, challenges this stylistic assessment). There is a chance that these are the words which Cato put in the mouth of the tribune, but it looks as if Cato was just referring to a hillock, not a rocky outcrop on a mountain.

An attempt at elevation of style is made clear by the use of *atque*, the most dramatic word for 'and' (HS 476); it is found only four times in the *De Agr.* as a copulative. Besides this only -*que*, not *et*, is used as a copula, and that to surfeit. The sentences are nearly all arranged on the pattern subject - (object etc.) - verb, varied only where style requires otherwise (in the last sentence *tribuno* has to come first because of the contrast, in the penultimate one *omnis Graecia* has to yield to the connective *propter eius uirtutes*). This is the order normally observed by legal and religious texts, Cato and historians; see on Quadrigarius 10 and for Caesar e.g. Eden, *Glotta* 40 (1962), 94 (though Caesar can vary when he thinks the context demands it; Panhuis, *Indog. Forsch.* 89 (1984), 154). The one verb in Cato not placed at the end of its clause, *decorauere* in (c), has been displaced to add a touch of artistry in word-order to this stylistically ambitious sentence.

Throughout this passage, and almost invariably in the *Origines* (so far as we have verbal quotations; exceptions frs. 7, 71), Cato uses the more elevated (Leumann 607; Löfstedt *PA* 37) form of the third person plural perfect active ending in -*ere*, as he generally does in the speeches too (exceptions 168, 192-3); in the *De Agr.* there are, naturally enough, only three 3rd person plural perfect active verbs (praef. 1 twice, 152.1), all in -*erunt*. Other early historians and orators, to judge from their fragments, vastly prefer *-erunt*. For the usage in the Caesarian corpus see Pascucci on *Bell. Hisp.* 23.2.

   (**a**) *ita euenit* is followed by a paratactic construction; cf. on *De Agr.* 157.2, HS 529. Another *euenit* in a different sense (as transmitted) follows (cf. on *De Agr.* pr.1), but the text involves the following problems: (1) the Romans knew perfectly well that a head wound is not necessarily fatal; (2) *uulnus euenit* is a strange combination; (3) the dative referring to a part of the body rather than a person is odd after this verb. All these problems are cured by Mommsen's conjecture, 'no wound turned out fatal'. I am not convinced by the interpretation of *capiti* by S. Goldberg, *Understanding Terence* (1986) 194, namely that the tribune was recognised because his face was uninjured; this does not seem to me to fit the immediate context of the phrase at all.

   saucius factus esset instead of *sauciatus esset* slightly lets down the stylistic level (J.P. Krebs - J.H. Schmalz, *Antibarbarus* (ed. 7, 1905) s.v. *facio*). This particular combination is found also in Cic. *Pro Tull.* 56, *Bell. Afr.* 70.5; *De Agr.* 157.3 is different.

   eumque seems to stand in an unduly emphatic position; so do the following *eum* and *isque*, but Cato could have avoided the former only at the cost of abandoning the final position of the verb, and if he had written simply *conualuitque* without expressed subject he would have blurred successive stages in the action. For the general type of connection see *Origines* 71 and on Calpurnius Piso 27. Still, a later writer would probably have written *sublatus tamen conualuit*; but at this stage Latin does not yet make much use of participles. For what it is worth, the only other narrative participle in the remains of the *Origines* is in fr. 101; *defetigatum* here is not such. *circumueniuntur, circumuenti...* in Gellius' narrative (3.7.14) of these events does not profess to be a verbal quotation of Cato, but in *De Agr.* 79 he does have *coquito...coctos eximito*. Note that the subject of *cognouere* and *sustulere* is taken for granted.

   uulneribus atque quod... The two causes for his exhaustion are given in asymmetrical form, an interesting example of the stylistic feature familiar later from Sallust and Tacitus and earlier from Thucydides.

   sanguen is also found in Speeches 211; *sanguis* does not appear in preserved Cato. See NW 1.243.

   (**b**) *postillā* (not elsewhere in Cato, and conceivably even here it should be *post illă*) is somewhat grander than *postea*. For *saepĕque* see on *De Agr.* 156.1.

   praehibuit = praebuit; *operam praebere* is quite common (*TLL* 9.2.666.65), o. *perhibere* is not found elsewhere. For *operam fortem* cf. Quadrigarius 7 and other instances in *TLL* 6.1. 1155.59; for *fortem atque strenuam* cf. *De Agr.* pr.4 (also Livy 38.41.3, Sen. *Ep.* 77.6 and more in Ogilvie on Livy 4.3.16), and for the the the coupling of adjectives Speeches 163.

   illoque facto...illos milites (and perhaps even a preceding *post illa*) shows the indifference to verbal repetition remarked on *De Agr.* pr.2; so does *illo facto -*

simile...fecit - factis - idem fecerat.

When one looks back over this sentence, it comes across as incoherent because thoughts of all kinds have been strung together paratactically and not in either logical or temporal order.

idem beneficium is thrust forward for emphasis (cf. p. 4). *ponas* = 'invest'; the combination with *beneficium* (for which cf. *TLL* 2.1881.29) is indicative of the attitude of the Romans towards conferring benefits. Cato prefixes a *sententia* to the moral of his story.

nimium, as very often particularly in old Latin, means 'very much', not 'too much' as in Speeches 58; *OLD* s.v. 2 and *nimis* 3a.

(c) *Leonides Laco...* as it stands is an anacoluthon, with the hanging nominative *Leonides* taken up by the genitive *eius*; cf. *De Agr.* 34.2 *ager rubricosus...ibi lupinum bonum fiet*, 51 and 133.1 *pulli qui nascentur, eos in terram deprimito*, Speeches 73 *serui, ancillae, siquis eorum sub centone crepuit*, Ennius III, VI, and see HS 29, 731, KS 2.586. It is hard to be sure how far we should ascribe this specifically to reverse attraction of the antecedent to the relative; for this see e.g. Speeches 159 *agrum quem uir habet tollitur* (quoted by DServ. on *Aen.* 1.573, another instance of the idiom), Plaut. *Amph.* 1009 *Naucratem quem conuenire uolui, in naui non erat* and HS 567. For occurrences in laws see de Meo 72 and now *Lex Irnitana* 69 (*JRS* 76 (1986), 170) *iique qui sententias laturi erunt...quisque eorum iuret.* We must certainly recognise the wish to give prominence to the name. Madvig's conjecture, at the cost of introducing a pleonasm between *quia...* and *propter eius uirtutes* (which Madvig also wished to alter to *propterea e. uirtutis*), removes the anomaly as seemingly too informal, but the parallels are strong, the occurrences in laws (and, if it is reverse attraction of an antecedent, in the mouth of Dido) indicate that 'informal' may not be the right description, and in any case the rest of the passage up to this point has not shown any great stylistic artistry. See the discussion of the problem by Calboli in E. Norden, *La Prosa d'Arte Antica* (1986) 1090.

However, Cato now tries to elevate the style with some flourishes. One is *claritudinis inclitissimae monumentis*, with which cf. *Origines* 63 *in maximum decus atque in excelsissimam claritudinem sublimauit*. Abstract nouns in *-udo* are popular in elevated contexts at this time (HS 744; Till 4, 57, 65 = 20, 99, 112), but, except for archaising writers, later went out of fashion; this one was replaced by *claritas* (note *inclitae claritatis* Val. Max. praef.). *inclitus* too is a mainly poetical word, used also by historians but not by Caesar, Nepos or Cicero; apart from here, the superlative is found only once each in Columella and Gellius (Livy uses *maxime inclitus*). Another is the assonant *gloriam atque gratiam* (for which see *TLL* 6.2.2064.26; an assonant pair in the sense discussed on *De Agr.* 141.2). His object seems to be ironical, to mock the extravagance of Greece in honouring Leonidas, and the same is the point of the following enumeration of honours, which is marked as epexegetic by the resumption of *gratiam* in *gratissimum* (the superlative matching *inclitissimae*). The word *historiis* (not found elsewhere in Cato) is itself Greek, and Greek words seem to have played a part in the creation of *elogium* (see on my *ML* 63.10); Cato could have used the Latin word *titulis*. *signa* means paintings or relief sculptures (*OLD* s.v. 12b-c) as contrasted with free-standing statues. The list is arranged so that the Latin words are bound together by alliteration and rise from 2 to 3 syllables, but are outweighed by the Greek words, each of 4 syllables; similarly on a larger scale the expansive sentence about Leonidas is followed by the much smaller one allotted to the Roman. However Cato's point is not fair, since according to Pliny *NH* 22.11 the tribune, whom he calls Calpurnius Flamma, was awarded the extremely rare honour of the *corona graminea*.

Leonides Cato uses the form of the name which he knew from Herodotus, not *Leonidas* (Cicero etc.) nor the latinized *Leonida*. Polybius 9.38.3 also uses - ης, and it is a variant (apparently with weaker support) at Diod. Sic. 11.4.2. Cato himself was proud of having fought at another battle of Thermopylae, in which he used his knowledge of the topography, no doubt derived from Herodotus, to find the path used by the Persians (Plut. 14). This among other things shows the falsity of allegations that he did not acquaint himself with Greek literature until late in life; his posture of anti-hellenism prevailed over the facts.

uirtutes 'glorious deeds'; the plural magnifies Leonidas as the Greeks saw him, whereas the tribune only got a singular *ex eius uirtute* (a) from Cato's Roman viewpoint.

omnis Graecia...decorauere For this ad sensum construction see Lex Furfensis 9 and HS 436-7, KS 1.22.

aliisque rebus Presumably poems; so Norden *Kl. Schr.* 558, who remarks that Cato did not have enough respect for the genre to name it.

id eius illustrates the tendency of pronouns to cluster (HS 400, KS 2.617).

parua pro factis 'small in proportion to his deeds'.

An excellent commentary on the Speeches of Cato was published by M. T. Sblendorio Cugusi in 1982; my notes are inevitably much indebted to this, and in this section I provide references to her numeration as well as to Malcovati's.

Origines 95 Peter = V 3 Chassignet = Speeches 163-9 Malcovati = 118-124 Sblendorio Cugusi = Gell. 6.3 passim.
Pro Rodiensibus

163 Scio solere plerisque hominibus rebus secundis atque prolixis atque prosperis animum excellere atque superbiam atque ferociam augescere atque crescere. quod mihi nunc magnae curae est, quom haec res tam secunde processit, nequid in consulendo aduorsi eueniat quod nostras secundas res confutet, neue haec laetitia nimis luxuriose eueniat. aduorsae res edomant et docent quid opus siet facto,

secundae res laetitia transuorsum trudere solent a recte consulendo atque intellegendo. quo maiore opere dico suadeoque uti haec res aliquot dies proferatur, dum ex tanto gaudio in potestatem nostram redeamus.

164 atque ego quidem arbitror Rodienses noluisse nos ita depugnare uti depugnatum est, neque regem Persen uinci. sed non Rodienses modo id noluere, sed multos populos atque multas nationes idem noluisse arbitror. atque haud scio an partim eorum fuerint qui non nostrae contumeliae causa id noluerint euenire, sed enim id metuere, si nemo esset homo quem uereremur, quicquid luberet faceremus, ne sub solo imperio nostro in seruitute nostra essent; libertatis suae causa in ea sententia fuisse arbitror. atque Rodienses tamen Persen publice numquam adiuuere. cogitate quanto nos inter nos priuatim cautius facimus. nam unusquisque nostrum, siquis aduorsus rem suam quid fieri arbitra[n]tur, summa ui contra nititur ne aduorsus eam fiat; quod illi tamen perpessi.

165 ea nunc derepente tanta beneficia ultro citroque, tantam amicitiam relinquemus? quod illos dicimus uoluisse facere, id nos priores facere occupabimus?

166 qui acerrime aduorsus eos dicit, ita dicit, hostes uoluisse fieri. ecquis est tandem uestrorum qui, quod ad sese attineat, aequum censeat poenas dare ob eam rem, quod arguatur male facere uoluisse? nemo, opinor; nam ego, quod ad me attinet, nolim.

167 quid nunc? ecqua tandem lex est tam acerba quae dicat: siquis illud facere uoluerit, mille minus dimidium familiae multa esto; siquis plus quingenta iugera habere uoluerit, tanta poena esto; siquis maiorem pecuum numerum habere uoluerit, tantum damnas esto? atque nos omnia plura habere uolumus, et id nobis impune est.

168 sed si honorem non aequum est haberi ob eam rem, quod bene facere uoluisse quis dicit neque fecit tamen, Rodiensibus oberit quod non male fecerunt, sed quia uoluisse dicuntur facere?

169 Rodienses superbos esse aiunt, id obiectantes quod mihi et liberis meis minime dici uelim. sint sane superbi: quid id ad nos attinet? idne irascimini, siquis est superbior quam nos?

163 in rebus *Gell. 13.25.14*
    quom *Haupt ap. Jordan*, quod *codd.*
    edomant *Price*, se domant *codd.*, saepe domant *Calboli*
166 uestrorum qui *excerpta Sciopii*, qui uestrorum *codd.*
167 atqui *codd. dett.*
168 oberit *anon. ap. Gronovium*, taberit *codd.*

In the Third Macedonian War the people of Rhodes began to waver in their allegiance to Rome, and eventually tried to mediate between Rome and King Perseus, but their envoys unfortunately arrived in Rome just after news had been received of the defeat and capture of Perseus in 168, which naturally annoyed the senate even though the Rhodians hastily substituted an unconvincing congratulatory speech for the one which they had intended to deliver. A proposal was actually put forward to declare war on Rhodes, but Cato delivered the speech here discussed in its favour, which he subsequently included in *Origines* V (see Astin 235). The narrative of the events surrounding the delivery of Cato's speech is found in Livy 45.20-25 (with reminiscences of Cato's words); see *CAH* 8.336-8, Astin 123, 273. Gellius quotes extensive fragments from the speech in order to refute criticisms of it made by Cicero's freedman Tiro. See the discussion by von Albrecht 11; the remains of this speech have been edited by G. Calboli (1978).

163

This was the exordium of the speech. It closely resembles another exordium, 122 M = 90 SC (probably earlier than this) *scio fortunas secundas neglegentiam prendere solere*. In each case Cato begins with a *sententia*, here underlined by an alliteration of *s*. In this fragment the *sententia*, the sentiment of which incorporates a thought of strongly Greek flavour, is followed by an application to the actual situation (with *haec res*), then another *sententia* (again with *secundae res* and *solent*) followed by another application (again with *haec res*). The logic of the passage is linked together by *rebus secundis -secunde* (see below on this) - *nequid in consulendo aduorsi - nostras res secundas - laetitia - aduorsae res - secundae res - laetitia - a recte consulendo*. After the first *rebus secundis* the order of noun and adjective indicating 'prosperity' or 'adversity' is reversed because a contrast is introduced.

secundis atque prolixis atque prosperis A striking accumulation of synonyms (Gell. 13.25.13 with reference to this passage comments on Cato's fondness for this; for the roots of the feature in Latin see on *De Agr.* 141.2 and p. 8, though by now it has clearly become a device for rhetorical emphasis (Scherer 214)), and of the connective *atque*, for which see on *Origines* 83; Marcus Aurelius ap. Fronto p. 34.19-21 remarks on Cato's partiality for this connective. HS 478 and 786 compare 21 M = 5 SC *cognoui atque intellexi atque arbitror* (with which cf. Apul. *Apol.* 25 *nosse atque scire atque callere*), see also 50, 128, 178, 185 M = 13, 93, 135, 139 SC. There are still three occurrences of this conjunction to come in this sentence, two of them connecting synonyms; Cato sees no reason to vary in the odd man out after *excellere* (cf. on *De Agr.* 1.3), and was probably attracted by the identity of rhythm *atque superbiam - atque ferociam* (to a minimal extent this supports Fraenkel's suggestion that Cato's fondness for *atque* may be influenced by rhythm). Thereafter in 164-9 there are six cases of *atque* (two of them connecting pairs, and another possibly open to faint doubt), three of *et* and one of *-que*; these numbers (including 163) accurately reflect the overall relative frequency of the copulative conjunctions in Cato's speeches.

prolixus is found in this sense ('flowing smoothly', from the root of *liqueo* etc.) also at Cic. *Ad Att.* 1.1.2, and nowhere else; it alliterates with *prosperis*. See on *De Agr.* 141 and p. 3 for the Latin roots of such alliteration.

superbiam...crescere Homoeoteleuton binds together each of these pairs. Note that, typically of Cato, the sentence ends in the shorter of two paired words; see p. 9.

quod is commonly followed by an epexegesis (HS 572), here given in the *ne*-clauses. At this date causal *quom* naturally takes the indicative; see on Gracchus 44d. Perhaps in Cato one does not even need to change the second *quod* (cf. on *De Agr.* pr.1). Others prefer to read *quo...quod*, comparing *quo maiore opere* below, but the comparative there makes a difference; causal *quo* is legitimate (see on Scipio 19), but is not found elsewhere in Cato (nor are *quare* and *quocirca*).

secunde This adverb is not found elsewhere and was clearly created by Cato for this context; for other such neologisms see on *De Agr.* 2.7.

eueniat...eueniat The figure of epiphora; cf. on Speeches 59.

laetitia...luxuriose Another alliterative pair. Both are agricultural terms, *laetus* referring to flourishing crops, *luxuriosus* to those which have gone to seed; cf. Cic. *De Or.* 3.155 *luxuriem esse in herbis, laetas segetes etiam rustici dicunt*, id. *Or.* 81, Colum. 3.12.3 *laetissimam (terram) luxuria...laborare*, Ovid *AA* 1.359 and Livian parallels quoted by Hertz in his apparatus to Gellius. *Laetamen* means 'manure', *laetificare* 'to fertilize'. The former is taken up in the next sentence, and that to Cato provides enough connection without any *nam* (cf. on *De Agr.* 157.7). Then at the end, uncharacteristically for Cato, it is varied to *gaudio*; see on 164 for another such variation.

aduorsae res...secundae res Classical style would have felt it unnecessary to repeat the second *res*; cf. p. 5.

edomant et docent, dico suadeoque Cato feels that for the moment the audience has had enough of *atque*. In the last sentence the heavy initial verbal ornamentation is brought to a down-to-earth conclusion. For *dico ut* see Bennett 1.213, *TLL* 5.986.69; here of course the combination with the synonym (cf. on *De Agr.* 141.2 and p. 8) *suadeo* helps.

quid opus siet facto See on *De Agr.* 2.6.

transuorsum trudere Another alliteration. Other writers prefer to couple less obtrusive verbs with this adjective (even Sallust *Jug.* 6.2 sticks to *agere*).

recte consulendo atque intellegendo takes up *consulendo* above; see on *De Agr.* pr.3 and p. 9.

maiore opere is the comparative of *magnopere*.

in potestatem n. r. 'regain self-control', *compotes nostri fiamus*.

164

This passage is organised so that topic (1) is introduced by *atque* and answered by *sed*, and topic (2) is also introduced by *atque* and answered by *atque...tamen* making the same point as *neque fecit tamen* in 168 (on the logical structure of this part see below). (1) is introduced by *arbitror...noluisse* and ended by *noluisse arbitror*, the order in the second case being due to the need to put the subject of the infinitive first for the sake of contrast. In (2) the charge which Cato is going to refute is introduced by *haud scio an* and ended by *arbitror*, the former showing a desire for variety of expression rare in Cato (see on 163 *laetitia - gaudio*). As well as these occurrences, the passage also has a *noluerint* and an *arbitrantur*; cf. on *De Agr.* pr.2.

    uti depugnatum est For the indicative see on *De Agr.* 1.6.

    nolo...neque Cf. HS 340 and on *De Agr.* 141.4.

    Persen For the declension of this name see NW 1.517-8; it is properly Perseus, but the diphthong *eu* hardly exists in Latin, whence *Achilles* = ᾿Αχιλλεύς etc.

    sed...sed The first links the sentences, the second follows on *non modo*.

    A *populus* has political organisation, a *natio* only a common ethnic origin.

    partim eorum fuerint For this construction see HS 46-7, KS 1.26.

    In the combination *sed enim* the latter keeps its original sense of assevera-tion (HS 508, KS 2.78); editors show by their punctuation that they have not grasped the logic of this passage, and do not realise that we here have the regular sequence *non A sed B*. Cato's argument is: in the case of some Rhodians the disloyalty was due not to any desire to humiliate us, but to fears for their own future status, in short concern for their liberty. This explains why *nostrae* is placed before its noun; it is because of the 'we - they' contrast. Had *libertatis suae causa* been closer to *non nostrae contumeliae causa*, Cato would have written *suae libertatis*.

    The construction of *id metuere...essent* has caused much unnecessary dispute. As it stands it is a perfect example of the order of clauses discussed on *De Agr.* 1.7, as Giré, *Ant. Class.* 48 (1979), 549 argues, with good parallels for the order *metuere si...ne*; in *Bell. Hisp.* 36.2 we have *si...timuit ne*. The only problem is the relationship of the clauses *si nemo esset* and *faceremus*, and the answer to that is that they are in asyndeton, like *si ei opus non apparet, dicit uilicus sedolo se fecisse* in *De Agr.* 2.2. If this seems too harsh, we might read *uereremur <ut>. uereor*, unlike *metuo*, implies an element of respect (see e.g. Cic. *Cato* 37).

    nemo homo implies either the fading of awareness that *nemo* is itself *ne homo* (Festus 162), or else a deliberate repetition of the *homo* element for emphasis; for the combination see HS 56-7, 205, Till 13 = 34.

    nostro...nostra An emphatic repetition.

    facimus An indicative in an indirect question, as at *De Agr.* 6.4; contrast ibid. 30 *cogitato hiemis quam longa siet* and for the variation see on *De Agr.* pr. 1. Such indicatives are quite common in early Latin after verbs like *cogitare* (KS 2.489.3a; e.g. Ter. *Haut.* 638); see p. 11.

    nos contrasts with *Rodienses*. The sequence of thought is: the Rhodians from self-interest may have been inclined to favour Perseus, but they did not give him any concrete aid. We Romans are much more cautious [heavy irony]; in such a situation we would not have let our own interests take second place, but the Rhodians allowed this to happen [by not giving material support to Perseus].

A classical writer might have felt *ne...fiat* superfluous.

165

ea...tanta beneficia The hyperbaton gives great emphasis.

ultro citroque is used adjectivally (see KS 1.218, HS 171); this is quite easy when the noun, like *beneficia* here, has strong verbal connections. The next sentence, like 168, shows the figure of *contrarium*, reasoning by contraries, highlighted by the chiasmus *uoluisse facere - facere occupabimus. quod...id* mean 'to wage war'.

166

Cato uses a similar argument in Speeches 197 M = 153 SC *tamen dicunt deficere uoluisse* (sc. *Lusitanos*).

dicit, ita dicit Cf. *De Agr.* pr. 2 *quom laudabant, ita laudabant.*

uestrorum For this form (contrast *nostrum* 164) see Leumann 465. This must depend on *ecquis*, though editors seem quite content with the manuscript order, which precludes this.

167

tam...quae For the consecutive relative see KS 2.298.

siquis...esto [repeated three times]. This is the figure of *complexio* (Lausberg 633). *uoluerit* here is not in any way to be related to the formula discussed on *De Agr.* 5.4 or any legal formulation (this against Daube 38-9); as a *reductio ad absurdum* Cato is simply distinguishing inclination from action, as in 168.

mille...multa esto Cf. the Lex Silia quoted by Festus 246 *eum quis uolet magistratus multare, dum minore parti familias taxat, liceto,* the Lex Bantina (Bruns 54 = *FIRA* 1.83 = Crawford 200 = Warmington IV 298) *sei quis mag(istratus) multam inrogare uolet, [quei uolet, dum minoris] partus familias taxsat, liceto* (cf. also Bücheler's translation of the Oscan part of this law in Bruns 50-1 = *FIRA* 1.164 = Crawford 281) and the Lex Gabinia Calpurnia de insula Delo 32 (Crawford 346) *eius familia pe[cunia...] minus dimi[diae partis...].* See too Fronto p. 93.7 *ut antiquitus multas inrogari mos fuit, mille minus dimidio.* It is disputed whether this means 'half of his property less 1000 sesterces' or 'a thousand sesterces, provided that that be less than half of his property'; Latinity decidedly favours the former interpretation. For *familia = patrimonium* see *TLL* s.v. 237.57, *RE* s.v. 1980-1; it is not plain what exactly is meant at *De Agr.* 138.

illud means 'such and such a thing', and similarly *tanta* and *tantum*; see HS 197. The latter use perhaps derived from instances preceding specification of the amount, cf. Bücheler's translation of the Oscan Lex Bantina, Bruns 50 = *FIRA* 1. 164 = Crawford 281, *multa tanta esto: n. MM.*

This book is not the place for discussion of the laws about holding of public land and grazing rights in force in Cato's day; see *CAH* 8.203, D. J. Gargola, *Lands,*

Laws and Gods (1995) 136. *maiorem* means 'than the law in a preceding clause has permitted'.

tantum damnas The accusative is unexpected in place of a judicial genitive or ablative. Alfenus *Dig.* 30.106 *si in testamento scriptum esset 'heres meus aureos centum Licinio damnas esto' neque adscripsisset 'dare', deberi legatum constat*, far from validating it, shows that it was unorthodox. Perhaps here too one should read *<dare> damnas*, but the accusative may be defended by that which indicates a fine after *condemno* (HS 76, de Meo 107 n. 67).

atque is here adversative in sense; see KS 2.22, Leo *AKS* 1.57. *atqui* is still rare in Plautus and is not found elsewhere in extant Cato. This sentence, incorporating a paradox, hints at an apprehension on Cato's part that the Roman desire to subjugate Rhodes was due to greed; see Gellius 7 and 52, Sall. *Cat.* 51.5 *postquam bello confecto de Rhodiis consultum est, maiores nostri, nequis diuitiarum magis quam iniuriae causa bellum inceptum diceret, inpunitos eos dimisere* (spoken by Caesar opposing the harsh punishment presently advocated by another Cato). Because of *poena* above, Malcovati wished to spell *inpoene*, as is somewhat uncertainly transmitted in Speeches 173; in fact Cato doubtless spelt the word so. *Poena* is a Greek loan word found as early as the XII Tables (it must have been taken into Latin before that); it originally means 'compensation', so that *impune* = νηποινεί, but soon acquired a more general sense, as here. The noun in its earliest occurrences is nearly always plural, as in 166 (*RE* suppl. 9.843), with only rare instances of the singular, as here and Plaut. *Capt.* 695 (XII Tables 8.3 is not a verbal quotation, but 8.4 with the genitive singular (Löfstedt *Synt* 1.128) is). See Norden *AAP* 254 n.2, Ducos 60, Wieacker (1988) 304 n.93. Lamacchia in *Studia Florentina A. Ronconi* (1970) 135 draws attention to combinations with the word which exactly mirror Greek expressions.

168

This fragment presents an *argumentum ex contrario* (Lausberg 394).

One could read *uoluisse <se>*, but see on *De Agr.* 2.2.

oberit is a perfectly satisfactory emendation; as Hertz explains, the reading of the mss. is probably a substituted variant, †(= *uel) aberit*.

quod...quia For this variation see HŠ 585-6, KS 2.384, *ML* 172.6-7 with my note; for *quia* introducing a substantival clause cf. Speeches 174 M = 218 SC, HS 586, KS 2.271, Bennett 1.130.

For the termination of *fecerunt* see on *Origines* 83.

uoluisse dicuntur (male) facere changes the word-order relative to *bene facere uoluisse quis dicit* because 'are said to have wished' has to receive stress as a double contradiction of 'actually did'.

169

obiectantes does not really differ from *obicientes*; see on *De Agr.* 157.7. *id obiectantes* is an instance of a construction extremely rare in early Latin, a present participle with a direct object; there is another case in Piso fr. 27 (p. 141).

quod...minime dici uelim Tarquinius Superbus gave an enduring negative undertone to the word; *debellare superbos*, as Vergil has it, is the Roman mission. Rhodians had a reputation for pride (Plaut. *Epid.* 300-1, Ter. *Eun.* 420 sqq., Diogenianus 5.18). *dico* sometimes has specific reference to criticisms (Mart. 7.18.1-2, *CIL* 11.6204).

sint sane superbi An alliterative *concessio* (on *De Agr.* pr.1). *superbior quam nos* takes up the notion of swelling pride due to prosperity from 163.

---

58 Malcovati = 42 Sblendorio Cugusi = Gell. 10.3.17
In Q. Minucium Thermum de falsis pugnis

dixit a decemuiris parum bene sibi cibaria curata esse. iussit uestimenta detrahi atque flagro caedi. decemuiros Bruttiani uerberauere, uidere multi mortales. quis hanc contumeliam, quis hoc imperium, quis hanc seruitutem ferre potest? nemo hoc rex ausus est facere: eane fieri bonis, bono genere gnatis, boni consultis! ubi societas? ubi fides maiorum? insignitas iniurias, plagas, uerbera, uibices, eos dolores atque carnificinas per dedecus atque maximam contumeliam, inspectantibus popularibus suis atque multis mortalibus, te facere ausum esse! set quantum luctum, quantum gemitum, quid lacrimarum, quantum fletum factum audiui! serui iniurias nimis aegre ferunt: quid illos, bono genere gnatos, magna uirtute praeditos, opinamini animi habuisse atque habituros dum uiuent?

59 Malcovati = 43 Sblendorio Cugusi = Gell. 13.25.12
In Q. Minucium Thermum de decem hominibus

tuum nefarium facinus peiore facinore operire postulas; succidias humanas facis, tantam trucidationem facis, decem funera facis, decem capita libera interficis, decem hominibus uitam eripis indicta causa, iniudicatis, indemnatis.

Q. Minucius Thermus was consul in 193, and the province of Liguria fell to his lot. He claimed to have subdued the Ligurians, and on his return home in 190 petitioned for a triumph, which however was denied to him through the opposition of Cato, expressed in two orations evidently both delivered in the senate. See Livy 37.46.1-2, Astin 59, *CAH* 8.115. The title of the first indicates that Cato accused him of inventing some of his victories, but the actual preserved fragment deals with an extraneous accusation.

58

dixit, iussit The verbs come first in order to focus attention on the doings of Thermus himself; cf. 173 (a). This placement is quite common in lively narrative (HS 403, Kroll 98, Scherer 107, KS 2.599); for initial placement generally cf. Dressler, *Indog. Forsch.* 83 (1969), 15.

decemuiris The town councilors, who were supposed to supply provisions when a Roman magistrate visited.

caedi sc. *eos*; the change of subject is as easy as at *De Agr.* 2.2, but here adds vivid brevity, produces symmetry and ensures that every word counts. Cf. Gracchus fr. 48-9 (with *uestimenta detracta sunt*) and many other cases of such abuses by Roman magistrates like Verres (see below); a parallel is drawn by Gellius in this chapter with Cic. 2 *Verr.* 5.161. Cato himself perhaps promoted a *lex Porcia de tergo ciuium* (Astin 22).

Bruttiani Natives of Bruttium who had defected to Hannibal and as punishment were forced to perform demeaning services for magistrates (Gellius 18, Paul. Fest. 31, Strabo 5.4.13.251, Appian *Hann.* 61); the juxtaposition with *decemuiros* underlines the indignity to the latter. The antithetical basis of the whole sentence is emphasised by the chiasmus *Bruttiani uerberauere, uidere multi mortales* and the alliteration of the verbs. The effective elasticity of the word-order contrasts strikingly with *Origines* 83.

multi mortales A stately alliterative combination, found as early as Naevius, *Bell. Poen.* 5 Morel; in prose it is used by Quadrigarius 76 and by Cicero and other classical writers. See the discussion by Gellius 13.29 with Ronconi, *Stud. Urb.* 49.1 (1975), 133, Oakley on Livy 6.16.4.

nemo...consultis An argument a fortiori. For *nemo* used adjectivally see KS 1.652, NW 2.520-2, *OLD* s.v. 5a. *Rex* carries its usual pejorative sense 'tyrant', and is emphasised by the 'Sperrung' which separates it from *nemo*; cf. on *De Agr.* 5.4.

bonis...consultis A tricolon which, as quite often in Cato, does not end with its longest item (cf. p. 9). For the phraseology cf. Ter. *Ph.* 115 *bonam bonis prognatam*, Quadrigarius 15 *summo genere gnatus* and 10.18 (p. 144), Plaut. *Epid.* 107, *Merc.* 969. *Genere gnatus* is an etymological figure (cf. on 59); to underline this Quadrigarius retains the archaic spelling *gnatus*. There is also polyptoton of *bonus. Boni consulere* means 'to reckon as creditable'; here it is transferred to a personal passive, as at Apul. *De Deo Socr.* 23 *sapiens boni consultus* (which of course is one of Apuleius' deliberate archaisms). Here the phrase corresponds to *magna uirtute praeditos* below. Cato now repeats his points in almost the same order: *uidere multi mortales - inspectantibus...multis mortalibus, ausus est facere - te facere ausum esse, bono genere gnatis - bono genere gnatos*; but the repeated *contumeliam* stands in different relative positions.

insignitas iniurias An alliterative combination; the adverb *insignite* is associated with *iniuria* four times in Plautus.

uerbera, uibices ('weals') is another alliterative pair (see p. 3 and on *De Agr.* 141), cf. Pliny *NH* 30.118 *uerberum uulnera atque uibices.*

inspectantibus This verb often implies watching without doing anything because of either indifference or, as here, helplessness. Outside Plautus, who uses the verb freely, there are only two occurrences before the end of the 1st century A.D. in which it is not employed in an ablative absolute present participle. Cf. Quadrigarius 10.37.

suis in strict grammar should be *eorum*, but the reflexive aptly suggests a close emotional link between the victims and the spectators.

facere This verb here, in *fletum factum* below and in 59 functions as a jack of all trades capable of governing a variety of objects; see on Quadrigarius 10.10-11 and HS 754-5.

quantum luctum...fletum This passage is recalled by Cic. 2 *Verr.* 1.76 *quid lacrimarum ipsum Neronem putatis profudisse? quem fletum totius Asiae fuisse, quem luctum et gemitum Lampsacenorum?* Cicero however breaks up Cato's series of nouns into separate sentences, in each of which a different person or community is named as experiencing grief, and thus presents more aspects. T. N. Habinek, *The Colometry of Latin Prose* (1985) 185-6 and 192-3 acutely compares this colon with the form of the *uersus quadratus* (see my *FLP* 478) in which anaphoric cola are self-contained within the metra; in fact *quantum luctum, quantum gemitum, quid lacrimarum <uidimus>* or the like would constitute such a *uersus quadratus*, followed by the beginning of another, *quantum fletum factum audiui.* This does not of course mean that Cato was consciously recalling this verse medium; it just means that he and the verse form independently employ stylistic means deeply rooted in old Latin. Cato says *quid lacrimarum* rather than *quot lacrimas* in order to retain quantitative equivalence with the other items, even though a plural partitive genitive other than *rerum* is rare after *quid*; Bennett 2.26, missing this instance, quotes only three others. Generally one may compare 28 M = 15 SC *tantum nauium, tantum exercitum, tantum <com>meatum.*

nimis aegre = aegerrime; see on *Origines* 83 (b). This is another argument a fortiori.

opinamini animi A doubtless accidental jingle; cf. *De Agr.* 115.1 *ueratri atri. animi* is a long way from the *quid* which governs it because *illos* with all its attributes has to be placed as early as possible for the contrast.

dum uiuent A characteristically short colon at the conclusion (see p. 9). For the indicative see on *De Agr.* 1.6.

59

This does not refer to the same ten men as 58, since those were not killed. There are four other brief and mutilated fragments of this speech; this one illustrates the rhetorical figure of *congeries* (Lausberg 406).

facinus...facinore is an instance of polyptoton; one may compare the proverbial *malum malo addere* and the like (Otto no. 1018 and *Nachträge* 59, 182; similar phrases in Seneca are collected by Landgraf, *ALL* 5 (1888), 185). 'In Latin literature what is most often increased is crime and gore' (Wills 192). The nouns are taken up by the verb *facis*, an etymological figure (see index s.v. and p. 8) for which cf. Haffter 34. *tuum* is emphatically placed; the whole responsibility is put on Thermus (cf. Quadrigarius 41).

postulas 'you look to', as commonly in early Latin (*OLD* 4).

succidias is normally applied to animals (cf. *Origines* 39); the paradoxical combination with *humanas* underlines the inhumanity. *Facis...facis...facis* (ingeniously followed by the compound *interficis*) illustrates the figure of epiphora (see on *De Agr.* 2.7); for the verb itself see on 58. The epiphora is interwoven with anaphora of *decem* in a rising tricolon. But this rising tricolon is followed (characteristically for Cato; see p. 9) by a falling one, *indicta causa, iniudicatis, indemnatis*; here one manuscript offers *incondemnatis*, but this reading is stemmatically quite impossible. Cato appears to have coined the word *iniudicatus* for the sake of the homoeoarchon, though the tricolon is still not quite symmetrical; for such coinages see on *De Agr.* 2.7. Such (often asyndetic) negative tricola have a long history, in the classical languages since *Iliad* 9.63; prose instances are Heraclitus 92 DK, Gorgias *Palamedes* 36, Plato *Phaedr.* 240a, Demosth. 4.36, 9.40, 25.52, Gellius 1.5.3. As some of these occurrences will show, the form is particularly suitable for denunciation. For Latin instances cf. Plaut. *Persa* 168, 408, *Rud.* 194, 652, Lucil. 600, Pliny *NH* 30.17. Note also Accius 364 *o ingratifici Argiui, inmunes Graii, inmemores benefici*.

capita libera is a phrase common in legal contexts (*TLL* 3.404.66), and thus highlights the illegality of Thermus' actions.

Fr. 173 Malcovati = 169 Sblendorio Cugusi = Fronto p. 90.15
De Sumptu Suo

(a) Iussi caudicem proferri ubi mea oratio scripta erat de ea re quod sponsionem feceram cum M. Cornelio; tabulae prolatae. maiorum bene facta perlecta; deinde quae ego pro re p. fecissem leguntur. (b) ubi id utrumque perlectum est, deinde scriptum erat in oratione: 'numquam ego pecuniam neque meam neque sociorum per ambitionem dilargitus sum'. 'attat, noli noli †scribere†', inquam, 'istud; nolunt audire'. (c) deinde recitauit: 'numquam <ego> praefectos per sociorum uestrorum oppida imposiui, qui eorum bona, liberos diriperent'. istud quoque dele; nolunt audire. (d) recita porro. 'numquam ego praedam neque quod de hostibus captum esset neque manubias inter pauculos amicos meos diuisi ut illis eriperem qui cepissent'. istuc quoque dele: nihil minus uolunt dici, non opus est recitato. (e) 'numquam ego euectionem dataui quo amici mei per symbolos pecunias magnas caperent'. perge istuc quoque uti cum maxime delere. **(f)** 'numquam ego argentum pro uino congiario inter apparitores atque amicos meos disdidi neque eos malo publico diuites feci'. enimuero usque istuc ad lignum dele. **(g)** uide sis quo loco res p. siet, ubi, quod rei p. bene fecissem unde gratiam capiebam, nunc idem illud memorare non audeo, ne inuidiae siet. ita inductum est male facere inpoene, bene facere non inpoene licere.

(b) cribere *suprascripto* s *cod.*; recitare *Haines (ed. Loeb 2.44), del. Leo GRL 476 n.3*

(c) numquam <ego> *A. Schaefer,* numquos *cod.*
  bona <coniuges> *Meyer,* liberos <seruos> *Castiglioni ap. Malcovati*
  istuc *Jordan*

(d) nihil minus *Jordan,* nihilominus *cod.*

(g) quo in loco *imprimit van den Hout, falso*
  ubi *Haupt (Opusc. 2.351),* uti *cod.*
  inpoene *bis manus prima,* inpune *bis corrector ut vid.*

This speech was attributed to 164 by P. Fraccaro, *Opusc.* 1.257, but that dating depends on the uncertain attribution to this speech of 174 M = 218 SC. This fragment quotes from Cato's earlier speech *De ea re quod sponsionem fecerat cum M. Cornelio* (203 M = 168 SC), but the date of that too is uncertain; Sblendorio Cugusi inclines to put it around 170 (see on (c)). It has been suggested that this speech is a reaction to an accusation of luxurious living before the censors; one possibility is the unfriendly censors of 159. Plut. 25 records that towards the end of his life Cato did relax his earlier austerity.

I have introduced subdivisions for ease of reference.

(a) *iussi* is placed first as in 58.

caudicem This form usually means 'block of wood'; elsewhere it means 'book' only at Sen. *Brev. Vit.* 13.4, where Seneca has to use it to explain the cognomen Caudex. Cato himself employs *codicillus* thrice in the *De Agr.* The plebeian *o* appears to have established itself in the colloquial diminutive before it did so in the primary form. Likewise Cato uses *caulis (De Agr.* 70.1 should probably be emended to this) but *coliculus.*

mea The emphatic position of this word was probably justified by some contrasting term in the preceding sentence.

sponsionem Cf. 206 M = 186 SC and Crook, *JRS* 66 (1976), 133.

prolatae...perlecta The omission of the auxiliary verb suits the quick movement of events. The second verb is taken up by the uncompounded form, an ancient method of expression (see on XII Tables 8. 1-2); the sense requires the revival of the compound in *perlectum.* As in Greek courts, an official *lector* (Cic. *De Or.* 2.223) or *recitator (Pro Clu.* 141) was provided for reading from documents.

The historic present (found elsewhere in Cato's speeches in 29-30 M = 17-18 SC) *leguntur* is taken up by *inquam*; then with *recita* (d) we are transported back into the actual court-room at the time, with Cato representing himself as playing a lively charade. G. Kennedy, *The Art of Rhetoric in the Roman World* (1972) 43, partly misled by the corrupt *scribere*, totally misapprehends what is going on ('Cato describes himself as seated in his study planning his speech and dictating to his slave').

 maiorum sc. *meorum*; for their *bene facta* see Plut. 1.1-2.

 deinde recurs in (b) and (c); see on *De Agr.* 157.9.

 fecissem One would have expected this to be a relative clause rather than an indirect question (if that is what it is; cf. on *esset* (d)).

 dilargitus - (c) *diriperent* - (d) *diuisi* - (f) *disdidi* There is much emphasis on spreading around corrupt profits.

 (b) *id utrumque* See KS 1.427.

 attat is a lively colloquial interjection; the duplication *noli noli* contributes to the same effect.

 istud here and in (c) changes to *istuc* in (d) - (f).

 (c) The following passages refer either to Cato's government of Sardinia as praetor in 198 or of Spain as consul in 195. In 171 he was one of the *patroni* of the Spaniards who obtained a senate decree *ne praefecti in oppida sua ad pecunias cogendas imponerentur* (Livy 43.2.12).

 inposiui The speeches show the same variation as the *De Agr.* (see on pr.1) in the perfect of this verb.

 bona liberos For the asyndeton bimembre see on *De Agr.* 2.2; some here emend (see the apparatus).

 (d) Cato expounded his views on this matter in his speech *De praeda militibus diuidenda* (224-6 M = 172-4 SC; undated). Livy 34.46.2-3 reports that in his Spanish triumph Cato shared the booty between his soldiers and cavalry, not members of his *cohors*; cf. Plut. 10.4-5.

 praedam...manubias Another descending tricolon (see p. 9). For the distinction between *manubiae* (the general's share of booty) and *praeda* see Gell. 13.25 (though the matter is controversial; E. M. Orlin, *Temples, Religion and Politics in the Roman Republic* (1997) 117). I do not know why Cato writes *captum esset* rather than *c. erat*; cf. on *fecissem* (a).

 amici here and in (f) refers to members of the *cohors*; see *TLL* 1.1908.60. Cato again uses the diminutive *pauculi* in 43 M = 12 SC; it is more invidious than the simple form.

 nihil minus is a much better emendation than *nihil eo minus* (H. Allen); good parallels are quoted by Sblendorio Cugusi and J. B. Hofmann, *Lat. Umgangssprache* (ed. 3, 1951) 208 n.9.

 (e) *euectio* is the right of using the horses of the *cursus publicus. symbolus* is the token of authenticity given by a seal-ring, here = 'by my authorisation'; the word is frequent in Plautus and must have made its way into Latin early.

dataui 'I was never in the habit of giving'; see on *De Agr.* 157.7. For *quo* without a comparative see on Twelve Tables 10.5. *uti cum maxime* is found at Ter. *Hec.* 115, Cic. *Ad Q. f.* 2.5.4 = 2.4.6.

(f) *uinum congiarium* is wine provided for a magistrate in the performance of his duties at public expense (cf. *cibaria* 58). Despite Cato's disapproval, the custom of giving a money equivalent must have started early, as it did with *salarium*. The adjective *congiarius*, found only here, soon had its neuter turned into a noun, as also happened to *merum* etc.

disdidi seems to be an artificial archaism for *dididi*; cf. *dismota* in the SC de Bacanalibus 30.

enimuero is combined with a jussive subjunctive by Fronto pp. 151.20, 193.4.

usque...lignum shows an unusual word order, but cf. Varro *LL* 7.28 *usque radices in Oscam linguam egit*, Hor. *Serm.* 1.5.82 *usque puellam / ad mediam noctem expecto*. If Cato recorded all his speeches on waxed wooden *codices* those must have been voluminous indeed.

(g) *sis* is another lively colloquialism.

fecissem The subjunctive is due to dependence on the infinitive; Bennett 1.312.

gratiam capiebam Cf. 155 M = 111 SC; *gratia* is contrasted with *inuidia*.

inpoene See on 167.

CHAPTER IV

SENATE DECREES

As it happens, both these decrees are embedded, at least in substance, in letters from Roman magistrates to the bodies concerned; for other senatorial decrees incorporated in such a framework see *RE* suppl. 6.807.30, Gelzer, *Hermes* 71 (1936), 279.

(a) SENATUS CONSULTUM DE BACANALIBUS

CIL 1 (ed. 2) 581 (cf. 1.2.4 p. 907) = 10.104 = ILLRP 511 = ILS 18 = FIRA 1 no. 30 = Bruns no. 164 = Gordon no. 8 and plate 6.8 = Warmington IV 254. There is a photo in A. Degrassi, *Imagines, ILLRP* (1965) 392.

[Q.] Marcius L. f., S(p.) Postumius L. f. cos. senatum consoluerunt n(onis) Octob(ribus) apud aedem (2) Duelonai. sc(ribendo) arf(uerunt) M. Claudi(us) M. f., L. Valeri(us) P. f., Q. Minuci(us) C. f. De Bacanalibus quei foideratei (3) esent ita exdeicendum censuere:
neiquis eorum Bacanal habuise uelet; sei ques (4) esent quei sibei deicerent necesus ese Bacanal habere, eeis utei ad pr(aitorem) urbanum (5) Romam uenirent, deque eeis rebus, ubei eorum uerba audita esent, utei senatus (6) noster decerneret, dum ne minus senatoribus C adesent quom ea res cosoleretur. (7) Bacas uir nequis adiese uelet ceiuis Romanus neue nominus Latini neue socium (8) quisquam, nisei pr(aitorem) urbanum adiesent, isque de senatuos sententiad, dum ne (9) minus senatoribus C adesent quom ea res cosoleretur, iousisent. censuere.
(10) sacerdos nequis uir eset; magister neque uir neque mulier quisquam eset. (11) neue pecuniam quisquam eorum comoinem habuise uelet; neue magistratum (12) neue pro magistratud neque uirum neque mulierem qui<s>quam fecise uelet. (13) neue posthac inter sed coniourase neue comuouise neue conspondise (14) neue conpromesise uelet, neue quisquam fidem inter sed dedise uelet. (15) sacra in oquoltod ne quisquam fecise uelet; neue in poplicod neue in (16) preiuatod neue exstrad urbem sacra quisquam fecise uelet, nisei (17) pr(aitorem) urbanum adieset,

isque de senatuos sententiad, dum ne minus (18) senatoribus C adesent quom ea res cosoleretur, iousisent. censuere.

(19) homines plous V oinuorsei uirei atque mulieres sacra ne quisquam (20) fecise uelet, neue interibei uirei plous duobus, mulieribus plous tribus (21) arfuise uelent, nisei de pr(aitoris) urbani senatuosque sententiad, utei suprad (22) scriptum est.

haice utei in couentionid exdeicatis ne minus trinum (23) noundinum; senatuosque sententiam utei scientes esetis - eorum (24) sententia ita fuit: 'sei ques esent quei aruorsum ead fecisent quam suprad (25) scriptum est, eeis rem caputalem faciendam censuere' - atque utei (26) hoce in tabolam ahenam inceideretis, ita senatus aiquom censuit; (27) uteique eam figier ioubeatis ubei facilumed gnoscier potisit, atque (28) utei ea Bacanalia, sei qua sunt, exstrad quam sei quid ibei sacri est, (29) ita utei suprad scriptum est, in diebus X quibus uobeis tabelai datai (30) erunt faciatis utei dismota sient. IN AGRO TEURANO.

The above numeration is that of the original lineation on a bronze tablet. There are a few errors of incision, but in my view only one, which I have indicated, where even the slightest doubt arises; I have eliminated the others.

Our knowledge of the Bacchanalian 'conspiracy' of 186 B.C. depends on Livy 39.8 - 19. Livy mentions the following relevant senatorial decrees:

(1) 14.5 sqq. Among other clauses *sacerdotes eorum sacrorum, seu uiri seu feminae essent, non Romae modo sed per omnia fora et conciliabula conquiri...edici praeterea et in urbe Roma et per totam Italiam edicta mitti, ne quis qui Bacchis initiatus esset coisse aut conuenisse sacrorum causa uelit neu quid talis rei diuinae fecisse. ante omnia ut quaestio de iis habeatur qui coierint coniurauerintue quo stuprum flagitiumue inferretur.*

(2) 18.7 *datum deinde consulibus negotium est ut omnia Bacchanalia Romae primum, deinde per totam Italiam diruerent, extra quam si qua ibi uetusta ara aut signum consecratum esset.*

(3) 18.8 *in reliquum deinde senatus consulto cautum est ne qua Bacchanalia Romae neue in Italia essent. si quis tale sacrum sollemne et necessarium duceret, nec sine religione et piaculo se id omittere posse, apud praetorem urbanum profiteretur, praetor senatum consuleret. si ei permissum esset cum in senatu centum non minus essent, ita id sacrum faceret dum ne plus quinque sacrificio interessent, neu qua pecunia communis neu quis magister sacrorum aut sacerdos esset.*

The first and second of these prescribe immediate action for suppression. Livy clearly separates the third from the second by *senatus consulto*, which would otherwise be pointless; no doubt the senate passed two decrees in rapid succession. This prescribes long-term measures for seeing that the cult should for the future (*in reliquum*) be kept on a tight rein. This inscription in 3-22 clearly gives the original text, or parts of it, of Livy's third decree in the frame of a letter from the consuls communicating it to local officials and instructing them how to proceed. The whole episode raises knotty historical questions which are outside the scope of this book; the most helpful discussions in relation to the inscription are by McDonald, *JRS* 34 (1944), 25; Tierney, *Proc. Royal Irish Academy, section C* 51 no. 5 (1947), 89; North, *PCPS* n.s. 25 (1979), 90. There is a recent massive discussion by J.-M. Pailler, *Bacchanalia* (1988), with a photo of the inscription in fig.2.

The spelling of this inscription is remarkably correct (e.g. *ei* and *ī* are carefully distinguished) and (with only a few of the most minor lapses) consistent; double consonants are spelt as single throughout, as is natural at this time. This, together with the presence of a few archaisms (some of them false), shows what a rigid format had been evolved by senatorial draftsmen.

1 *consoluerunt* contrasts with *cosoleretur* in the text of the decree, which however also has *censuere*. Official language seems to have wavered in the choice of third-person perfect endings; *CIL* 1 (ed. 2) 402 = 9.439 has *consuluere...censuere*, but 1.1511 and 1525 = *ILS* 5344 and 5396 in a dedication formula have *coerauerunt...probauere. aedem* is a more modern form than *aidem*, which would have been used in the text of the decree.

2 *Duelonai* = *Bellonae*, a clear archaism. The genitive termination is no doubt disyllabic (hence there is no clash with *aedem*).

scribendo arfuerunt Senior members of the senate would help to draft resolutions; see *RE* suppl. 6.801.42. Those named here had been consuls 197-5 B.C. The form *ar* (Leumann 155, Sommer 264) is consistently applied in this document for *ad*.

quei foideratei esent sc. *eis*; see on Cato *De Agr.* pr. 4. It is very unlikely that *foideratei* here means 'devotees bound together by an oath'. But it is also very unlikely that Tiriolo in Bruttium, where the inscription was found, had anything to do with any *ciuitas foederata*. The word seems to refer generally to Italian peoples other than Roman citizens and members of Latin colonies (Pailler 286-91), i.e. the *socii* of 7.

3 *neiquis* (Leumann 64, Wachter n. 744) but *nequis* twice below and *ne, neue* consistently. This (found also on the law in *FIRA* 1.168 = Bruns 121 = Crawford 212 = Warmington IV.442.32) is a false archaism based on the analogy of *seiquis*.

Bacanal habuise uelet For the last two words see on Cato *De Agr.* 5.4. *Bacanal habuise* = 'keep a shrine of Bacchus'; the noun is generally, though not invariably, so used in the singular, and appears also in the plural in 28. By contrast *de Bacanalibus* 2 means 'concerning Bacchic festivals'.

ques (also 24) is a regularly formed third declension plural of *quis*, contrasting with the relative *quei*. See Leumann 472, Sommer 438.

4 The position of *sibei* shows that *quei deicerent necesus ese* is to be regarded as one colon; brief accusative and infinitive constructions often do not constitute a separate colon.

necesus The termination of this form (see NW 2.181-2), which is modernised by Livy quoted above, seems to be due to the analogy of *opus*. Livy adds more specification of the circumstances which would make cult observance necessary, using a traditional formula to be compared with the oath (p. 103) *auspiciumue quod sine piaculo praeterire non liceat.*

eeis Nominative plural; Leumann 427, Sommer 419.

6 *noster* contrasted with local senates.

res cosoleretur For this construction see *FIRA* 3.474 = Bruns 375 = Warmington IV 278 col. 3.10 and KS 1.337.

7 *Bacas uir* An eloquent conjunction; one might compare Plaut. *Merc.* 821 *uxor uirum si clam domo egressa est*. Initiation of men is presented as a novelty by Livy 39.13.8-9, though it was already present in the Etruscan variety of Bacchic cult (ibid. 8.5); the senate accepts this with restriction. The object comes before the subject in order to provide a rubric, like *sacra* 15; one may note that both of these come at the beginning of a line.

adiese, adiesent = adiisse, adiissent, cf. 17 and on 13. *uelet* is the only verb in 3-22 not at the end of a grammatical clause, but it is at the end of a colon; the subject needs a separate colon for specification and amplification.

nominus See on the Letter to the Tiburtines (p. 101).

8 *quisquam* emphatically resumes *quis* at the end of the clause.

senatuos For this form see Leumann 442, Sommer 389.

9 *iousisent* Plural (so also 18) because *is de senatuos sententiad* is felt to be synonomous with *is senatusque*: cf. Altenburg 518, HS 434, KS 1.27-8.

10 *sacerdos nequis uir eset* Only a woman is to be allowed to hold this position (cf. Livy 39.13.8); the Greek *antistes sacrorum* in Etruria (id. 39.8.3-4) had set a bad precedent.

magister The masculine includes the feminine. This title belongs to the chief lay administrator; the senate evidently thinks that to have such an official, as in a *collegium*, would entail a dangerously tight organisation. Livy (quoted above) specifies *magister sacrorum.*

11 *comoinem* The adjective is emphatically separated from its noun because the communality constitutes the essence of what is forbidden. The reference of *eorum* is rather vague (whereas in 3 it means *foederatorum*), no doubt 'the devotees of Bacchus'.

neue...fecise uelet This seems to be the converse of *magister...eset* (nobody is to be elected, and nobody is to elect); it is hard to see why they do not stand together. *magistratus* = a structure involving a *magister* or *magistri*, just as *CIL* 6.2239 speaks of *magistratus collegi Bonae Deae*, meaning the status of having held office as one of her *magistrae. promagistri* are known among the Arval Brothers.

13 It is not clear either from the spacing or an interpunct (I cannot see one on the photographs, but they are often tiny and faint on this inscription) whether the engraver meant *posthac* or (which is quite correct in itself on the principle explained on 16) *post hac*.

inter sed is, strictly speaking, illogical in a sentence with singular object and verb. In the personal pronouns the ablative *-d* spread to the accusative; at least this is the simplest interpretation, though it causes discomfort to grammarians (Sommer 411, Leumann 461).

coniourase...conpromesise The words *conuouere* (*conuoti* is glossed by Paul. Fest. 37 as *isdem uotis obligati*) and *conspondere* (this quoted by Varro *LL* 6.70 from Naevius) barely exist outside this SC; *conpromittere* survives in a technical sense, 'to submit by agreement to an arbitrator'. Here we have a strained attempt, typical of legal style, to pile up virtual synonyms (*consensise* might have been added; Plaut. *Pseud.* 539) in order to cover all eventualities; see p. 8, Altenburg 491, Löfstedt *Synt* 2.315. Taken together, Cic. *Pro Clu.* 148 and 157 suggest that Sulla in his law *de sicariis et ueneficiis* combined *coire conuenire consentire*; see too *censuit consensit consciuit* in the fetial formula, Livy 1.32.13. *conpromesise* seems to show the old spelling with *e* for *ei* (Leumann 63-4, Sommer 73); Sommer 588 sees this as parallelled by *adiese* etc. (see on 7), but they are properly *ĭ* and dissimilation is relevant. Wölfflin, *Sitzb. bay. Akad* 1896.187 wished to read *conprome<i>sise*; in fact the tablet has *conprome.sise*, and Wachter n.688 thinks he sees an erased *i* under the interpunct. Formally this word is a double compound (HS 284), but in reality *promittere* is felt to be a simple verb. The presentation of the cult as a *coniuratio* by the senate was intended to scare (E. S. Gruen, *Studies in Greek Culture and Roman Policy* (1990), 47).

15 *oquoltod* (= *oc(c)ulto*) is a false archaism, since the *qu* has no etymological justification (HS 54*, Wachter §121a).

ne quisquam Until this point the drafters have used *quisquam* only with *neue* or *neque*, otherwise *ne quis*, last in 10; since then there have been four occurrences of *quisquam*, which here and in 19 prevails.

poplicod (cf. the Letter to the Tiburtes) is the original derivative from *pop(u)lus*; the orthodox view that the later *publicus* is due to the influence of *pubes* is challenged by Wachter 384-5. The Lex Acilia has *poplicus* (very old-fashioned by then) four times, *puplicus* three; there is also *poblicus* (*CIL* 1.397). On the other side Ernout - Meillet, *Dictionnaire étymologique* deny that there ever was a real word *poplicus* and see this as just an etymologising spelling of *publicus* (with *puplicus* as a half-hearted attempt at the same).

16 *neue exstrad urbem* A corresponding phrase *neue in urbid* or the like (cf. *ne...Romae neue in Italia* in Livy's third decree) has been omitted because it is not relevant to the recipients of this letter (Fraenkel [see on 22] 380 = 458). Pailler's suggestion (184-5) that we punctuate *uelet, neue...preiuatod; neue exstrad...* makes no essential difference. *exstrad* (cf. 28) has an ablative *-d* because it is in origin the ablative feminine singular of the adjective *exter* (sc. *parte*), and similarly *suprad* thrice below from *superus*. The same applies to *aruorsum ead* 24 (cf. *aduersus hac*

Festus 246, *aruorsu hac* in *FIRA* 3.224 = Bruns 283 = Warmington IV 154), which means 'in a confrontational manner starting from this point' (Leumann 483); *posthac* (13) etc. are formed on the same principle. The spelling *xs* in *exstrad* contrasts with that of *exdeicere* (twice).

19 *homines...fecise uelet* Because of the drop-by-drop method of expression, this starts off as if intended to be *homines plous V...ne uelent*, but then reverts to the standardised form *ne quisquam...uelet*. Transposing into hypotactic form one might say 'in assemblies of more than five people in total, men and women, no-one is to perform ceremonies'. *homines plous V* also shows a form based on a paratactic apposition (HS 110; Calboli *ANRW* 2.29.1.53), but it has to contend with the hypotactic *minus senatoribus C* thrice above; the two collide in 20 *uirei plous duobus, mulieribus plous tribus*. Note the distinction between *homines* and *uirei*.

oinuorsei = **oinuuorsei* with *u* written just once (see my note on *ML* 188.389) = *uniuersi*. The appearance of *atque* (and twice *atque utei* in the last paragraph) in a senatorial decree is surprising (otherwise *-que* makes six appearances). It is found several times before *ob*, and *recte atque ordine* alternates with *recte et ordine*. Apart from that, it appears in the SC de Ludis Saecularibus (Bruns 191 = *FIRA* 1.274 *atque etiam*). The recently discovered *SC de Cn. Pisone patre* has two such occurrences. In a draft decree in Cic. *Phil.* 14.36-8 there is one *atque ita* (to avoid an ambiguous *itaque*) amid a welter of *-que*.

20 *inter ibei* = *interibi*; the usual sense is 'meanwhile', but here it seems to mean 'in that company'.

21 The consuls apparently now begin to abbreviate, omitting *censuere* and employing the compressed phrase *de praitoris senatuosque sententiad*, in which *sententia* strictly applies only to the senate. *utei suprad scriptum est* is no doubt part of the same abbreviation. In view of *nominus* above, the expansion should perhaps be printed *pr(aitorus)*.

22 So far all has been reasonably plain sailing, but confusion of thought and expression now sets in, first stressed and acutely analysed by Fraenkel, *Hermes* 67 (1932), 369 = *KB* 2.447; his article provoked discussions by Keil, ibid. 68 (1933), 306; Krause and Gelzer, ibid. 71 (1936), 214 and 278; Accame, *RFIC* 16 = 66 (1938), 225; Dihle, *Hermes* 90 (1962), 376; Heilmann in *AINIΓMA, Festschr. H. Rahn*, ed. F. R. Varwig (1987) 241. My notes do not attempt to follow all the details of this discussion, but simply put forward what seems to me to emerge as an economical explanation for the peculiarities.

Until now the consuls have been quoting from the senatorial decree framed by professional draftsmen; now they are telling the local officials what they have to do, and, being more used to the sword than the pen, do so in an incoherent way. They begin with the jussive *utei...exdeicatis* (cf. on Cato *De Agr.* 1.2); then with *-que* (not quite as unstylish here as in Cato *Origines* 83b) they proceed to *senatus aiquom censuit utei scientes esetis sententiam suam atque hoc incideretis* (except that, having started off in *guttatim*-style with the rubric *senatuos sententiam*, they retain the genitive of the noun in place of my hypotactic-style *suam*). Finally they return, with another *-que*, to their own orders to the local officials, who are to act as their agents in executing the commission given by the senate to the consuls in its second decree to dismantle (Livy modernises *dismota sient* to *diruerent*) the shrines.

haice = haec, couentionid = contione. trinum n(o)undinum is the period covering three market days, a statutory interval in various legal and political situations, in this case the period ensuring public awareness of the decree. It is disputed whether it means the period covering three intervals between one market day and the next, i.e. 24-5 days (so e.g. A. K. Michels, *The Calendar of the Roman Republic* (1967) 191; G. Radke, *Fasti Romani* (1990) 8-9; Primavesi in C. Neumeister (ed.), *Antike Texte in Forschung und Schule, Festschr. W. Heilmann* (1993) 125) or a period of variable length covering three market days from any starting point, giving a minimum of 17-18 days (so Lintott, *CQ* 15 (1965), 281, who on 284 remarks about this passage 'it is more plausible to imagine a *contio* being held and the contents of the decree announced on three market-days than throughout three weeks'). The phrase appears to be a genitive plural from a nominative singular *nundinum* (so Primavesi, and Szemerényi in *Vir Bonus Discendi Peritus, Studies...O. Skutsch, BICS* suppl. 51 (1988), 130; B. Löfstedt, *Eranos* 56 (1958), 112). Primavesi thinks that we have a Grecising genitive of the time within which, which seems very unlikely to me. I think that in this case the composers intended 'in the assemblies regularly held during the time covering three market-days' (similarly, but by a different route, Primavesi), and that in most occurrences an ellipse of *spatium* or the like is to be assumed (for similar ellipses with expressions of distance see Caes. *BG* 1.25.5, Cic. *Ad Att.* 3.7.1, 5.16.4 *castra...aberant bidui*). The closest parallel to this occurrence is in the Fragmentum Tarentinum 23 (Crawford 212 = *CIL* 1 (ed. 2) 2924) *quom ex hac] l(ege) trinum nundinum contenuo palam prodixerit nondinisq(ue)/[tertiis...accusatio prosc]ripta propositaque apud forum fuerit* (supplements uncertain).

exdeicatis Left to themselves the consuls do not observe the general practice of the drafters of putting the verb at the end of its clause (see on 7).
23 *scientes esetis* Cf. on Cato *De Agr.* pr.4 and Plaut. *Poen.* 1038, Ter. *Andr.* 508, 775 *ut(tu) sis sciens.* As Löfstedt *PA* 246 remarks, this is clearly more emphatic than *ut sciretis*, and combines with the 'energetic, voluntative character' of the sentence. The participle is still felt as verbal, not adjectival, since it governs a direct object. Fraenkel compares ὑμᾶς εἰδέναι βουλόμεθα in the SC reported to the people of Oropus (*FIRA* 1. 260 = Bruns 181) and ἵνα πᾶσιν ᾖ γνωστόν in the fifth Cyrene edict of Augustus (*FIRA* 1.410). It is another sign of literary inexpertness that *senatuos sententiam* refers not to the preceding (21) occurrence of the phrase but to the following parenthesis (and a parenthesis too is surprising in a formal context like this). Fraenkel remarks that *sententia* normally refers to a whole decree (cf. *RE* suppl. 6.801.17), and that its application here to just a part is unheard of; this is perhaps not a huge stumbling-block. *eorum = senatorum*, taken out of *senatuos*.

24 *aruorsum ead* See on 16; for *quam* cf. Plaut. *Trin.* 176.

eeis...censuere 'proceedings for capital offence must be taken against them'. According to Livy 39.18.3-4 those who had just been initiated and had taken the oaths of 'conspiracy' without actually committing any unlawful action were imprisoned, whereas those who had committed such crimes *eos capitali poena adficiebant* (sc. *consules*, carrying out the *quaestio* mandated to them by the senate in ch. 14.6-8). In the light of this, it seems that the consuls in drafting this letter have carelessly introduced a provision of Livy's first decree, and *suprad scriptum est* does not refer to anything in this text, especially as it relates to past transgressions, whereas, as remarked above, 3-22 are concerned with the provisions for the future of Livy's third decree. Similarly in 29 *ita utei suprad scriptum est* the vague *sei quid ibei sacri est* is doubtless an abbreviation of a phrase used in the second decree (but not quoted by the consuls) which is represented more fully and accurately by Livy. *caputalem* in place of *capitalem* is an artificial retrograde formation (Leumann 80).

26 Cf. Bruns 179 = *FIRA* 1.257 = Warmington IV 450 *uteiq[ue Q. Lutatius, M. Aemilius cos. a(lter) a(mboue)]...litteras ad magistratus...mitta[nt, senatum uelle et] aequom censere ea ita fieri* ; so also on the Tabula Siarensis 22 (see next note). *hoce* contrasts with the plural *haice* in 22; there the plural gathers together all the preceding details, a notion less prominent here (cf. on Cato *De Agr.* 141.2).

27 *facilumed* Since adverbs in *-e* from 1st-2nd declension adjectives were originally instrumental forms, they are not strictly entitled to the ablative *-d* (Leumann 426, Wachter n. 695), which however they acquired quite early. *potisit* = *potis sit* spelt as one word and therefore with a single consonant; Leumann 525, Sommer 532. Cf. Pliny *Ep.* 8.6.13 *senatusque consulta de iis rebus facta in aere inciderentur idque aes figeretur ad statuam loricatam diui Iulii.* The Tabula Siarensis 20-27 (Crawford 518) ordains that a decree in honour of Germanicus is to be inscribed on bronze, that copies are to be sent to municipia and coloniae, and that provincial governors are to see that it be displayed; similarly the end of the *SC de Cn. Pisone patre* (see on 19). For the injunction of engraving on bronze see Williamson, *Class. Ant.* 6 (1987), 179; the provision for public display (for which the more specific formula *unde de plano recte legi possit(ur)* was subsequently framed; ibid. 172 n.49, Crawford 20) would also of course have been in the decree, but the consuls drift back into giving an order themselves.

28 *exstrad quam si* is a phrase for indicating legal exemptions (KS 2.460, HS 595); Livy reproduces it. See on 24. *sacri* means 'duly consecrated by the rites of recognised Roman religion'.

29 *in diebus X quibus* For the construction cf. KS 1.356, Bennett 2.298; there are several occurrences of such phrases in the Tabula Heracleensis and the Lex Ursonensis, and in Greek versions of a law (*FIRA* 1.127-8, Crawford 242-4).

tabelai 'despatches' containing this letter.

30 *sient* contrasts with the *sit* implicit in *potisit* 27; for *dismota* see on Cato Speeches 173f. This is more forceful than the usual *faciatis ut dimoueantur*; it underlines that the job is to be completed by the end of the time-limit. *IN AGRO TEURANO* is written in larger letters than the rest and perhaps by a different hand; it also lacks the ablatival *-d* applied in the rest of the inscription, which therefore is an archaism (and also in *facilumed*). It is clearly a consignment note indicating the destination of this copy. The place is otherwise unknown, but presumably its name survives in Tiriolo, the find-spot of the inscription.

(b) AD TIBURTES

CIL 1 (ed. 2) 586 = 14.3584 = ILLRP 512 = ILS 19 = Inscr. Ital. 4.1.3 = Bruns 170-1 = FIRA 1.247-8 = Warmington IV 260

L. Cornelius Cn. f. pr(aetor) sen(atum) cons(uluit) a.d. III nonas Maias sub aede Kastorus.

Scr(ibendo) adf(uerunt) A. Manlius A. f., Sex. Iulius....., L. Postumius S(p.) f.

Quod Teiburtes u(erba) f(ecistis) quibusque de rebus uos purgauistis, ea senatus animum aduortit ita utei aequom fuit; nosque ea ita audiueramus ut uos deixistis uobeis nontiata esse. ea nos animum nostrum indoucebamus ita facta esse propterea quod scibamus ea uos merito nostro facere non potuisse, neque uos dignos esse quei ea faceretis, neque id uobeis neque rei poplicae uostrae oitile esse facere. et postquam uostra uerba senatus audiuit, tanto magis animum nostrum indoucimus, ita utei ante arbitrabamur, de eieis rebus af uobeis peccatum non esse. quonque de eieis rebus senatuei purgati estis, credimus, uosque animum uostrum indoucere oportet, item uos populo Romano purgatos fore.

This inscription belongs probably to 159 B.C.; it reports to the people of Tibur, who had heard that their acts had been misrepresented, a senatusconsultum concerning them, turning the third persons of the decree into second. It is a good specimen of business-like Latin, not concerned to vary phraseology such as *animum inducere* (a weighty and formal phrase, cf. Scipio 30; the same notion could be expressed by use of *(per)suadeo*).

Pre-classical spellings which are readily comprehensible are not re-marked.

sub aede Kastorus For the temple of Castor as a meeting-place for the senate see Taylor and Scott, *TAPA* 100 (1969), 557; as they note, *sub* instead of *in* is hard to explain. The termination *-us* in the genitive of the third declension is quite common in inscriptions with the names of gods (Leumann 435, de Meo 96-7); see also *nominus* in the SC de Bacanalibus 7.

quod uerba fecit (fecerunt, facta sunt)...de ea re ita censuerunt is the traditional beginning of a SC.

quibusque The syntax slips, and *-que* seems superfluous; bureaucratic language is inclined to fall into stiff mumbo-jumbo. Something similar seems to lie behind the Greek of the SC relating to Thisbe (*FIRA* 1.243, Bruns 166).

ea (nos)...facta esse The pronoun is placed first, with a long hyperbaton, for connection.

poplicae See on SC de Bacanalibus 15.

oitile i.e. *utile.*

uostra is placed before its noun because of the implicit contrast with rumours heard indirectly from others.

eieis This spelling is not found elsewhere (and the singular *eiei* only on *CIL* 1 (ed. 2) 583).

af For this form see B. Vine, *Studies in Archaic Latin Inscriptions* (1993) 175; Giacomelli, *Acme* 41.1 (1988), 129.

quonque See Leumann 215.

purgati contrasts with the *ei* spellings found elsewhere in this inscription, and in fact seems to be the earliest occurrence of this spelling for etymological *ei.*

CHAPTER V

MILITARY OATHS

Gell. 16.4.2-4 = Cincius fr. 13-14 Huschke = 13 Seckel - Kübler

(2) (in libro eiusdem Cincii De Re Militari quinto ita scriptum est: cum dilectus antiquitus fieret et milites scriberentur, iusiurandum eos tribunus militaris adigebat in uerba haec:)

C. Laelii C. fili consulis L. Cornelii P. fili consulis in exercitu decemque milia passuum prope furtum non facies dolo malo solus neque cum pluribus pluris nummi argentei in dies singulos; extraque hastam, hastile, ligna, pom<a>, pabulum, utrem, follem, faculam si quid ibi inueneris sustulerisue quod tuum non erit, quod pluris nummi argentei erit, uti tu ad C. Laelium C. filium consulem Luciumue Cornelium P. filium consulem siue quem ad uter eorum iusserit proferes aut profitebere in triduo proximo quidquid inueneris sustulerisue [in] dolo malo, aut domino suo, cuium id censebis esse, reddes, uti quod recte factum esse uoles.

(3) (militibus autem scriptis dies praefiniebatur quo die adessent et citanti consuli responderent; (4) deinde ita concipiebatur iusiurandum ut adessent, his additis exceptionibus:)

nisi harunce quae causa erit: funus familiare feriaeue denicales quae non eius rei causa in eum diem conlatae sint quo is eo die minus ibi esset, morbus sonticus auspiciumue quod sine piaculo praeterire non liceat, sacrificiumue anniuersarium quod recte fieri non possit nisi ipsus eo die ibi sit, uis hostesue, status condictusue dies cum hoste; si cui eorum harunce quae causa erit, tum se postridie quam per eas causas licebit, eo die uenturum aditurumque eum qui eum pagum uicum oppidumue delegerit.

2 quidquid *flor.*, quod quid *codd.*, quom quid *Huschke fere*, quo quid *Seckel - Kübler*

This Cincius is almost certainly not identical with the annalist L. Cincius Alimentus; the language of the antiquarian writings adduced under this name is not archaic, and in the preceding section Gellius quotes a fragment from this same book of Cincius mentioning the Hermunduli, who were apparently unknown to the Romans until late in the first century B.C. A terminus ante quem is provided by Verrius Flaccus' use of his works; his writings may be approximately placed around the 30's B.C. See E. Rawson, *Intellectual Life in the Late Roman Republic* (1985) 247.

Various problems relating to these fragments are discussed by Hinard in *Au miroir de la culture antique, mélanges...R. Marache* (1992) 287, but his conclusions seem fragile to me.

2

C. Laelius and L. Cornelius Scipio Asiaticus were consuls in 190 B.C., in which year one consular army was reinforced and another was raised for the war against the Aetolians and Antiochus (Livy 37.2.2-4). This oath is summarised by Polybius 6.33.2 μηδὲν ἐκ τῆς παρεμβολῆς (camp) κλέψειν ἀλλὰ κἂν εὕρῃ τι, τοῦτ' ἀνοίσειν ἐπὶ τοὺς χιλιάρχους, cf. 10.16.6 περὶ δὲ τοῦ μηδένα νοσφίζεσθαι μηδὲν τῶν ἐκ τῆς διαρπαγῆς ἀλλὰ τηρεῖν τὴν πίστιν κατὰ τὸν ὅρκον ὃν ὀμνύουσι πάντες ὅταν ἀθροίσθωσι πρῶτον εἰς τὴν παρεμβολὴν ἐξιέναι μέλλοντες εἰς τὴν πολεμίαν.

dolo malo A legal term, 'with malice aforethought' (cf. on Cato *De Agr.* 2.2).

nummi argentei A vague term which here no doubt means a sestertius.

hastile is a spear-shaft (here waiting to be lopped from a tree) as opposed to the complete *hasta*. *ligna* is firewood; *utrem* and *follem* are leather sacks, the former for transporting wine, the latter dry goods (cf. Nepos *Eum.* 8.7 *utris atque etiam culleos*). Torches would be needed for moving around the camp at night.

inueneris is εὕρῃ in Polybius.

uti tu...proferes This seems to combine *proferes* and *uti proferas* (see p. 10), but a future tense seems much more appropriate to an oath than a jussive, and one must wonder if *uti* is just a dittography.

quem ad For this order of preposition and relative see KS 1.585, *TLL* 1.473.11.

uter 'either of the two'; *OLD* s.v. 3, KS 1.648.

uti...uoles For this legal formula cf. the Lex de repetundis 30, 65, 67-8 (*FIRA* 1.92, 97-8, Bruns 64, 69, Crawford 61, 72, Warmington IV 338, 360).

4

Unlike the former oath, Cincius has reported this in indirect speech, changing second persons into third. This oath too is referred to by Polybius 6.26.2-4 (soldiers swear to turn up except in case of ὀρνιθεία and τὰ ἀδύνατα).

feriae denicales Days set aside for the purification of the family of a deceased person. In the Lex Ursonensis (cf. p. 19) 95 *morbus sonticus, uadimonium, iudicium, sacrificium, funus familiare feriaeue denicales* are also excuses for a magistrate *quo minus adesse possit* in judicial proceedings; note that in the oath *quo minus* have still not coalesced. A *morbus sonticus* is 'any serious disease considered as excusing a person from attendance at a lawcourt and other public duties' (*OLD*). This appears in the Twelve Tables, II 2 (*morbus sonticus...aut status dies cum hoste* are reasons for postponement of legal proceedings).

ipsus is rarely found in prose (a 'law of Numa' quoted by Paul. Fest. 6, twice in Cato (*De Agr.* 70-1), the orator Titius quoted by Macrob. *Sat.* 3.16.16 (for the sake of the clausula); never in inscriptions).

status...hoste See above and Plaut. *Curc.* 5 *si status condictus cum hoste interuenit dies* in a military metaphor (this together with Polybius establishes the basic antiquity of this oath, though it may have been modified over time). Cic. *De Off.* 1.37 explains that according to archaic usage *hostis* here means *peregrinus*, and that the notion 'enemy' was then conveyed by *perduellis* (see also Varro *LL* 5.3 *eo uerbo dicebant peregrinum qui suis legibus uteretur*). Cf. too Festus 314 *status dies uocatur qui iudicii causa est constitutus cum peregrino, eius enim generis ab antiquis hostes appellabantur quod erant pari iure cum populo Romano, atque hostire ponebatur pro aequare* (followed by a quotation of the *Curculio*). Benveniste 75 sqq. however argues that while the ancient sources are correct in their connection with *hostire* 'to requite', and that the word means a stranger enjoying equal rights with Roman citizens, it was not synonymous with *peregrinus* but referred to the system of mutual obligation inherent in *hospitium*. See also Bettini and Borghini in *Linguistica e Antropologia* (1983) 303; F. de Martino, *Storia della costituzione Romana* (ed. 2, 1973) 2.17. The older view was that *hostis* developed its later meaning because in primitive society any stranger is a potential enemy. Here the old sense, frozen in this formula, collides with the new in *hostesue*.

postridie quam See HS 602, KS 2.355. This is taken up by *eo die*, which is natural enough in the style which thinks in small units. But I cannot help suspecting that *die* is interpolated and that *eo* 'thither' has been adjusted by Cincius from *huc* of the direct speech, like *ibi (esset)* above.

delegerit 'made subject to levy'; usually the object is not the district, but the men levied (*TLL* 5.1.457.1). A levy itself is *dilectus*.

CHAPTER VI

RELIGIOUS TEXTS

This chapter is to be read in conjunction with the commentary on Cato *De Agr.* 141. There are other religious formulae in Livy 1.24 and 32, which seem to be antiquarian reconstructions of the second century B.C. (see Ogilvie's commentary, and on the other side Dumézil 90); with (a) too no doubt 'the old ritual' [used against Etruscan cities in Rome's early days] 'was deliberately refurbished and given a new application' (Ogilvie 674).

(a) Macrob. *Sat.* 3.9.6-11

(uidendum ne quod nonnulli male aestimauerunt nos quoque confundat, opinantes uno carmine et euocari ex urbe aliqua deos et ipsam deuotam fieri ciuitatem. nam repperi in libro quinto Rerum Reconditarum Sereni Sammonici utrumque carmen, quod ille se in cuiusdam Furii uetustissimo libro repperisse professus est. (7) est autem carmen huius modi quo di euocantur cum oppugnatione ciuitas cingitur:)

Si deus, si dea est cui populus ciuitasque Carthaginiensis est in tutela, teque maxime, ille qui urbis huius populique tutelam recepisti, precor uenerorque ueniamque a uobis peto ut uos populum ciuitatemque Carthaginiensem deseratis, loca templa sacra urbemque eorum relinquatis, (8) absque his abeatis, eique populo ciuitatique metum formidinem obliuionem iniciatis, propitiique Romam ad me meosque ueniatis, nostraque uobis loca templa sacra urbs acceptior probatiorque sit, mihique populoque Romano militibusque meis propitii sitis. si <haec> ita feceritis ut sciamus intellegamusque, uoueo uobis templa ludosque facturum.

(9) (in eadem uerba hostias fieri oportet auctoritatemque uideri extorum, ut ea promittant futura. urbes uero exercitusque sic deuouentur iam numinibus euocatis, sed dictatores imperatoresque soli possunt deuouere his uerbis:)

107

(10) Dis pater Veiouis Manes, siue uos quo alio nomine fas est nominare, ut omnes illam urbem Carthaginem exercitumque quem ego me sentio dicere fuga formidine terrore compleatis, quique aduersum legiones exercitumque nostrum arma telaque ferent, uti uos eum exercitum eos hostes eosque homines, urbes agrosque eorum et qui in his locis regionibusque, agris urbibusque habitant abducatis lumine supero priuetis, exercitumque hostium, urbes agrosque eorum quos me sentio dicere, uti uos eas urbes agrosque, capita aetatesque eorum deuotas consecratasque habeatis ollis legibus quibus quandoque sunt maxime hostes deuoti. (11) eosque ego uicarios pro me fide magistratuque meo, pro populo Romano exercitu legionibusque nostris do deuoueo, ut me meamque fidem imperiumque, legiones exercitumque nostrum qui in his rebus gerundis sunt bene saluos siritis esse. si haec ita faxitis ut ego sciam sentiam intellegamque, tunc quisquis uotum hoc faxit ubiubi faxit, recte factum esto ouibus atris tribus. Tellus Mater teque Iuppiter obtestor.

8 ciuitatique *Serv. ad Aen. 2.244*, ciuitati *Macrob.*

   propitiique *Huschke (1.15 Seckel - Kübler)*, proditique *codd.*, proditi<s>que *Schilling ap. J. Collart (ed.), Varron, Grammaire antique et stylistique latine (1978) 181*

   propitii *Bergk, Philol. 32 (1873), 567*, praepositi *codd. (non* propositi*), quod frustra defendit Ramminger, MH 43 (1986),197*, praesentes propitii *O. Weinreich, Religionsgesch. Studien (1968) 19 (-20) n.5*

   <haec> *E. Fraenkel, Horace (1957) 237*

   ut sciamus sentiamusque *hic Fraenkel, post* praepositi sitis *codd.*

10 [et] *Engelbrecht, WS 24 (1902), 483*

11 exercitu *Courtney*, exercitibus *codd.*

   <te> Tellus *Huschke 16*

This passage is full of problems, which are discussed with notable impartiality by E. Rawson, *JRS* 63 (1973), 168. First is that of authority. We do not know enough about Serenus Sammonicus, an antiquary killed in 211 A.D., to assess his reliability, and the Furius on whom he draws cannot be securely identified; he is usually thought to be L. Furius Philus, cos. 136 B.C. and a friend of Scipio Aemilianus, but that man is not known to have written anything. However, Rawson makes a case for tracing back some of the material to respectable sources. Second, we have no record that any Carthaginian cults were transferred to Rome in 146 B.C.; Fraenkel proposed to see an allusion to such a transfer in Hor. *Odes* 2.1.25-7, but, as Rawson shows, it is doubtful if he is right. One might rather adduce *Culex* 370-1 *Scipiadasque duces, quorum deuota triumphis / moenia †rapidis† Libycae Carthaginis horrent* as evidence for the *deuotio*, but even if that is the allusion few would regard the author of the *Culex* as a historical authority. One might therefore be inclined to regard all this as a pseudo-antiquarian concoction (so Wissowa 384 n.6, Latte 125 n.2, 346 n.4), but its reliability received a boost with the publication of *Ann. Epigr.* 1977.816 = *CIL* 1.2954, which reads as follows:

Serueilius C. f. imperator
hostibus uicteis, Isaura Vetere
capta, captiueis uenum datis,
sei deus seiue deast quoius in
tutela oppidum Vetus Isaura
fuit...uotum soluit.

This, found at Isaura in Cilicia, shows P. Servilius (*RE* s.v. 1814) Vatia Isauricus during his siege of Isaura in 75 B.C. performing a rite of *euocatio* in vocabulary very like that reported by Macrobius (and apparently dedicating a temple to the deity at Isaura rather than at Rome; see M. Beard and others, *Religions at Rome* (1998) 1.133); note that Servilius was a *pontifex* (Cic. *Har. Resp.* 12). One may conclude that, whether the rite was actually performed in 146 or not, the formulations presented by Macrobius (with specific references to Carthage deleted if need be) are in substance authentic.

7 *si deus, si dea est* A typical formulation in Roman cult intended to cover all bases as an acknowledgement of the limitations of human knowledge about divine powers; see Appel 80, Wissowa 38, Latte 54, Dumézil 43, Alvar *Numen* 32 (1985), 236 sqq. (esp. 247, 254), Oakley on Livy 7.26.4 and note *CIL* 6.2099 = *ILS* 5047 *siue deo siue deae in cuius tutela hic lucus locusue est.* It was sometimes supposed that cities kept secret the name of their tutelary deity so that (s)he could not be evoked (see Appel 81). In a treaty between Hannibal and Philip of Macedon the unnamed δαίμων Καρχηδονίων is identified by M. L. Barré, *The God-List in the Treaty between Hannibal and Philip V* (1983) with Astarte; he also adduces (68) the *genius Carthaginis* on *CIL* 3.993 = *ILS* 3923 (from Dacia). DServ. *Aen.* 2.351 mentions a shield dedicated *genio urbis Romae siue mas siue femina* (for this deity see Wissowa 179, Latte 240, *RE, genius* 1166). It is unclear what distinction the Romans have in mind between the *deus - dea* and the *ille* (Alvar has a very unlikely explanation); to avoid this difficulty Dumézil 469 n.11 takes *si deus...* to mean 'all the gods and goddesses who...' Le Gall in *L'Italie préromaine...mél. Heurgon* (1976) 522 n.15 oddly takes *maxime* as vocative.

urbis huius Carthage, before which the Roman general is standing; some interpreters seem wrongly to refer it to Rome.

precor...peto Again sacral pleonasm; cf. *precor quaesoque* in Cato *De Agr.* 141.2, *uos precor ueneror ueniam peto feroque* in the *deuotio* formula of Decius (Livy 8.9.7), Appel 121 and 142, Latte 183 n.4, Hickson 50-51. For the use of *ueneror* and *uenia* in such contexts see Szantyr, *Gymn.* 78 (1971), 26 (this passage on 44), Dumézil 421. The alliteration of *p* and *u* is striking; so is the rising tricolon.

8 *absque* i.e. 'and from'; this combination is found nowhere else because of potential confusion with the compound word *absque* 'without'. Here *abeatis* clarifies the sense; for similar clarification see on *inuisus* Cato *De Agr.* 141.2.

obliuionem 'bewilderment'.

propitiique This seems more convincing than Schilling's suggestion, though he compares Livy 5.21.5 *Veientes ignari se iam a suis uatibus, iam ab externis oraculis proditos.*

acceptior probatiorque is the same type of sacral pleonasm as *deuotas consecratasque* 10, and also *sciamus intellegamusque* 8, *sciam sentiam intellegamque* 11.

mihi...meis is like *mihi domo familiaeque nostrae* in Cato 141.2.

ut sciamus intellegamusque The subjunctive in such phrases (cf. 11) appears to be secondary and due to misunderstanding as if a consecutive clause were intended; the indicative, as in 10 *quos me sentio dicere* (see there) is the original. Fraenkel's constitution of the text is corroborated by 11. For *uoueo facturum* without subject-accusative cf. Cato *De Agr.* 2.2.

The *deuotio* is not the curse pronounced over the defeated city, but belongs to an earlier stage in which it has not yet been subdued. The ritual has been discussed in detail by Versnel, *Mnem.* 29 (1976), 365; it represents a unique development of the rite in which a Roman general devotes himself and takes much from the formulae then employed, but also has to introduce some innovation. For the *Culex* see above.

10 *Veiouis* The etymology of this name indicates the Jupiter who disappoints expectations, since the prefix *-ue* conveys that the function expressed in the stem of the word is conducted badly or in undesirable fashion (Latte 81); therefore he is a suitable god to invoke when one desires the defeat of an enemy.

siue...nominare The point of this common expression is much the same as that of *siue deus siue dea*; see Appel 76, Wissowa 37 n.4, Latte 62, Norden *AT* 144, van der Horst in R. van den Broek and others, *Knowledge of God in the Graeco-Roman World* (1988) 38, S. Pulleyn, *Prayer in Greek Religion* (1997) 100-102.

ut See p. 10. The structure of the sentence (I have to adjust it a little) is (1) *ut...compleatis* (2) *utique qui aduersum...priuetis* (3) *utique exercitum...deuoti.* In (2) and (3) the objects are put first for emphasis and then picked up by demonstratives, (2) *eum...homines*, (3) *eas urbes agrosque*; cf. Altenburg 492.

illam urbem Carthaginem This is intelligible enough if one envisages the Roman general pointing out Carthage from a distance, but Norden *AAP* 63 n.1 suggests that the formula given to him contained only *illam urbem*, signifying 'the relevant city' (HS 182; add e.g. Sen. *Ep.* 59.2) and meant to be replaced by a specific name, in this case Carthage. Cf. Livy 1.32.10 *populum illum (quicumque est, nominat).* C. O. Thulin, *Italische sakrale Poesie und Prosa* (1906) 56 in fact deleted *Carthaginem.*

quem ego me sentio dicere Another precaution against divine misunderstanding; cf. Varro *LL* 7.8, Norden *AAP* 55-7 and 85-7, Appel 146-7. See above for the secondary introduction of the subjunctive into such clauses when headed by *ut.*

fuga formidine terrore The desire to maintain the alliterative pair (Wölfflin 261) takes precedence over that for a rising tricolon. The expression belongs to the class identified by Leo *AKS* 1.173 (see also Timpanaro *RIFC* 116 (1988), 274), in which for the sake of rhythm a third item is added to a cohesive pair. Cf. *hostes...terrore formidine morteque adficiatis* in the *deuotio* formula of Decius, Livy 8.9.7.

et Engelbrecht points out that -*que* is elsewhere invariable in these prayers and that here *quique* would have been expected. But the inhabitants need to be an item on their own (*homines* does not mean this, but 'men' in the military sense; *OLD* s.v. 5), and *et* 'and moreover' (see on Cato *De Agr.* 5) is not unsuitable.

agris urbibusque The reverse order is observed in the other three occurrences of this pair. By contrast *legiones exercitumque...exercitibus legionibusque...legiones exercitumque* shows a perfect chiastic pattern (cf. on Cato *De Agr.* 141.2 and p. 6) which is upset only by the inexplicable plural *exercitibus*.

locis regionibusque is yet another sacral pleonasm (HS 787).

abducatis sc. *uobiscum ad inferos.*

capita aetatesque For this combination in curses cf. Plaut. *Rud.* 375 *uae capiti atque aetati tuae*, 1346 *ut te...Venus eradicet, caput atque aetatem tuam*, Ter. *Hec.* 334. It looks as if these maledictions may be derived from solemn curses.

ollis contrasts with *illam* above. The two forms stand beside each other in the Lex Templi Furfensis; for *ollis legibus* see too the altar-dedications there adduced (p. 114).

quibus...deuoti Cf. Cato Speeches 173e *uti cum maxime*. For the word-order *quibus q. sunt...deuoti* see J. N. Adams, *Wackernagel's Law and the Placement of the copula esse* (1994; *PCPS* suppl. 18) 44, who remarks a tendency for the relative pronoun to attract the auxiliary verb in periphrastic tenses.

11 *uicarios* For the concept of substitution in this context see Versnel 387 sqq.; even in the usual type of *deuotio* the general could substitute any citizen soldier for himself (Livy 8.10.11).

fide magistratuque See Enn. *Ann.* 102 with Skutsch's note, *TLL, fides* 679.6; observe also Sabidius quoted by Schol. Ver. on *Aen.* 10.241 (Funaioli *GRF* 111) *im<periumque> fidemque m<eam seruent>* (sc. *milites*), said by a general taking the auspices.

exercitu See above on *agris urbibusque* and cf. Livy 8.9.8 *pro re p. <populi Romani> Quiritium, exercitu legionibus...*, though the text there is uncertain.

siritis This form is common in prayers (Norden *AAP* 131-2, Hickson 54, 88), cf. Cato *De Agr.* 141.2 and on 'Cornelia' (d).

ut...intellegamque See on 8; Plaut. *Truc.* 545 *sentio atque intellego*, etc. (Norden *AAP* 86).

quisquis...esto For this precautionary phrase see Appel 148-9, for *facio* with ablative = 'sacrifice' *OLD* s.v. 24b.

Tellus Huschke's emendation seems obvious, but there are enough instances of this particular form of ἀπο κοινοῦ placing of the pronoun to give us pause (Leo *AKS* 1.99-100). One must however wonder if the figure would be too artificial for this context.

(b) CIL 1 (ed. 2) 756 = 9.3513 = ILLRP 508 = ILS 4906 = Bruns 105 = FIRA 3.225 = Gordon 19 and plate 11.

Discussion by Laffi (sometimes far-fetched) in *La Cultura Italica* (1978) 121, with plate (better than Gordon's) after p. 129. There is another photograph in A. Degrassi, *Imagines, ILLRP* (1965) 382. The numbers in the following text are those of the stone's lineation.

(1) L. Aienus L. f. Q. Baebatius Sex. f. aedem dedicarunt (2) Iouis Liberi Furfone a. d. III idus Quinctileis L. Pisone A. Gabinio cos. mense flusare (3) †comula.teis† olleis legibus illeis regionibus, utei †extremae undae quae† lapide (4) facta hoiusque aedis ergo uteique ad eam aede(m) scalasque lapide †structuendo† (5) columnae stant citra scalas ad aedem uersus stipitesque aedis huius tabula(6)mentaque. utei tangere sarcire tegere deuehere defigere †mandare† ferro oeti (7) promouere referre <liceat, idque facere ius> fasque esto. sei quod ad eam aedem donum datum donatum dedicatum(8)que erit, utei liceat oeti uenum dare. ubei uenum datum erit, id profanum esto. uenditio (9) locatio aedilis esto quem quomque ueicus Furfens(is) fecerit, quod se sentiant eam rem (10) sine scelere sine piaculo <uendere locare>, alis ne potesto. quae pequnia recepta erit, ea pequnia emere (11) conducere locare dare, quo id templum melius honestius seit, liceto. quae pequnia ad eas (12) res data erit, profana esto, quod d(olo) m(alo) non erit factum. quod emptum erit aere aut argento (13) ea pequnia, quae pequnia ad id templum data erit, {quod emptum erit} eis rebus eadem (14) lex esto quasei sei dedicatum sit. sei qui heic sacrum surupuerit, aedilis multatio esto (15) quanti uolet; idque ueicus Furf(ensis) m(aior) pars fifeltares sei apsoluere uolent siue condemnare (16) liceto. sei quei ad huc templum rem deiuinam fecerit Ioui Libero aut Iouis genio, pelleis (17) coria fanei sunto.

3 quae *an* ouae *lapis incertum*; extrema fundamenta sunt *Dessau*
5 humus *lapis*
7 <liceat, idque facere ius> *Mommsen*
9 sentiunt *lapis*
10 <uendere locare> *Mommsen*
13 {quod emptum erit} *del. H. Jordan, Hermes 7 (1873), 210 = Krit. Beitr. (1879), 261*

A very provisional translation is as follows:

> Lucius Aienus, son of Lucius, and Quintus Baebatius, son of Sextus, dedicated the temple of Jupiter Liber at Furfo on 13 July in the consulship of Lucius Piso and Aulus Gabinius, in the month of flowers (OR of Flora), specifying (?) those regulations and those boundaries, according as the outermost foundations (?) constructed of stone for the purpose of this temple, and as, towards that temple and the staircase constructed of stone, columns on this side of the staircase leading towards the temple and the piles and roofing of this temple stand. Let it be allowed to touch, repair, cover, carry away, piledrive, clean out, use iron, push forward, contract, and let this be permissible under human and divine law. If any gift be given, presented, dedicated to that temple, be it permitted to use or sell it. When it has been sold, let it be secular. Let the sale or leasing be in the hands of whatever aedile the village of Furfo has elected, so far as they feel that they are selling or leasing that object without crime or impiety; no-one else is to have this power. Be it permitted with the money that is received to buy, hire, put it out at interest or make a gift of it so that the temple may be improved and beautified. Money contributed for those purposes is to be secular, insofar as there is no fraud involved. Anything bought with the money, bronze or silver, given to that temple, those things should be subject to the same regulations as if it had been dedicated. If anyone here steals a consecrated object, the aedile is to have the power of fining in whatever amount he sees fit; and if the village of Furfo [*fifeltares* ?] by majority vote wishes either to acquit or condemn, this is to be allowed. If anyone performs sacrifice at this temple to Jupiter Liber or to the Genius of Jupiter, the skins and hides are to belong to the shrine.

Mommsen regarded this as the most carelessly cut inscription he had ever met. It comes from Furfo, a hamlet of the Vestini about 60 English miles ENE of Rome, and bears a considerable resemblance to the *leges* of altars at Narbo and Salonae (Bruns 285-7 = *FIRA* 3.228-30), which both refer for unspecified provisions to the *lex* of the ancient altar of Diana on the Aventine (also referred to on on *Inscr. Ital.* 4.1.73, an altar to Bona Dea); this, together with the evident antiquity of the language and formulations, justifies inclusion of this inscription in this book despite the consular date of 58 B.C. Note that *-que* is the only copulative conjunction employed.

(2) For the cult of Iuppiter Liber or Libertas see *CIL* 1 (ed. 2) ad loc., Wissowa 120, Latte 70.

Quinctileis This is not an inconsistent way of representing what would in classical Latin be *ī* in both the second and third syllables; each spelling is etymologically correct both here and in *deiuinam* 16. Nevertheless there are clear inconsistencies in this matter: *quei* and *qui*, *sei* and *siue*, *quanti* and *Liberi* (the etymologically correct spelling of the genitive singular) but *fanei. eis* in 13 might represent *īs*.

mense flusare (Flusare) Cf. *mesene flusare* on a dialect inscription from the same region (Vetter no. 160 = Conway no. 248). This may derive from *flos* (occasionally spelt *flus* on inscriptions; *TLL* 6.1.932.77) or from Flora (Oscan *Flusa*; Vetter 21, 147 = Conway 46, 175; the latter also has *Fluusasiais* = *Floralibus*). See *RAC, Flora* 1124-5. It is natural to suppose that an original *flosaris* became *floraris* through rhotacism and then *floralis* through dissimilation, though linguists argue about this; see further Wachter 414.

Radke, *Rh. Mus.* 106 (1963), 313 points out that July in Italy is too late to be the month of flowers, and that if it is assumed that the Roman calendar in 58 B.C. was three months out of tune with the natural year, 13 July will be 13 April Julian, the date of the *natalis* of the temple of Jupiter Libertas on the Aventine (Latte l.c.). This cannot be right because the Roman calendar was certainly nowhere nearly so much out of joint in 58 B.C. (Laffi 125 n.12; P. Brind'Amour, *Le Calendrier romain* (1983) 49-51 and 303). Yet Radke's observation is botanically sound; the Floralia were celebrated at the end of April and the beginning of May, and *Anth. Lat.* 395.24 puts *florales fugas* in June, whether that means 'the rout of Flora' or 'the withering of flowers' (see *MH* 45 (1988), 48-9). I suspect that we have to reckon with dislocation of not the Roman calendar but that of Furfo.

(3) *olleis legibus illeis regionibus* A noteworthy instance of inconsistent spelling (see above on the *deuotio*, p. 111); the composer or ordinator began by maintaining the form of the antique prescription, but then slipped into that of his own time. A *regio* (*OLD* 4; add Livy 1.18.7, Cic. *Nat. Deor.* 2.9) is a boundary line fixed around a *templum* defined by an augur; the same thing happens with the institution of a physical temple (Livy 1.10.6 *templumque his regionibus quas modo animo metatus sum dedico*). The bounds are defined by the following *utei*. Cf. the altar dedications, *hanc aram...his (ollis) legibus hisque (ollisque) regionibus dabo dedicaboque quas hic hodie (palam) dixero, uti infimum solum huius(que) arae est*. The relative clause there suggests that for the first corruption here we might read *noncupateis* (= *nuncupatis*), cf. Norden *AAP* 47. Dessau's emendation of the second seems right with the possible exception of *sunt*; it may be that *stant* serves zeugmatically to all the subjects *fundamenta, columnae, stipites, tabulamenta* (see below for the construction of the last two).

(4) *hoiusque* = *huiusce*; but note the spelling *huius* restored below. For the *-que* see Sommer 424, 450 (and at Cato *de Agr.* 139 Victorius emended *harumque* to *harumce*, rightly for the sense); Sommer sees it as due to the influence of *quoiusque*.

structuendo (the third letter is uncertain; Laffi 130 n.33). This must conceal *structas* (Laffi 132 compares *FIRA* 3.240 = Bruns 363 *structio scalaris*), but that can hardly be the whole answer.

(5) *citra* is hard to interpret because we do not know the viewpoint taken, outwards from the *cella* (which seems to be meant by *aedem*) or inwards towards it; the positioning of the stone in its original site would have made this plain. It seems to me that *ad eam aede(m) scalasque* and *ad aedem uersus* simply repeat each other;

that it would be pointless to specify columns (i.e. those supporting the pediment) at the top of the steps as a *regio*; and that we should therefore think of a colonnade leading towards the temple and take the second viewpoint for *citra*, which would imply that this inscription was not built into the temple itself. *CIL* 9.3523 from another site nearby refers to construction of a *fanum porticus ala* complex; it is unfortunate that archaeology gives no help at Furfo.

stipites are piles driven into the ground (cf. Iavolenus *Dig.* 19.1.18 and Festus 314 *stipes, fustis terrae defixus*); as Festus shows, this item correlates with *defigere* in the next sentence. *tabulamentum* (found elsewhere only as a variant at Frontin. *Strat.* 1.7.1) probably, as Mommsen thought, refers to the wooden roof of the temple and correlates with the following *tegere*. Laffi 133 n.39 mentions another interpretation which seems very unlikely to me. The words have been construed in the following ways:

(a) they are governed by *ad*; but it is not likely that one would specify a colonnade leading towards the foundation piles and roof of the temple.

(b) one should end the sentence after *uersus* and make them the object of *tangere* etc. But these verbs clearly refer to the whole building (as on the Narbo inscription); there would be no point in specifying repairs just to these two items.

(c) they are governed by *dedicarunt* 1; this is wildly improbable.

(d) I therefore take them as subjects of the zeugmatic *stant*. This implies that the *regiones* are defined both horizontally and vertically.

(6-7) <*liceat*> at least is essential in order to give functions to *utei* (see p. 10) and *(fas)que*, but the longer addition is probable; cf. the Narbo inscription *si quis tergere ornare reficere uolet...ius fasque esto. ius* would link with *sine scelere* below, *fas* with *sine piaculo*.

tangere is specified because often the sacred may not be touched; Livy 29.20.10 *tacta ac uiolata*, *CIL* 8.11796 = *ILS* 4908 (a statue) *neue ab alio quo [nisi ab eis o]mnibus quibus ornandum tergendumue erit contingatur*, Festus 348, Serv. *Aen.* 7.776, Livy 5.22.5.

sarcire refers to the walls, *tegere* to the roof; cf. the common *sarta tecta* (*OLD tego* 2b, Mommsen 2.450 n.3). For *mandare* the best correction seems to be Huschke's *emendare* (*Jahrb. kl. Phil., suppl.* 5 (1877), 860), a word applied to construction by Pliny *NH* 36.121, Pliny *Ep.* 10.39.6; Orelli's *mundare* would suggest no more than sweeping out the temple.

ferro oeti (= *uti*; so below, and cf. *oitile* in the letter to the Tiburtines, p. 101). Most religious ceremonies have roots that predate the Iron Age, so iron is generally not admitted into sacral surroundings (and the same applies to magic). Cf. Macrob. *Sat.* 5.19.11-13 and expiations in the Acta Fratrum Arvalium (p. 131 Henzen), and see Ruggiero *ferrum* 59-60, Frazer on Ovid *Fasti* 5.441, my note on Juv. 6.441-3. However an exception has to be made for workmen's tools.

promouere referre 'push forward' (cf. Cic. *Ad Q.f.* 3.1.2) 'and contract'; e.g. the foundations might need buttressing or realignment if they bulged.

(7) *ad eam aedem* Here and in 13 *ad id templum* the preposition in effect conveys a dative sense; see HS 220 and Kroll, *Glotta* 22 (1934), 13.

quod...donum The hyperbaton is in the service of alliteration; in inscriptions we often meet‑*d(onum) d(at) d(icat) d(edicat)*. Cf. Wölfflin 257.

(8) *oeti* Cf. Plut. *Tib. Gracchus* 15.6 (τοῖς τῶν θεῶν ἀναθήμασι) χρῆσθαι...ὡς βούλεται τὸν δῆμον οὐδεὶς κωλύει.

(9) *aedilis* Probably one of those municipal 'nominell magistratischen, sachlich sacerdotalen Aedilen' of whom Mommsen 2.479 n.1 speaks. We do not know how Furfo was administered, nor what position the two dedicators named at the beginning of this inscription held.

fecerit The stone has *fecernt* with the last two letters ligatured, so perhaps we should read *fecerint*, with plural verb after a collective noun (see on Cato *Origines* 83c).

quod se sentiant For *quod* with subjunctive = 'so far as' see HS 572-3, Bennett 1.295. Norden *AAP* 54-6 quotes weak parallels for the present indicative offered by the stone, but himself wants to read the subjunctive as a better match for the following *quod dolo malo non erit factum*; he also compares *quod magmentum nec protollat* in the altar inscriptions (*nec = non*, cf. on Cato *De Agr.* 141.4). Unlike the mood, the ad sensum plural causes no problems (Norden 55 n.1), though one notes the singular *uolet* 15.

(10) *alis = alius* (Leumann 471, Sommer 442, *TLL* 1.1623.49).

(11) *ea pequnia emere...dare* The ablative suits the first two verbs; with the second two one has to understand an accusative, so that the contrast *conducere* 'hire' and *locare* 'put out at interest' will be defective (it will still be defective if one maintains an ablative and interprets *locare* as 'put out a contract'). For *dare* cf. the next sentence.

(10) Cf. *CIL* 11.944 = *ILS* 4909 *sine scelere sine fraude*.

(11) *honestius* 'more handsome' (*OLD* 4a). The asyndeton bimembre is characteristic (see below 16 and on Cato *De Agr.* 2.2).

seit (contrast *sit* 14) suggests that this phrase originated when the pronunciation *sīt* was still current (Leumann 111, SP 104).

(12) *quod* again = 'so far as'. A future indicative with *posse* is quite common in this construction (KS 2.308, 453); see also Lex Acilia 73 (*FIRA* 1.99, Bruns 71, Warmington IV 364, Crawford 73) *ea omnia, quod ex hace lege factum non erit, faciant*.

quod emptum erit...(13) eis rebus For this natural equivalence of the neuter gender and *res* see HS 431-2, KS 1.63; as for the number, *quod* has a collective sense. The neuter prevails again with *dedicatum* 14.

(13) *aere aut argento* The two metals used for currency (gold coinage had not yet been introduced); *ea pequnia* is epexegetic to this, and then the antecedent is repeated in the relative clause (see on Piso 27). The previous two sentences have

shown different patterns: *quae pequnia...ea pecunia, quae pequnia* followed by no demonstrative.

ad id templum See above 7.

eadem...(14) quasei See HS 674, *TLL* 7.1.199.59 and for *quasei sei* HS 675, KS 2.454.

aedilis multatio esto The same type of formulation as *manus iniectio esto* XII Tables 3.2. Cf. *FIRA* 3.223 = Bruns 283 = Warmington IV.154 *eius piacli moltaique dicator[ei] exactio est[od]*, and *FIRA* 1.167 = Bruns 120 = Warmington IV.438.6 *eiusque pequniae magistratus...petitio exactioque esto*.

(15) *idque* For the construction of this Laffi compares *FIRA* 3.508 = Bruns 403. 42-3 *quei controuorsias Genuensium ob iniourias iudicati aut damnati sunt*; it appears to be some kind of accusative of respect. Perhaps the analogy of the accusative of neuter pronouns indicating the charge after *accusare* (*TLL* 1.352.9) has had some influence.

ueicus Furf(ensis) maior pars Altenburg 500, Norden *AAP* 42-5 and Laffi 141 produce good parallels for this type of partitive apposition; see also the lex Acilia 60 (Bruns 68 = *FIRA* 1.60 = Warmington IV 354 = Crawford 71), Plaut. *MG* 93 and HS 428-9 (add now the Lex Irnitana 73 (*JRS* 76 (1986), 172) *quos decuriones conscriptiue municipi eius pars maior probauerit*).

fifeltares This has not been satisfactorily explained; the attempt of Laffi 141 is unconvincing.

sei...siue See HS 670; for the spelling see on 2 above.

(16) *huc = hoc*; so in the dedication of the cooks of Falerii (*ML* 2.5).

genio For the *genii* of gods see my note on *ML* 155 and *RAC, genius* 60; this is apparently the first mention.

pelleis Nom. plur. (Leumann 440, Sommer 382); this is in asyndeton bimembre (cf. 11 above) with *coria*.

(c) Marcellus Empiricus, *De Medicamentis* 15.11 = R. Heim, *Incantamenta Magica (Neue Jahrb. kl. Phil. suppl. 19, 1893)* no. 40 p. 476

exi, <si> hodie nata, si ante nata,
si hodie creata, si ante creata;
hanc pestem, hanc pestilentiam,
hunc dolorem, hunc tumorem, hunc ruborem,
has toles, has tosillas,
hunc panum, has panuclas,
hanc strumam, hanc strumellam,
hac religione euoco educo excanto
de istis membris medullis.

<si> *Heim*
hac religione *Bernays ap. Heim*, hanc religionem *uel* relegionem *codd.*

Charms against ailments are recorded by Cato, Varro and Marcellus. Stylistically this, which is intended to counter *synanche* (sore throat), is much the most interesting; all that one can tell about its dating is that it is older than Marcellus, who wrote at the beginning of the fifth century A.D., but it so clearly reproduces the forms of antiquity that it merits inclusion in this book. The parallellism, assonance (note *nATA, creATA*), exhaustive enumeration are all typical of religious formulation (and notoriously it is very hard to draw a firm line between religion and magic, though in a subtle analysis Addabbo, *Civiltà Classica e Cristiana* 12 (1991), 14 remarks some differences in application of the stylistic means); the first two lines are bound to remind us of *si deus, si dea es*. No copulative conjunction occurs here. The nouns are mostly paired, with the second member expanded from the first; this expansion takes priority over appropriateness to the context in *pestilentiam*, and *membris medullis* too is not wholly suitable, but rather a means of indicating the whole body within this stylistic framework. There are also two assonant tricola, and bicolon and tricolon combine in 5-7. It is perhaps worth while to suggest that Catullus had formulae of this nature in mind when he wrote *o di...eripite hanc pestem perniciemque mihi* (76.20) in a passage dominated by medical metaphors.

toles (originally **tonsles*) is the base form on which the diminutive *to(n)sillae* is created (Festus 356), *panus* and *panucla* seem to refer to some kind of tumor (these words are better treated in Lewis and Short than in *OLD*), *struma* is a glandular swelling.

euoco educo excanto is compared by Appel 142 with *demando deuoueo desacrifico* in a curse (his no. 54).

CHAPTER VII

ORATORS

(a) SCIPIO AEMILIANUS

In general see A. E. Astin, *Scipio Aemilianus* (1967).

fr. 17 Malcovati = Gell. 6.12.5
Aduersus P. Sulpicium Galum

nam qui cotidie unguentatus aduersus speculum ornetur, cuius supercilia radantur, qui barba uulsa feminibusque subuulsis ambulet, qui in conuiuiis adulescentulus cum amatore cum chirodyta tunica inferior accubuerit, qui non modo uinosus sed uirosus quoque sit, eumne quisquam dubitet quin idem fecerit quod cinaedi facere solent?

v.l. aduersum

This speech was perhaps delivered when Scipio was censor in 142 and conducted a severe *recognitio equitum*.

All these items form part of the traditional characterisation of the effeminate man and sexual invert, and as such are part of the stock arsenal of oratorical abuse (W. Süss, *Ethos* (1910) 249; A. Richlin, *Garden of Priapus* (ed. 2, 1992) 96, with this passage oddly placed on 93). Mirrors were supposed to be used only by women, not by he-men; cf. my note on Juv. 2.99 and Sen. *NQ* 1.17.2 *ad speculum barbam uellere*. For depilation see Blümner 269 and 438-9, *RAC Effeminatus* 633; for tunics with sleeves Blümner 207, Marquardt 551. This last item is contemptuously designated by a Greek term rather than the Latin *manicata, manuleata*; cf. Lucilius 71 *chirodyti aurati*. For *unguentatus* see my note on Juv. 2.41. Shaving of the eyebrows is decried by Cic. *Pro Rosc. Com.* 20.

cum...cum in different senses, 'in the company of...wearing'; cf. on fr. 30 init. and on Cato *De Agr.* pr.1.

inferior accubuerit This would be the position occupied by disreputable women under the republic, when respectable women did not recline at table with the men; cf. Livy 39.43.3, Cic. *Ad Fam.* 9.26.2. This charge therefore implies passive homosexuality.

uīrosus is used by Afranius 62, Lucilius 282. In the same book, the themes of which cannot be established in detail but seem to have been generally erotic, Lucilius 264-5 has *rador subuellor desquamor pumicor ornor / expolior pingor*, which looks as if he had the words of his friend Scipio in mind, especially as the word *subuellor* (the force of the prefix is not clear to me) is found only in these two passages. Scipio is probably punning not only on *uinosus* but also implicitly on *uīrosus*, 'venomous, fetid'.

eumne For the prolepsis see on Cato *De Agr.* 1.4. There are comparable sexual euphemisms with *solere* in Plaut. *Cas.* 1011, *Pseud.* 780.

fr. 19 - 20 = Gell. 6.11.9, 2.20.6
Pro se contra Ti. Claudium Asellum de multa ad populum

omnia mala probra flagitia quae homines faciunt in duabus rebus sunt, malitia atque nequitia. utrum defendis, malitiam an nequitiam? an utrumque simul? si nequitiam defendere uis, licet. si tu in uno scorto maiorem pecuniam absumpsisti quam quanti omne instrumentum fundi Sabini in censum dedicauisti, si hoc ita est, qui spondet mille nummum? si tu plus tertia parte pecuniae paternae perdidisti atque absumpsisti in flagitiis, si hoc ita est, qui spondet mille nummum? non uis nequitiam, age malitiam saltem defende. si tu uerbis conceptis coniurauisti sciens sciente animo tuo, si hoc ita est, qui spondet mille nummum?

abinsumpsisti *codd. priore loco*, sumpsisti *cod. unus altero*
iurauisti *Hertz*, periurauisti *Meyer*

ubi agros optime cultos atque uillas expolitissimas uidisset, in his regionibus excelsissimo loco grumam statuere <oportere> aiebat, inde corrigere uiam, aliis per uineas medias, aliis per roborarium atque piscinam, aliis per uillam.

loco grumam *Madvig*, locorum (mu) *codd.*
<oportere> *Courtney*

As censor in 142 Scipio had deprived Ti. Claudius Asellus of his horse, but Scipio's colleague L. Mummius restored Asellus to equestrian status (see Astin 326-7). Asellus became tribune in 140 and prosecuted Scipio for his conduct as censor: Lucil. 394 *Scipiadae magno improbus obiciebat Asellus / lustrum illo censore malum infelixque fuisse* (these words are recalled by Cic. *De Or.* 2.268). The *infelicitas* perhaps consisted of a plague in 142 (Astin 176 n.1).

19

Scipio begins with a *diuisio* (Lausberg 393) which presents Asellus with a dilemma. The first sentence shows a rising tricolon of near synonyms and ends with a striking homoeoteleuton which matches with each other the two equally indefensible charges. Then the two charges are put in corresponding form. Gellius explains that *nequitia* means 'prodigality'.

(pecuniam) absumpsisti The manuscripts have clearly combined two variants; *insumpsisti* is discouraged by the deliberate recurrence of *abs.* below and the fact that *insumere* is not attested before Cicero.

in censum dedicare means to declare as one's property for census purposes; it is not clear whether the noun should be in the accusative or, as at Varro *LL* 5.160 (at Cic. *Pro Flacc.* 79 the ms. has *incensa*), the ablative.

qui spondet... 'Who pledges 1000 sesterces on your innocence?' *Qui* and *quis* were not originally differentiated as interrogative adjective and pronoun, and *qui* continues to be preferred before *s*; see HS 540-1, *OLD* s.v. *qui (1)* 4a.

plus...perdidisti One can envisage the vehemence with which Scipio spat out the alliterating *p* in this sentence.

uerbis conceptis See on Cato *De Agr.* 141.4. *coniurauisti* is elsewhere so used only at [Ov.] *Her.* 21.135, where it is open to suspicion; Timpanaro ap. Kenney, *CQ* 29 (1979), 421 interprets 'I have shared in no oath with my mind'. We are left with the choice between supposing (a) that Scipio ventured on a linguistic experiment for the sake of an assonance, or (b) that a scribe's eye or mind has wandered to the preceding word. I favour (b) with Meyer's emendation, since otherwise the sentence does not specifically charge Asellus with anything; though one must admit that an assonance would go well with the weightily pleonastic polyptoton *sciens sciente.* Cf. Plaut. *Asin.* 562 *ubi uerbis conceptis sciens...peiieraris, Pseud.* 1056-7; Cic. *Pro Clu.* 134 quotes Scipio himself as using the phrase *uerbis conceptis peierasse.*

sciens (see *OLD* s.v. 2) is often used in legal contexts = 'deliberately' (Appel 148, M. Kaser, *Ausg. Schr.* (1976) 1.243). Cf. also Fronto p. 115.10 *libens scienti animo,* where Hauler doubtfully read the first word as *sciens.*

20

Gellius specifies that this comes from Scipio's fifth speech against Asellus.

uidisset An exceptionally early appearance of the iterative subjunctive, of which there are only scattered examples before Livy (indeed some deny totally its existence in early Latin). See Bennett 1.338, Handford 176, HS 354.

gruma A surveying instrument; see *kl. Pauly* and *Der Neue Pauly* s.v. *groma*, O. A. W. Dilke, *Roman Land Surveyors* (1971) 15-16, 50 (plate), 66-70.

aiebat is sometimes understood 'he ordered'; the word however does not possess this meaning. Yet it seems to be right for the general sense, as 'he said' is not; my addition, which could easily have fallen out because of homoeoteleuton, introduces the right sense. Cima's *auebat* (*BFC* 8 (1902), 283) is rather weak.

roboraria (the word is not found elsewhere) is explained by Gellius to mean game-preserves (*uiuaria*) with timber fences; for such see Colum. 9.1.3. Elsewhere we do not hear of game-preserves and fish-ponds until about 50 years later than this.

fr. 30 = Macrob. *Sat.* 3.14.6
Contra legem iudiciariam Ti. Gracchi

docentur praestigias inhonestas, cum cinaedulis et sambucis psalterioque eunt in ludum histrionum, discunt cantare, quae maiores nostri ingenuis probro ducier uoluerunt; eunt, inquam, in ludum saltatorium inter cinaedos uirgines puerique ingenui. haec cum mihi quispiam narrabat, non poteram animum inducere ea liberos homines nobiles docere, sed cum ductus sum in ludum saltatorium, plus medius fidius in eo ludo uidi pueris uirginibusque quinquaginta, in his unum (quo me rei publicae maxime miseritum est) puerum bullatum, petitoris filium non minorem annis duodecim, cum crotalis saltare, quam saltationem pudicus seruulus honeste saltare non posset.

histrionium *Meyer*
quispiam *Meyer*, quisquam *codd.*
vv. ll. quingenta, quingentis
quo *et* pudicus *Courtney*, quod *et* impudicus *codd.*

The *lex iudiciaria* in question was evidently a sequel to Gracchus' agrarian legislation, giving the land-commissioners powers to adjudicate on the status of land in dispute (Livy periocha 58; Astin 239-40; E. S. Gruen, *Roman Politics and the Criminal Courts* (1968) 58). Appian *BC* 1.19.78 (see Gabba's note) mentions Scipio's attack on this law in a speech in the senate in 129 B.C. after the death of Gracchus. It must have ranged widely over what he saw as the harmful effects of all of Gracchus' legislation in bringing Asian luxury and degeneration closer to Rome with the annexation of Pergamum and the use of its revenues; see *CAH* 9.7-8. Music and dancing, though frowned upon by strict moralists, nevertheless seem to have been quite widely taught at Rome; see S. F. Bonner, *Education in Ancient Rome* (1977) 44, H. I. Marrou, *History of Education in Antiquity* (English transl., Mentor

Books, 1956) 332. Cf. Sen. *Contr.* 1 pr. 8 *cantandi saltandique obscena studia tenent effeminatos*; Horace *Odes* 3.6.21 *motus doceri gaudet Ionicos / matura uirgo* (here *matura* has come under suspicion, but is defended by Scipio's *non minorem annis duodecim*), Quintil. 1.10.31 *psalteria et spadices etiam uirginibus probis recusanda*. Scipio's presumed point is reinforced by the fact that harp-like stringed instruments had strong Asiatic associations; see my note on Juv. 3.63-5.

   cum cinaedulis et psalteriis For the syllepsis of *cum*, which with the first noun is equivalent to *inter cinaedos* below, cf. HS 831-2, Lausberg 702, 707.1 and on fr. 17. For what that is worth, this is the only occurrence of *et* in Scipio's fragments; there are four each of *-que* and (in Catonian vein) of *atque*. The fundamental sense of *cinaedus* (the diminutive here reinforces the scorn) is 'dancer' (see Lucil. 32, my note on Juv. 6.O.19, A. Corbeill, *Controlling Laughter* (1996) 136-7, McGing, *Hermathena* 143 (1987), 77, *RAC* s.v. *Effeminatus* 638, Perpillou-Thomas *ZPE* 108 (1995), 228). Polyb. 5.37.10 has κιναίδους ἄγειν καὶ σαμβύκας; did Scipio recall words of his friend? Despite Scipio's scorn here, it seems to emerge from Lucil. 1140 (unfortunately the passage is desperately corrupt) that he had a *cinaedus* in his entourage. *cum cinaedulis...eunt in ludum* is chiastically reversed when repeated, *eunt in ludum inter cinaedos*; cf. Cic. *Har. Resp.* 8 *de religionibus sacris [et] caerimoniis est contionatus...Clodius: P., inquam, Clodius sacra et religiones neglegi...questus est.* This is a variety of the figure of *redditio* (Lausberg 626). *uirgines puerique* on repetition is also chiastically reversed to *pueris uirginibusque*.

   docentur...cantare shows a Catonian-style falling tricolon.

   ludum histrionum Meyer's emendation is supported by *ludum saltatorium* below, but Sen. *Ep.* 70.20 has *in ludo bestiariorum* before 22 *in ludo bestiario*.

   ducier This form of the infinitive was probably already an archaism to Scipio, who is contrasted with Laelius' fondness for archaisms by Cicero (*Brut.* 83) and who has *censeri* in fr. 14; he uses it because he is speaking of the *maiores*. It is the last occurrence of this form in oratory. See Lebek 49.

   Livy 1.35.3, where the same emendation as here has been made, seems to be the only support for such a use of *quisquam*.

   For *animum inducere* with accus. and inf. cf. the letter to the Tiburtines (p. 101) and Bennett 1.379.

   liberos homines nobiles The meaning is clear despite the formal ambiguity of the *aio te, Aeacida, Romanos uincere posse* type.

   medius fidius A colloquial interjection, found e.g. in Cato Speeches 176 M and 18 times in Cicero's speeches.

   in eo ludo A later writer might have said *ibi*, but for this type of connection see p. 7 and on Ennius XI.

   quo 'Wherefore'; cf. *OLD* s.v. *quo (2)* 1a. I cannot understand what the syntax of *quod* would be. For the deponent *miseritum est* see HS 416, KS 1.469.

bullatum i.e. free-born, contrasted with the *pudicus seruulus*; see Palmer, *AJAH* 14 (1989, publ. 1998), 1 sqq. (esp. 26).

I cannot make sense out of *impudicus*; it would strangely imply that it would be "respectable" for an *impudicus seruulus* to perform certain dances. For my emendation cf. *uirginibus probis* in Quintilian quoted above. A *seruulus* may be granted more licence than an *ingenuus*, but even a slave who was *pudicus* (the adjective emphatically placed) could not keep that reputation if he performed such a dance.

Scipio's fragments show some stylistic features which recall Cato and (in 17 and 19) the same vehemently aggressive tone, accentuated by rhetorical devices like anaphora (17), figures involving repetition of sounds and polyptoton (19). 30, not being directed against an individual, displays indignation rather than vituperation. Despite an instance of the figure of *redditio*, it is less formally structured and shows a certain approach to the level of mundane narrative (note the colloquial *medius fidius*); the indignation comes through mainly in the careful choice of vocabulary, which pits Greek against Roman and traditional Roman values against degeneracy from them. Scipio's discretion in the application of stylistic devices certainly constitutes an advance over Cato.

(b) C. SEMPRONIUS GRACCHUS

Fr. 26-8 Malcovati = Gell. 15.12
Ad populum cum ex Sardinia rediit

Versatus sum in prouincia quomodo ex usu uestro existimabam esse, non quomodo ambitioni meae conducere arbitrabar. nulla apud me fuit popina, neque pueri eximia facie stabant, sed in conuiuio liberi uestri modestius erant quam apud principia.

ita uersatus sum in prouincia uti nemo posset uere dicere assem aut eo plus in muneribus me accepisse aut mea opera quemquam sumptum fecisse. biennium fui in prouincia; si ulla meretrix domum meam introiuit aut cuiusquam seruulus propter me sollicitatus est, omnium nationum postremissimum nequissimumque existimatote. cum a seruis eorum tam caste me habuerim, inde poteritis considerare quomodo me putetis cum liberis uestris uixisse.

itaque, Quirites, cum Romam profectus sum, zonas, quas plenas argenti extuli, eas ex prouincia inanes rettuli: alii uini amphoras quas plenas tulerunt, eas argento repletas domum reportauerunt.

26 astabant *Castiglioni apud Malcovati*
27 nationum *quibusdam suspectum*

In 126 Gracchus went to Sardinia as quaestor, and after staying there for two years spontaneously returned to Rome, no successor having been appointed because the optimates wished to keep him out of the way. The censors on this pretext wished to deprive him of his horse, but he vigorously defended himself in a speech before them and another before the people. Plut. 2.9-10 professes to give a summary of the former, part of which is more or less identical with fr. 28; this may mean either that Gracchus repeated himself or that Plutarch confused the two speeches (he mentions only the one). His self-defence was so successful that he was elected tribune for 123.

26

astabant might be right, but *stabant* adds an extra hint of prostitution; see my note on Juv. 10.172.

liberi uestri Not identical with the *pueri*, but potential clients of such. The sons of the audience (cf. 28) experienced less temptation at Gracchus' table than they did at military headquarters, which seems to imply a hit at Gracchus' commander L. Aurelius Orestes.

modestius esse See on Cato *De Agr.* 4.

27

biennium and Plutarch's (4) τριετίαν are just different ways of counting the same period of time.

propter me sollicitatus est by a member of my entourage acting for me.

nationum...existimatote Between them Löfstedt *Synt* 2.204 and Haffter *WS* 69 (1956), 370 have thrown much light on this clause. It rises from a word of three syllables to one of six, employing to that end (1) the word *nationum*, which looks a little odd in this setting, but is not clearly wrong and is certainly of the right length (2) the double superlative *postremissimum*, which has been specifically coined to fit this context (its later occurrences in Apul. *Apol.* 98, where see Butler - Owen, and Tertull. *De Cultu Fem.* 2.1 do not have this justification; see Leumann 499) (3) the weighty form *existimatote*; the second person plural of the 'future' imperative, generally rare, tends to be reserved for special effects like this. All this is reinforced by the homoeoteleuton of -*um*.

eorum refers to the body of people of which an individual member is indicated by *cuiusquam*.

cum...uixisse An inductive argument (Lausberg 419-20).

28

This fragment is built around an elaborate series of antitheses.

zonas is a word which quickly naturalized itself; in Plautus it already has a Latinized form *sona*. Since ancient clothes had no pockets, it was usual to carry money in the belt.

eas For the resumptive pronoun see p. 4 and on Cato *De Agr.* 5.3.

extuli...rettuli...tulerunt...reportauerunt This shows an interesting solicitude for variety. The first and third exemplify the ancient idiom of following a compounded by an uncompounded form (see p. 2); the prefix in the second and fourth matches that in *repletas*, the right verb to denote replenishment. For the conversion of wine-jars into piggy-banks cf. Mart. 6.27.6 and the *Aulularia* of Plautus.

44 M = Gell. 11.10
Dissuasio legis †Aufeiae†

(**a**) Nam uos, Quirites, si uelitis sapientia atque uirtute uti, etsi quaeritis, neminem nostrum inuenietis sine pretio huc prodire. omnes nos qui uerba facimus aliquid petimus, neque ullius rei causa quisquam ad uos prodit nisi ut aliquid auferat. (**b**) ego ipse, qui aput uos uerba facio uti uectigalia uestra augeatis quo facilius uestra commoda et rempublicam administrare possitis, non gratis prodeo; uerum peto a uobis non pecuniam sed bonam existimationem atque honorem. (**c**) qui prodeunt dissuasuri ne hanc legem accipiatis, petunt non honorem a uobis, uerum a Nicomede pecuniam; qui suadent ut accipiatis, hi quoque petunt non a uobis bonam existimationem, uerum a Mitridate rei familiari[s] suae pretium et praemium; qui autem ex eodem loco atque ordine tacent, hi uel acerrimi sunt, nam ab omnibus pretium accipiunt et omnis fallunt. (**d**) uos, cum putatis eos ab his rebus remotos esse, impertitis bonam existimationem; legationes autem a regibus, cum putant eos sua causa reticere, sumptus atque pecunias maximas praebent, item uti in terra Graecia, quo in tempore tragoedus gloriae sibi ducebat talentum magnum ob unam fabulam datum esse, homo eloquentissimus ciuitatis suae Demades ei respondisse dicitur 'mirum tibi uidetur si tu loquendo talentum quaesisti? ego ut tacerem decem talenta a rege accepi'. item nunc isti pretia maxima ob tacendum accipiunt.

(a) quaeretis *Madvig dubitanter (Adv. Crit. 2.601)*
(c) dissuasum *Wackernagel*
  tacent *codd. dett.*, placent *primarii (eadem corruptela Gell.17.9.4)*
  sacerrimi *Bernays ap. Hertz*

The name Aufeius is extremely rare, and nobody so called is known ever to have held office at Rome. The only emendation which has anything to support it is Hill's

(*CR* 62 (1948), 112) *Aquiliam*, which will put the law in connection with the settlement of Asia by M'. Aquilius after the suppression of the revolt of Aristonicus; we still do not hear anything of its purport. From what Gracchus says we infer that ambassadors from Mithridates V King of Pontus, and Nicomedes III King of Bithynia were in Rome. Aquilius had presented part of Phrygia to Mithridates as a reward for his assistance in suppressing the rebellion of Aristonicus, but was forced to buy it back (Appian *Mithr.* 2.12, Justin 37.1.2, 38.5.3). Nicomedes, whose father had also helped against Aristonicus, clearly desired the same territory and tried to prevent the passage of this law, which was evidently in favour of Mithridates. For various interpretations of these events see *CAH* 9.34-5 and 79, D. Magie, *Roman Rule in Asia Minor* (1950) 1043, A. N. Sherwin-White, *Roman Foreign Policy in the East* (1984) 88-9 and in *JRS* 67 (1977), 7-8. Gracchus himself opposed the law because it would deprive the Roman treasury of revenues which he wished to use.

In this fragment Gracchus employs the conjunction *et*, which appears to have been his preferred copulative conjunction, thrice and, in Catonian vein, *atque* four times, in each occurrence linking nouns of related sense (so also in fr. 22 *auaritiam atque stultitiam*; in fr. 32 it links a pair of verbs). He is here seeking a weightier and more sententious effect than in the other fragments in this selection. This passage also shows much Catonian-style word-repetition. I have sub-divided it for easier reference.

(**a**) *si...inuenietis* Even though you are looking for impartial advisors, if you consider carefully you will not find that any of us answers to this description. *uirtus* is employed here in a very unusual way for which I have no good parallel.

(**b**) *uestra commoda* Your communal interests, contrasted with those of corrupt individuals; hence the emphatic placing of the possessive.

(**c**) *dissuasuri* For this date this is a very remarkable use of the future participle; see HS 390 and E. Laughton, *The Participle in Cicero* (1964) 119. Though the use really only establishes itself in Augustan times, there are parallels in *Bell. Afr.* 25.4, 65.2, Sall. *Hist.* 2.71 and a possible (Laughton 120) one in Cic. 2 *Verr.* 1.56. This is perhaps sufficient defence against Wackernagel's (1. 286) conjecture.

gratis should no doubt be written *gratiis*.

bonam existimationem atque honorem These terms are split in the next sentence so that the partisans of Nicomedes reject *honor* and those of Mithridates *bona existimatio*. In that sentence *non honorem...pecuniam* shows chiastic ABBA order, while *non a uobis...praemium* reverts to ABAB order.

Mitridate see Hertz's note for this spelling.

pretium et praemium is an alliterative pair (cf. on Cato *De Agr.* 141); see Quadrigarius 41 and other instances in *TLL* 10.2.713.19.

ex eodem ordine et loco Cf. Ter. *Eun.* 234 *quendam mei loci atque ordinis.* This implies that all who take the positions indicated are optimates.

acerrimi in this clause gives a good oxymoron, but seems not to suit the following clause well. For *sacer* 'abominable' see *OLD* s.v. 2c.

(d) *cum* 'since', still with the indicative (cf. on the 'Letter of Cornelia' b), though Gracchus has the subjunctive in 27 and 49. See Kroll 82, Handford 170.

pecunias 'sums of money'; see *TLL* s.v. 942.62.

item...item (nunc) Cf. Plaut. *Ps.* 869-72; here the second *item* is a conjecture (Seyffert, *BPW* 6 (1886), 1087).

terra Graecia It is quite a common form of expression in early Latin to follow a general designation with a specification, e.g. *uentus auster*; cf. KS 2.568 and Till (see p. 41) 9, 82-3 = 27, 137-8, Hache 11, Altenburg 491. Scipio the elder ap. Gell. 4.18.3 = fr. 3 M has *terra Africa*, and in addition to the examples quoted by KS (one of which is Cato Speeches 187 M) *terra Italia* is found repeatedly in *CIL* 1 (ed. 2) 585 (the *lex agraria* of 111 B.C.). For the opposite order see Skutsch on Enn. *Ann.* 309.

quo in tempore Classical usage would have omitted *in*; cf. Metellus Numidicus fr. 6 Malcovati *in eo tempore...in quo*, the 'Letter of Cornelia' (d) and on Piso 27.

tragoedus A tragic actor, not a tragic poet. In the identical anecdote referred to Demosthenes rather than Demades he is named as Aristodemus (see *RE* s.v. no. 10; Gell. 11.9.2) or Polus ([Plut.] *Vit. Decem Oratorum* 848b).

talentum magnum The Attic silver talent = 6000 drachmae; see Stöckert on Plaut. *Aul.* 309.

Demades was famous both for his apophthegms (F. Blass, *Die attische Beredsamkeit* (ed. 2, 1893) 3.272) and his venality (Dinarchus 1.89, 104; Plut. *De Cupid. Divit.* 5).

loquendo talentum quaesisti - ut tacerem decem talenta accepi The parallel arrangement underlines the contrast.

fr. 47-9 = Schol. Bob. in Cic., Pro Sulla 26 (p. 81.18 Stangl) + Gell. 10.3.3-5
De legibus promulgatis

si uellem aput uos uerba facere et a uobis postulare, cum genere summo ortus essem et cum fratrem propter uos amisissem, nec quisquam de P. Africani et Tiberi Gracchi familia nisi ego et puer restaremus, ut pateremini hoc tempore me quiescere, ne a stirpe genus nostrum interiret et uti aliqua propago generis nostri reliqua esset, haud <scio> an lubentibus a uobis impetrassem.

nuper Teanum Sidicinum consul uenit. uxor eius dixit se in balneis uirilibus lauari uelle. quaestori Sidicino M. Mario datum est negotium uti balneis exigerentur qui lauabantur. uxor renuntiat uiro parum cito sibi balneas traditas esse et parum lautas fuisse. idcirco palus destitutus est in foro eoque adductus suae ciuitatis nobilissimus homo M. Marius. uestimenta detracta sunt, uirgis caesus est. Caleni, ubi id audierunt, edixerunt ne quis in balneis lauisse uellet cum magistratus Romanus ibi esset. Ferentini ob eandem causam praetor noster quaestores abripi iussit: alter se de muro deiecit, alter prensus et uirgis caesus est.

quanta libido quantaque intemperantia sit hominum adulescentium, unum exemplum uobis ostendam. his annis paucis ex Asia missus est qui per id tempus magistratum non ceperat, homo adulescens pro legato. is in lectica ferebatur. ei obuiam bubulcus de plebe Venusina aduenit et per iocum, cum ignoraret qui ferretur, rogauit num mortuum ferrent. ubi id audiuit, lecticam iussit deponi, st<r>uppis quibus lectica deligata erat usque adeo uerberari iussit dum animam efflauit.

49 ex Asia *suspectum*

These passages are discussed by von Albrecht 33; there are three other small fragments of this speech. Despite D. Stockton, *The Gracchi* (1979) 120, 222 it seems to me most likely that this speech belongs to Gracchus' second tribunate in 122, when his influence with the plebs was beginning to wane and various laws which he promulgated failed to secure passage. Fr. 47 shows distinct insecurity.

47

This fragment is clearly from the exordium, the part of the speech where tension has not yet built up; hence the elaborate periodic structure which takes its time, in contrast to the spare, quick-moving narrative of 48-9.

quisquam must refer only to male descendants (F. Münzer, *Röm. Adelsparteien und Adelsfamilien* (1920) 273). The *puer* is probably the παιδίον of C. Gracchus mentioned by Plut. 15.2 (Münzer 268; ignored in the elaborate discussion by Stockton 30 n.32); others take him to be a surviving son of Tiberius. On the whole question see Astin, *Scipio Aemilianus* 319-20. For the word *familia* see on the 'Letter of Cornelia' (c).

propago 'offspring' is a metaphor from the propagation of plants by layering, and Gracchus, who stresses the idea of family continuity, probably still feels it as a poetic metaphor, cf. Trag. inc. 103 *qui nostrum porro propagat genus* in a family tree with *propagatus* 101, perhaps rendering the metaphor of ἔβλαστε Eur. *Iph. Taur.* 3. Otherwise it seems to be found before Gracchus only in Pacuv. 20. Here *a stirpe* incorporates the same metaphor.

48

Where Cato in similar circumstances is emotional (Speeches fr. 58), Gracchus allows the enormity of the proceedings to emerge from a cool and matter-of-fact presentation, with the facts recounted in curt and (apart from *idcirco*) asyndetic style.

renuntiat The pivotal action is put in the historic present.

destitutus 'set up'; *TLL* s.v. 762.18.

suae...Marius The word-order is noteworthy. *suae* is placed emphatically to stress that the dignity of a quaestor in Teanum Sidicinum matches that of a consul at Rome. His name is held back because it is less important than his station.

uestimenta detracta sunt Cf. Cato l.c.

ne quis...uellet See on Cato *De Agr.* 5.4.

uirgis caesus est is repeated from above to emphasise the setting of a pattern of iniquity by the consul.

One will note in this fragment the indifference to repetition of the word *balneae*, which could easily have been avoided.

49

his annis paucis 'within the last few years'; see *TLL* 6.2721.9, S. Lundström, *Abhinc und Ante* (1961) 19, 46-8.

ex Asia is open to suspicion. Mommsen 2.681 n.3 takes it to signify an envoy of a Roman official in Asia. Otherwise we have to consider emendation: *Venusiam* Jordan, *ex <s.c. in> Asiam* Hertz. The holding back of *homo adulescens pro legato* to the end forcefully adds an evaluation to the purely factual statement of the first part of the sentence. *Pro legato* becomes an official title of rank at the end of the first century B.C.

homo adulescens brings the general *hominum adulescentium* above down to a particular instance.

The connection by *is, ei* (see p. 7) and the repetition of *iussit* in the last sentence maintain the simple, matter-of-fact style of 48. This appears to be the first reliable reference to use of a litter by a Roman man. The *struppi* seem to be the straps by which the carrying-poles were attached to the litter, perhaps the same as the *lora* in Mart. 2.57.6; cf. *asseribus deligatis* Q. Curtius 4.3.15. *lectic(ul)a* is applied to a bier in Nepos *Att.* 22 and occasionally elsewhere (*RE* s.v. 1107). On this occasion the curtains were obviously closed. Cf. Cic. *Phil.* 2.106 *operta lectica latus per oppidum est ut mortuus.*

lecticam...lectica Classical style would consider the second superfluous.

usque adeo dum a. efflauit For the construction see HS 615; *animam efflare* is a stately phrase even on its occurrences in Plautus (*Pers.* 638, *Trin.* 876).

fr. 61 = Cic. *De Or.* 3.214, Quintil. 11.3.115

quo me miser conferam? quo uortam? in Capitoliumne? at fratris sanguine redundat. an domum? matremne ut miseram lamentantem uideam et abiectam?

at f. sanguinem redundat *cod. Laudensis Cic.*, at f. sanguine madet *codd. mutili Cic.*, ad f. sanguinem *Quintil.*
lamentantem *mutili*, lamentantemque *Laudensis*

This evidently comes from a speech delivered in the final days of Gracchus' life. It constitutes a famous example of the figure *dubitatio* (Lausberg 776). Another famous example had been produced in Latin before Gracchus by Ennius, *Medea* 217 Jocelyn: *quo nunc me uertam? quod iter incipiam ingredi? / domum paternamne, anne ad Peliae filias?* (translating Eur. *Med.* 502-3); this is quoted (217) soon after Gracchus by Cicero, also as an example of pathos. Von Albrecht 50 points out that in Euripides as in Gracchus each suggestion is immediately refuted, whereas Ennius blurs the clarity of this, but the Gracchan pattern is usual in the many examples both before and after Ennius, e.g. Demosth. 28.18, Ter. *Ph.* 185-6, Cic. *Pro Murena* 88 (closely imitating Gracchus; a comparison in von Albrecht). For other instances see Jocelyn's note, Bonnet *REA* 8 (1906), 40, Bömer on Ovid *Met.* 8.113, Tarrant on Sen. *Ag.* 649 (add Heliodorus 6.7.5). Cic. *De Or.* 3.214 stresses the effect of Gracchus' delivery here; see below.

quo me...uortam A double anaphoric question, as in Ennius (where Euripides had had only νῦν ποῖ τράπωμαι;).

sanguine redundat gives a clausula preferable to either *sanguinem r.* (which is is not a very likely construction; see *OLD, redundo* 2c) or *sanguine madet*; see below. In any case the picture is forceful; twelve years have not wiped out the blood.

matrem is prominently placed to match *fratris* and underline the sorrows of the whole family.

lamentantemque et abiectam would be too poetical; *-que...et* is not found in prose before Sallust.

Von Albrecht 35 has a valuable discussion of Gracchus; see also N. Haepke, *C. Semproni Gracchi...Fragmenta* (1915).

As an orator Gracchus had a reputation among the Romans for force and vehemence; *fortis ac uehemens orator existimatur esse* says Gellius 10.3.1 in introducing 48-9. Yet as we read most of the fragments of his speeches (61 being an exception), what strikes us is their matter-of-fact presentation and logical argumentation, not any emotionality; see for instance the fine restrained irony of fr. 44. This is so even when the situation seems to invite an outburst of rhetorical πάθος, as in 47-9, which contrast strongly with Cato 59 and Cicero's rendition of such occurrences in the *Verrines*. Gellius remarks the same:

in tam atroci re ac tam misera atque maesta iniuriae publicae contestatione ecquid est quod aut ampliter insigniterque aut lacrimose atque miseranter aut multa

copiosaque inuidia grauique et penetrabili querimonia dixerit? breuitas sane et
uenustas et mundities orationis est (4).

    haec quidem oratio super tam uiolento atque crudeli facinore nihil profecto
abest a cotidianis sermonibus (6).

    siquis est tam agresti aure ac tam hispida quem lux ista [i.e. of Cicero 2
Verr. 5.161] et amoenitas orationis uerborumque modificatio parum delectat, amat
autem priora [i.e. Gracchus] idcirco quod incompta et breuia et non operosa, sed
natiua quadam suauitate sunt quodque in his umbra et color quasi opacae uetustatis
est, is, siquid iudicii habet, consideret in causa pari M. Catonis, antiquioris hominis,
orationem [fr. 59], ad cuius uim et copiam Gracchus nec adspirauit. intellegat,
opinor, Catonem contentum eloquentia aetatis suae non fuisse et id iam tum facere
uoluisse quod Cicero postea perfecit (15-16).

    In the last quotation Gellius rightly draws attention to the reduction of the
narrative in Cato in favour of the *questio* also prominent in Cicero. On the printed
page Gracchus' coolness does actually succeed because it hints that behaviour like
this is nowadays unremarkable; but this is caviar for the general where most orators
would have been trying to set the mob howling. What bridges this seeming
disjunction between style and reputation must be, as von Albrecht suggests,
delivery (*actio*). It was well known that Gracchus devoted great attention to this
(von Albrecht 48), and in quoting fr. 61 Cicero (*De Or.* 3.214) particularly stresses
the effect which the delivery had on the audience, making even Gracchus' enemies
weep. See J. David in *Demokratia et Aristokratia* (ed. C. Nicolet, 1983) 103.

    The second most striking feature of Gracchus' oratory is that he has moved
beyond Scipio in attention paid to clausula-rhythms, and shows a great step towards
the Ciceronian norms. In 27 he may have chosen the form *existimatote* partly for the
sake of the clausula – ⏑ – – – ⏑ , one of Cicero's favourites; we even find the *esse
uideatur* variation of this in 44 *mirum tibi uidetur* and probably in 61 *sanguine
redundat*; instances of other rhythms favoured by Cicero are 61 *me miser conferam*
and often, 27 *quomodo me putetis* (on the assumption that Gracchus did not
pronounce *quomodŏ*). Moreover the dichoree is frequent when not (as in the last
example) preceded by a cretic, e.g. 26 *arbitrabar*; it was such a clausula (*comprobauit*)
when uttered by the later orator C. Carbo that evoked admiring applause from the
audience (Cic. *Or.* 214). Even where the ends of his cola do not strictly conform to
these norms (and Cicero *Or.* 233 shows how one of them in fr. 24 could have been
improved), Gracchus avoids the unrelieved series of longs which had thudded at the
end of so many of Cato's sentences.

    Speaking of clausulae Cicero *Or.* 212 says *unum est secuta Asia maxime,
qui dichoreus uocatur*; this has been put together with Cicero's statement (*Brut.*
100) that the instructor of Gracchus in rhetoric was Menelaus of Marathus in
Phoenicia to produce the facile classification of Gracchus as an 'Asianist' orator.
This is a categorization which would have had little meaning in Rome at the time

of Gracchus; he certainly would not have thought in terms of an Atticist - Asianist antithesis, and it is hard to pinpoint anything in his style as particularly 'Asianist'. His use of short cola in parallelism and repetition of words relate him much more strongly to traditional Latin style. Let Wilamowitz have the last word (*Hermes* 35 (1900), 36-7 = *Kl. Schr.* 3.258): 'die asianischen Klauseln der periodisierten Rede haben in Rom in der Gracchenzeit ihren Einzug gehalten...Also ist freilich die römische Rhetorik ohne jede Unterbrechung von der hellenistischen Tradition beherrscht worden; wenn man das asianisch nennen will, mag man's tun'.

CHAPTER VIII

THE 'LETTER OF CORNELIA'

AD C. GRACCHUM
Cornelius Nepos fr. 59

(Verba ex epistula Corneliae Gracchorum matris ex libro Cornelii Nepotis de Latinis historicis excerpta;)

(a) Dices pulchrum esse inimicos ulcisci. id neque maius neque pulchrius cuiquam atque mihi esse uidetur, sed si liceat re publica salua ea persequi. sed quatenus id fieri non potest, †multo tempore† multisque partibus inimici nostri non peribunt atque uti nunc sunt erunt potius quam res publica profligetur atque pereat.

(eadem alio loco:)

(b) Verbis conceptis deierare ausim, praeterquam qui Tiberium Gracchum necarunt, neminem inimicum tantum molestiae tantumque laboris quantum te ob has res mihi tradidisse; quem oportebat omnium eorum quos antehac habui liberos, partis eorum tolerare, atque curare ut quam minimum sollicitudinis in senecta haberem, utique quaecumque ageres, ea uelles maxime mihi placere, atque uti nefas haberes rerum maiorum aduersum meam sententiam quicquam facere, praesertim mihi, cui parua pars uitae restat. (c) ne id quidem tam breue spatium potest opitulari quin et mihi aduersere et rem publicam profliges? denique quae pausa erit? ecquando desinet familia nostra insanire? ecquando modus ei rei haberi poterit? ecquando desinemus et habentes et praebentes molestiis desistere? ecquando perpudescet miscenda atque perturbanda re publica? (d) sed si omnino id fieri non potest, ubi ego mortua ero petito tribunatum; per me facito quod lubebit cum ego non sentiam. ubi mortua ero, parentabis mihi et inuocabis deum parentem. in eo tempore non pude<bi>t te eorum deum preces expetere quos uiuos atque praesentes relictos atque desertos habueris? ne ille sirit Iuppiter te ea perseuerare, nec tibi tantam dementiam uenire in animum. et si perseueras, uereor ne in omnem uitam tantum laboris culpa tua recipias uti in nullo tempore tute tibi placere possis.

Cic. *Brut.* 211 refers to Cornelia's letters as extant, but the source from which this letter comes must give us pause. Why would Nepos quote it in a work with this title? We are not justified in simply rejecting our information; Plut. *Tib. Gracchus* 21 quotes Nepos (fr. 51 Marshall) as giving information involving C. Gracchus, but, as d'Errico (*AFLN* 10 (1962-3), 23) suggests, it could come from a life of Brutus among the Roman generals. In addition one must ask whether Nepos, contrary to his own practice and that of ancient historical writers in general, would be likely to reproduce a document verbally (N. Horsfall, *Cornelius Nepos* (1989) 41 and in *Athen.* 65 (1987), 231); it is true that in this respect biography operates by different rules from those of history, but in this case the argument still has force. One is bound to suspect that Nepos had occasion to quote this letter from the text of some historian, as suggested by Instinsky, *Chiron* 1 (1971), 189, in which case it is a free composition by that historian (see on Quadrigarius 41). Instinsky also argues that the view here presented of the Gracchi is that of the optimates (see below), though otherwise there is nothing in the letter which is demonstrably anachronistic or out of character; arguments to the contrary are hair-splitting, subjective and indecisive. It is therefore a successful composition by someone who took sides in the controversy whether Cornelia supported her younger son or not (Plut. *C. Gracchus* 13). C. Kappler, *Über die unter dem Namen der Cornelia überlieferten Brieffragmente* (1905) 75 (who himself holds the letter genuine) points to the annalist Fannius, who changed from a supporter of C. Gracchus to an opponent, that is if he is identical with the consul of 122, a matter about which there is much controversy (see Shackleton Bailey, *Ciceros's Letters to Atticus* vol. 5 appendix ii; Cassola *Vichiana* 12 (1983), 86).

The dramatic (or real) date is 124 B.C., the year in which C. Gracchus was a candidate for his first tribunate. Cornelia is presented as writing a letter because she retired to Misenum after the death of Tiberius (Oros. 5.12.9; cf. Plut. *C. Gracchus* 19); she had evidently returned to Rome by the time Gaius delivered fr. 61, unless he is being melodramatic rather than literal. The singular *epistula* in the title shows that what we have consists of two quotations from the same letter. I have subdivided for ease of reference.

It is noticeable that *atque* is much preferred to *et* or *-que*; this is one of the rhetorical techniques used to hammer home the message. The other most striking one is the fourfold anaphora of *ecquando*.

(a) *dices* This is the figure of *occupatio* (Lausberg 855). 'Cornelia' lends weight to her assent to this proposition by expanding *pulchrum* into *neque maius neque* *pulchrius* (cf. Cato Speeches 163). Some out of many parallels for the sentiment are quoted in my note on Juv. 13.180.

atque 'than' in a negative sentence; see HS 478, KS 2.20, *TLL* 2.1084.38.

ea 'these objects' vaguely.

multisque...potius 'It will be far preferable for our enemies not to perish and to continue as they now are'; *multis partibus = multo* (*TLL* 10.1.453.23). But I cannot see how *multo tempore* can fit in, and think that these words must be corrupt or lacunose; however Bergk's *malo temperes* is very ill adjusted to the context.

profligetur atque pereat The synonym pairing is underlined by the alliteration.

(b) *uerbis conceptis* See on Cato *De Agr.* 141.4; this is often combined with *iurare, peierare* and the like by Plautus (see also on Scipio 19). *deiero* is an archaic word which throughout the first centuries B.C. and A.D. is found only once each in Varro and Mela.

Tiberium Gracchum This does not look like the way in which a mother would name her son to his brother, but perhaps it can be explained as an attempt to attach an eternal stigma to his assassins; note however that in similar circumstances Plut. *C. Gracch.* 4.3 makes Gaius refer to his brother just as Tiberius.

tantum laboris The phrase is repeated in (d); the sense is 'tribulation'.

has res His candidacy for the tribunate.

eorum...eorum The antecedent is attracted into the relative clause leaving behind a demonstrative pronoun; cf. HS 564 and Munro on Lucr. 1.15. Then, in *guttatim* style, the pronoun is repeated for clarity, as e.g. at [Sall.] *Ep. ad Caes.* 1.3.4 *ea quae..., ea.*

tolerare i.e. *sustinere.*

senecta This noun developed from an adjectival use (like other adjectives such as *merum*) in the phrase *senecta aetas*; this is its first occurrence in prose, and it remains mainly poetical.

meam placed before its noun is self-assertive.

mihi has no syntax. I propose to read *praesertim cum mihi parua*; for the indicative after *cum* 'since' cf. Gracchus 44d. It should however be noted that the manuscript authority for the word *restat* is dubious, especially since already in Terence *praesertim cum* invariably takes a subjunctive.

rem p. profliges This phrase is repeated from (a). This sentence may be a statement rather than a question.

(c) *denique quae* Normally *denique* would follow the interrogative (cf. Enn. *Ann.* 327 *quae denique pausa*, a certain emendation) except when it closes a list of questions; I think that the words should be reversed here.

familia Cf. Gracchus 47; an air of family pride is imparted.

modus ei rei haberi Cf. Plaut. *Poen.* 238 *modus omnibus rebus...optumum est habitu.*

desinemus...desistere This pleonastically combines two constructions: (1) *desinemus et habentes et praebentes molestias* (2) *desistemus molestiis*; for such pleonasm see Löfstedt *Synt* 2.158, HS 348, 791, 797. *desino* with participle is apparently calqued on παύομαι; moreover *exhibere molestias* would be much more usual than *prae(hi)bere*, so it looks as if this too is calqued on πράγματα ἔχειν καὶ παρέχειν.

   perpudescet...publica For this construction cf. Plaut. *Bacch.* 379 *puditumst factis quae facis.* Instinsky 187-8 points out that *miscenda atque perturbanda re p.* is the vocabulary applied by the optimates to the Gracchi and other agitators; he might have added *insanire* (*TLL* 7.1.1828.28, 1831.9, 1834.56; Taldone *Boll. Stud. Lat.* 23 (1993), 8) and *profligare rem p.* (Cic. *De Or.* 3.3).

(d) *ubi ego mortua ero...ubi mortua ero* The first occurrence stresses the involvement of Cornelia's feelings, so it needs the emphatic pronoun. The gist of the repetition could be given simply by *tum* (though the thought of death suitably introduces the apodosis), so the pronoun is no longer needed. *cum ego non sentiam* implies a decided opinion on the common quandary *si etiam inferis sensus est* (see my note on *ML* 199A.39) and suggests that when Gracchus calls on his *deus parens* he will be performing an empty ritual, even though this weakens the force of 'Cornelia's' argument.

   deum parentem From the republic elsewhere only *diui (dei) parentum* is known (Latte 98 n.2); *diuos parentes* at Catull. 64.404 is probably a corruption of *penates* due to 400. These expressions have no feminine, and in fact the singular too is unique; in the following sentence Cornelia passes into a generalising masculine plural. *parentare* probably originally meant the same as *inuocare parentem* (H. Wagenvoort, *Studies in Roman Literature* (1956) 293, who compares *indigitare, uenerari*; on 295 he adduces Verg. *Aen.* 5.47 *diuinique ossa parentis*).

   in eo tempore Cf. *in nullo tempore* below and on Gracchus 44, Piso 27.

   preces expetere Cf. Plaut. *Rud.* 259 *preces...expetessunt,* CIL 6.32336 *preces posco*; but probably not Catull. 68.65 *iam prece Pollucis, iam Castoris implorata* (-ate codd.), though it does parallel the genitive here. All these (they seem to be a kind of internal accusative) are quoted by Jordan, *Hermes* 15 (1880), 533; see too Löfstedt *Synt* 1.259.

   relictos...habueris This form of expression, for which see KS 1.763, HS 319, de Meo 99, eventually becomes the periphrastic perfect of the Romance languages. Cato *De Agr.* 2.1-2 shows the base from which this development starts; see Jacob in Callebat 373 n.17 for the idiom in technical treatises like Cato (e.g. 5.6, 143.3).

   ne ille sirit Iuppiter Cf. Plaut. *Curc.* 27 *nec me ille sirit Iuppiter,* Pliny *Ep.* 2.2.2 *illud enim nec di sinant,* Petron. 112.7 *nec istud...di sinant,* Curtius 10.6.20 *nec di sierint,* Ciris 239 *quod nec sinat Adrastea* (these and more quoted by Löfstedt *Synt* 1.339), all these with the archaic *nec = non* (see on Cato *De Agr.* 141.4), which is already modernised to *ne* by Plautus according to his mss. at *Bacch.* 468, *Merc.*

613. For *ille*, which in such contexts must originally have been accompanied with a deictic gesture up to heaven, cf. Ogilvie on Livy 1.24.8 and Fordyce on Verg. *Aen.* 7.110.

      perseuerare For the internal accusative after this verb see *OLD* s.v. 1c.

CHAPTER IX

HISTORIANS

In the case of these writers, comparison with parallel passages in Livy will illuminate stylistic features. This chapter is to be read together with Cato *Origines* 83 (p. 74).

(a) L. CALPURNIUS PISO

Annales III 27 Peter = 37 Forsythe=Gell. 7.9.2-6

Livy 9.46. 1-2 and 9

Cn. Flauius, patre libertino natus, scriptum faciebat, isque in eo tempore aedili curuli apparebat quo tempore aediles subrogantur, eumque pro tribu aedilem curulem renuntiauerunt. [aedilis] qui comitia habebat negat accipere, neque sibi placere qui scriptum faceret, eum aedilem fieri. Cn. Flauius Anni filius dicitur tabulas posuisse, scriptu sese abdicasse, isque aedilis curulis factus est.

idem Cn. Flauius Anni filius dicitur ad collegam uenisse uisere aegrotum. eo in conclaue postquam introiuit, adulescentes ibi complures nobiles sedebant. hi contemnentes eum assurgere ei nemo uoluit. Cn. Flauius Anni filius id arrisit, sellam curulem iussit sibi adferri, eam in limine apposuit nequis illorum exire posset utique hi omnes inuiti uiderent sese in sella curuli sedentem.

eodem anno Cn. Flauius Cn. filius scriba, patre libertino, humili fortuna ortus, ceterum callidus uir et facundus, aedilis curulis fuit. inuenio in quibusdam annalibus, cum appareret aedilibus fierique se pro tribu aedilem uideret neque accipi nomen quia scriptum faceret, tabulam posuisse et iurasse se scriptum non facturum.

ad collegam aegrum uisendi causa Flauius cum uenisset, consensusque nobilium adulescentium qui ibi adsidebant adsurrectum ei non esset, curulem adferri sellam eo iussit ac <de> sede honoris sui anxios inuidia inimicos spectauit.

[aedilis] *L. Lange, Mommsen; alii alia*
hi (omnes)] ii *codd. recc.*

141

Flavius was curule aedile in 304 B.C.; see T. R. S. Broughton, *Magistrates of the Roman Republic* 1.168, 3.92.

isque...eumque The paratactic style of narrative is reminiscent of Cato *Origines* 83 and shows the same change to an indefinite subject (*renuntiauerunt - sustulere*); note also *isque* at the end of this paragraph. The second paragraph shows a similar style with *eo...eum...ei...eam* (cf. Ennius III); Livy replaces this with temporal subordination and an organised period. Cf. Kroll, *Glotta* 22 (1934), 9 and HS 186.

scriptum faciebat He was a *scriba*; for *scribae aedilicii* see *RE, scriba* 852.50. *Scribae* were respectable enough (they had to be free, but not necessarily free-born; Martina, *Labeo* 26 (1980), 165-7, Purcell *PBSR* 51 (1983), 137, Cohen in C. Nicolet (ed.), *Des Ordres à Rome* (1984) 55), but wage-earners (*mercenarii*) and therefore (W. Kunkel, *Staatsordnung und Staatspraxis der röm. Republik* (1995) 5) regarded as unfit to hold a magistracy unless they gave up their *scriptus*. For *scribae* who did achieve a political career see Cohen 58 n.160 and T. P. Wiseman, *New Men in the Roman Senate 139 B.C.- A.D. 14* (1971) 72. The phrase *scriptum facere* recurs below; Livy avoids the repetition by using *scriba* at this point.

in eo tempore Cf. Sempronius Asellio fr. 7 *tum in eo tempore* (with which cf. Lucr. 3.862), Letter of 'Cornelia' (d) and on Gracchus 44. Note the repetition of the antecedent in *quo tempore*; see Lex Furfensis 13, HS 563, KS 2.283, Pascucci 12, de Meo 87, Calboli in Callebat 622. This feature has its origin in legal style, where the need for clarity calls for the removal of all ambiguity in the reference of relative pronouns (some instances in Gaius are 1.13, 4.37 and 137); Caesar, who also places great store on clarity, is particularly fond of the idiom (Eden, *Glotta* 40 (1962), 87-8; Odelman 148). Adams, *Indog. Forsch.* 81 (1976), 87 prefers to see it as a result of the change from the placing of relatives before their antecedent (see on Cato *De Agr.* 141.2-3) to the placing after.

subrogantur 'are elected in place of the retiring aediles'.

pro tribu Livy, who means Piso by *in quibusdam annalibus*, takes this obscure phrase from him. W. B. Anderson notes on Livy (similarly Kunkel o.c. 75) 'possibly the returning officers, in announcing to the presiding magistrate the result of the voting in the individual tribes, used a formula in which occurred the words *pro tribu*, followed by the name of the particular tribe whose vote was being reported, e.g. *pro tribu Aemilia Cn. Flauium refero*'. The subject of *renuntiauerunt* will be the tellers. See also the *Lex Ursonensis* (p. 19) 101 *quicumque comitia magistratibus creandis subrogandis habebit, is ne quem eis comitis pro tribu accipito neue renuntiato neue renuntiari iubeto qui...*

qui comitia [sc. *tributa*] *habebat* This would be not an aedile, but a consul or praetor, hence *aedilis* has to be emended; *RE, comitia* 703.32, G. W. Botsford, *The Roman Assemblies* (1909) 292 and 465.

negat 'refuses', cf. KS 1.675, *OLD* s.v. 4; it is worrisome that the other instances are poetical and not pre-Augustan. For the following *neque* cf. *neue* Quadrig. 41 and on Cato *de Agr.* 141.4. For *non accipere* in this context see Kunkel o.c. 74.

Anni filius Ann(i)us is a rare praenomen; see O. Salomies, *Die röm. Vornamen* (1987) 92. Flavius is given this filiation not only by Piso (twice), but also by Cic. *Ad Att.* 6.1.8, Pliny *NH* 33.17. Somehow it must have become canonical; I am reminded of *Circa Solis filia*, for which see Fraenkel *EPP* 93 with addenda 407 ('L'aggiunta del nome del padre sembra servire in entrambi i casi ad accrescere la solennità del passo'). Livy, drawing on another source before he turns to Piso, calls him *Cn. filius.*

dicitur follows the name of Flavius also in the second paragraph; Cichorius (*RE, Calpurnius* 1393.59) sees in this a sign of the scrupulousness with which Piso reported anecdotes as such.

tabulas on which he was recording the proceedings.

collegam aegrotum Sallust *Hist.* 1.127 took this phrase from here. This is the only clause in this extract which does not end with a verbal form; Piso's word-order otherwise conforms to the formula 'subject first, verb last'. That is because the adjective is not merely attributive but conveys 'because he was sick'.

uisere For the purpose infinitive after a verb of motion see HS 344-5 (quoting *uenio uisere* from Varro), Bennett 1.419 (quoting two instances of this from Plautus and two of *ire uisere* from Terence); KS 1.681 add an occurrence of *ire uisere* from Gellius. It can be seen that this is standard usage with *uisere.* Livy prefers a more regular construction. This is the regular phrase for visiting the sick; *uenio* quite often serves for *eo* because of the tendency to replace short forms (Löfstedt, *Synt* 2.40).

eo = ad eum; see HS 208-9, *TLL* 7.2.481.15 and on Cato *De Agr.* 5.3. This sentence is an inexact way of saying '<he found> some young men of station sitting there'. The next sentence shows a remarkable anacoluthon, for which see HS 143 and Kroll, *Glotta* 22 (1934), 9. The writing here is decidedly careless.

ibi takes enclitic position, on the same principle as the relative pronoun may; see on Cato *De Agr.* 157.7.

contemnentes eum See on Cato Speeches 169.

L. Calpurnius Piso as tribune in 149 passed the first law against extortion; he was consul in 133, and later opposed C. Gracchus and was attacked by him. His history reached to at least 146 B.C. Cicero calls his style *exilis* (*Brut.* 106, *De Leg.* 1.6; cf. *De Or.* 2.51-3), a uerdict totally supported by this fragment. The archaist Gellius puts the best face he can on this and (11.14.1) speaks of his *simplicissima suauitas*; he introduces this extract as *perquam pure et uenuste narrata.* One will note in particular that the only copulative employed is *-que* (and this is the only one which appears in the other admittedly very scanty fragments quoted directly from Piso), that the word-order is standardised, and that the only characterising adjective

employed is *inuiti*, which seems very colourless when compared with Livy's *anxios inuidia*. There is also much repetition of the same vocabulary and concepts.
See in general G. Forsythe, *The Historian L. Calpurnius Piso Frugi* (1994).

b) Q. CLAUDIUS QUADRIGARIUS

Annales III 27 Peter = 37 Forsythe =   Livy 7.9.8 - 10.13 20
Gell. 7.9.2-6

cum interim Gallus quidam nudus praeter scutum et gladios duos torque atque armillis decoratus processit, qui et uiribus et magnitudine et adulescentia simulque uirtute ceteris antistabat. is maxime proelio commoto atque utrisque summo studio pugnantibus manu significare coepit utrisque quiescerent. pugnae facta pausa est. extemplo silentio facto cum uoce maxima conclamat, si quis secum depugnare uellet uti prodiret. nemo audebat propter magnitudinem atque inmanitatem facies. deinde Gallus inridere coepit atque linguam exsertare. id subito perdolitum est cuidam Tito Manlio, summo genere gnato, tantum flagitium ciuitati adcidere, e tanto exercitu neminem prodire.

is, ut dico, processit neque passus est

tum eximia corporis magnitudine in uacuum pontem Gallus processit et quantum maxima uoce potuit 'quem nunc' inquit 'Roma uirum fortissimum habet, procedat agedum ad pugnam, ut noster duorum euentus ostendat utra gens bello sit melior'. diu inter primores iuuenum Romanorum silentium fuit, cum et abnuere certamen uererentur et praecipuam sortem periculi petere nollent.

tum T. Manlius L. filius, qui patrem a uexatione tribunicia uindicauerat, ex statione ad dictatorem pergit; 'iniussu tuo' inquit, 'imperator, extra ordinem nunquam pugnauerim, non si certam uictoriam uideam: si tu permittis, uolo ego illi beluae ostendere, quando adeo ferox praesultat hostium signis, me ex ea familia ortum quae Gallorum agmen ex rupe Tarpeia deiecit'. tum dictator 'macte uirtute' inquit 'ac pietate in patrem patriamque, T. Manli, esto. perge et nomen Romanum inuictum

(line numbers: 5, 10, 15, 20, 25, 30)

uirtutem Romanum ab Gallo turpiter spoliari. scuto pedestri et gladio Hispanico cinctus contra Gallum constitit. metu magno ea congressio in ipso ponti utroque exercitu inspectante facta est.

ita ut ante dixi constiterunt, Gallus sua discipulina scuto proiecto cantabundus; Manlius animo magis quam arte confisus scuto scutum percussit atque statum Galli conturbauit. dum se Gallus iterum eodem pacto constituere studet, Manlius iterum scuto scutum percutit atque de loco hominem iterum deiecit; eo pacto ei sub Gallicum gladium successit atque Hispanico pectus hausit; deinde continuo umerum dextrum eodem concessu incidit neque recessit usquam donec subuertit, ne Gallus impetum icti haberet. ubi eum euertit, caput praecidit, torquem detraxit, eamque sanguinulentam sibi in collum inponit. quo ex facto ipse posterique eius Torquati nominati sunt.

iuuantibus dis praesta'. armant inde iuuenem aequales; pedestre scutum capit, Hispanico cingitur gladio ad propiorem habili pugnam. armatum adornatumque aduersus Gallum stolide laetum et (quoniam id quoque memoria dignum antiquis uisum est) linguam etiam ab inrisu exerentem producunt. recipiunt inde se ad stationem; et duo in medio armati spectaculi magis more quam lege belli destituuntur, nequaquam uisu ac specie aestimantibus pares. corpus alteri magnitudine eximium, uersicolori ueste pictisque et auro caelatis refulgens armis; media in altero militaris statura modicaque in armis habilibus magis quam decoris species; non cantus, non exultatio armorumque agitatio uana sed pectus animorum iraeque tacitae plenum; omnem ferociam in discrimen ipsum certaminis distulerat. ubi constitere inter duas acies tot circa mortalium animis spe metuque pendentibus, Gallus uelut moles superne imminens proiecto laeua scuto in aduenientis arma hostis uanum caesim cum ingenti sonitu ensem deiecit; Romanus mucrone subrecto cum scuto scutum imum perculisset totoque corpore interior periculo uolneris factus insinuasset se inter corpus armaque, uno alteroque subinde ictu uentrem atque inguina hausit et in spatium ingens ruentem porrexit hostem. iacentis inde corpus ab omni alia uexatione intactum uno torque spoliauit, quem respersum cruore collo circumdedit suo. defixerat pauor cum admiratione Gallos: Romani alacres ab statione

2 *v.1.* duo

31 ut dico] ilico *Mommsen ap. Hertz*

67 usque *Wölfflin (ALL 15 (1908), 15) dubitanter*

obuiam militi suo progressi 75 gratulantes laudantesque ad dictatorem perducunt. inter carminum prope \<in\> modum incondita quaedam militariter ioculantes Torquati cognomen 80 auditum; celebratum deinde posteris etiam familiaeque honori fuit.

The comparison between the accounts of Quadrigarius and Livy has been a time-honoured exercise of Latin scholarship; most discussions are listed by S. P. Oakley, *Commentary on Livy Books VI - X* (1997-8) 2.114 (note that some quote the Latin inaccurately), others are

Leeman 78.

Ronconi, *Stud. Urb.* 49.1 (1975), 135.

Richter in *Livius, Werke und Rezeption, Festschr. E. Burck* (1983), 62.

Murgia in W. Schuller (ed.), *Livius* (1993), 100.

Not all of the valuable points made by these scholars are incorporated here, since many of them concern ethos rather than style and Livy rather than Quadrigarius. Livy 6.42.5 himself acknowledges Quadrigarius among his sources, though he dates the event differently (Quadrigarius is meant by *antiquis* l. 38). My commentary was written before Oakley's appeared, and I have made no alterations except in adding references to his.

It is noticeable that Quadrigarius' preferred copulative is *atque*, whereas in Livy, who has this only in 66 (and *ac* 44), *que* vastly predominates. Quadrigarius places his verbs at the end of clauses and sentences (cf. on Cato *Origines* 83), and few clauses and sentences do not end with a verb or strongly verbal word like *cantabundus* 56; the exceptions are *coepit utrisque* 9 (where however the next and final word does end the sentence with a verb), 13-15, 16-17 (where the name has to be held back for dramatic effect), 67. The length and complexity of his sentences also shows much less variety than Livy; the four-word sentence in 9-10 is unique, and 10-13 shows the greatest degree of subordination in the piece.

2 *gladios duos* This detail is intended simply to emphasise the frightfulness of the Gaul; no use of it is made in the narrative (*gladium* 64).

torque Quadrigarius hints in advance at the point of the story; Livy prefers to keep this in reserve.

5 *simulque* sets off the moral from the physical qualities.

6 *is* The simple narrative connection by pronouns reappears in 16 and 31; cf. also *eo pacto* 63. See however on 35. In this passage, which is largely asyndetic, connection where it is found is made either by these pronouns or by temporal

adverbs (see on Ennius *Euhemerus*), except in 68-9.

maxime is placed in a surprisingly prominent position. Perhaps it should be <*cum*> *maxime*, 'at the very moment when the battle was in full swing' (cf. Plaut. *Amph.* 427 *legiones quom pugnabant maxume*); since the combination indicates simultaneity, naturally it is more often combined with a present than a past participle, but see Sen. *De Ben.* 7.27.1. The 'excerpta Sciopii' offer *maximo*.

8-9 *significare...quiescerent* See on Cato *De Agr.* 5.2. Livy rightly feels that the version of Quadrigarius is unrealistic here. The repetition of *utrisque* from 7 is rather inartistic, but that of *coepit* (here and 15) usefully marks actions spread over some time.

10-11 *facta...facto* For the generalised use of this verb cf. 37 and on Cato Speeches 58; the repetition here is not very obtrusive and helps connection. The word-order *facta pausa est* is standard (KS 2.603, HS 405).

11 *cum* An archaic and vulgar use of the preposition (KS 1.510, HS 259-60, *TLL* 4.1369.40). Intensifying adjectives like *magnus* usually precede their noun, but their superlatives, like *maxima* here, not infrequently follow (J. Marouzeau, *L'Ordre des mots* 1 (1922) 94). Livy removes both features with *quantum maxima uoce potuit* (3).

12 *uti* The position of this is explained by the idiom noted on Cato *De Agr.* 1.7. Livy puts the challenge in more vivid direct speech, and makes it nationalistic rather than personal.

15 *facies* The occurrence of both this form of the genitive and of *facii* in Book I of Quadrigarius is noted by Gell. 9.14.3 = fr. 30; fr. 41 shows the third form *fidei*. For the form in *-es* see Leumann 447, Sommer 396-8, for the use of an alternative on Cato *De Agr.* pr.1.

16 *linguam exsertare* Livy tones down the frequentative, which reinforces the implication of *coepit* (see on 8-9), to the root form *exerentem* (39; see Murgia l.c. 101 with n. 61), and also feels obliged to apologise for recording this uncivilised gesture. He postpones the detail so that Manlius' motive for volunteering is no longer pique.

16-7 *id...perdolitum est* A unique usage; *perdoluit* would be normal. It looks as if Quadrigarius is here coining a fake archaism on the analogy of e.g. *miseritum est* (Scipio 30).

cuidam A remarkable contrast with the precise identification given by Livy, who is concerned to link his narrative backwards (7.4-5) and forwards to the day when Manlius would punish his own son for fighting a duel contrary to orders (8.7). *summo genere gnato* (for which see on Cato Speeches 58) contents Quadrigarius, by whom the point of the identity of the Roman is held back until the end; at this stage it is almost as unimportant as that of the Gaul (*quidam* 1).

18-20 The second colon really explains the first, but Quadrigarius prefers anaphora rather than subordination in order to convey the indignation of Manlius.

Livy feels obliged (10-12) to give a more honourable motive than fear why the challenge was generally declined.

31 *ut dico* Quadrigarius has not been saying this; he is using the phrase rather inartistically to call attention to a picture which he has in his mind, even if he has not communicated it to the reader. *Bell. Hisp.* 4.2 *ut supra scripsimus* might be parallel, but in the unsophisticated style of that work it might mean *quos supra memorauimus*. The context of *ut supra demonstrauimus* ibid. 25.7 is too mangled for any certainty. The verb *processit* repeats the action of the Gaul (3), whereas the challenge and its response (13, 20) use *prodire*; Livy, who makes the audience interact much more, prefers to vary with *producunt* (40).

33 *spoliari* seems to be adequately defended by the phrase *spoliare dignitatem* (*OLD* s.v. *spoliare* 5c).

33-4 *gladio Hispanico cinctus* Quadrigarius places words in agreement beside each other, adjective after noun (the same applies to *scuto pedestri - pedestre scutum*); Livy (34) has the less mechanical order *Hispanico cingitur gladio* (the finite verb also changes from description to action). For such word-order in Livy see Oakley 1.730. Ethnic adjectives in *-icus* are often applied to 'technical specialities' (Leumann 338); but the Spanish sword is an anachronism at this date (see Oakley ad loc. and *kl. Pauly, gladius* 804.38). Livy underlines the point by adding *ad propiorem habili pugnam* (reinforced still more in 49), perhaps with Enn. *Ann.* 239 (where see Skutsch) in mind.

35 Quadrigarius gives precedence to the dramatic *metu magno* over his usual practice of initial placement of the subject and over the possibility of pronominal connection (see on 6) by placing *ea* first. For the same reason he puts *magno* in the less usual position (cf. on 11) after its noun.

36 *ponti* This form of the ablative does not seem to occur elsewhere in this word, but has abundant analogies. The variant *ponte* has weaker support.

37 For *inspectante* see on Cato Speeches 58. This and *pugnantibus* 8 are the only present participles in Quadrigarius, who in this respect contrasts with Livy's abundant and varied use.

54 *ita ut ante dixi* in 2-3 (the Gaul) and 33-5 (Manlius). Quadrigarius now embarks on an antithesis initially designed to specify their contrasting postures, but in the second limb he drifts from description to narrative and from partitive apposition to a finite verb (cf. p. 5; to a degree Cato *De Agr.* 4 is analogous). The repetition of *consisto* from 35 is inartistic.

55 *sua* is emphatically placed because of the antithesis between the Gaul's mechanical and the Roman's improvisatory tactics (*animo magis quam arte confisus*). Livy changes the focus to present Manlius on the contrary not as employing random brute force but as a model of disciplined Roman tactics (note how he here (61) substitutes *Romanus* for Quadrigarius' *Manlius*). *scuto proiecto* has the relationship noted on 33-4 to Livy's (58) *proiecto laeua scuto*.

56 *cantabundus* This word is found elsewhere only at Petron. 62. The

formations in -*bundus* are favoured in historical style (first in Quadrigarius, then Sisenna 55-6), though they are too colourful for Caesar; Quadrigarius 78 has the unique *hinnibundus*. Livy 50 applies the detail negatively to make it into a characterisation of the Roman.

54-70 It is particularly noticeable here how Livy in contrast to Quadrigarius employs subordination and periodic structure.

61 *scuto scutum* Wills 196 remarks this in the context of his category of 'battle polyptoton'; see also Oakley's note.

59-62 *iterum...iterum...iterum* Quadrigarius, at the cost of repetitions, prolongs the fight to create suspense. To Livy the repetitions seem pointless, and he prefers to magnify the Roman superiority by an instant victory. *eodem pacto...eo pacto* does not seem to me to have any stylistic point; at least Quadrigarius varies *percussit* 58 with the historic present *percutit* 61. M. Erren, *Einführung i. d. röm. Kunstprosa* (1983) 157 n.3 takes *deiĕcit* as present; for this spelling see my note on Cicero 17.7 *FLP* (where one reference should be to Sommer 486).

62 *hominem* is faintly colloquial in place of *eum*: HS 198 (the use is not as late as they imply), KS 1.618, *TLL* 6.2882.13, Pepe, *Helikon* 15-16 (1975-6), 410-11, Pascucci on *Bell. Hisp.* 18.1. In these circumstances a tinge of contempt is often implied.

63-5 'He got beneath the enemy's' (*ei*; dative of disadvantage) 'Gallic broadsword' (Livy 63-5 explains the point more carefully) 'and with his Spanish <sword> drained the blood from his chest'. *Gallicum* here means 'of Gallic type' (cf. on 33-4), not 'belonging to the Gaul', and is placed before its noun because of the contrast; Livy 22.46.5 elucidates the differences between the two types of sword.

65 *hausit* Given that Vergil *Aen.* 10. 313-4 has *gladio... latus haurit* (note also Lucr. 5. 1324 *latera ac uentres hauribant*), and that the metaphor is derived from *Il.* 13.508, 14.517, 17.314 (διαφύσσω, the probability must be great that Quadrigarius is here adapting a floscule from Ennius. Livy 66-7 uses the same verb with the same object as Lucretius (= ἔντερα in Homer), an object which fits more precisely into the narrative than Quadrigarius' *pectus* (the same concern makes him add *imum* 62); this might suggest that Livy saw an advantage in keeping closer to an Ennian prototype. See Pianezzola in *Scritti in onore di C. Diano* (1975), 311; West, *CQ* 59 (1965), 275; Tarrant on Sen. *Ag.* 890.

66 *concessu* seems to be defended by *equitum concessum* in *Bell. Hisp.* 25.7. *successu* (Damsté) takes up *successit* and may perhaps be parallelled by a variant at Caes. *BG* 2.20.2 (Verg. *Aen.* 12.616 at least predominantly means 'success'); other emendations are unsatisfactory. In 64-7 we have three derivatives of *cedo*.

67 *usquam* seems a little weak, though one may compare Cic. *Phil.* 1.1 *nec uero usquam discedebam*; for Wölfflin's *usque donec* (which would bring the verb *recessit* to the colon-end, as is usual in Quadrigarius) cf. Cato *De Agr.* 156.5 and

TLL 5.1.2003.62. The purpose clause too seems a weak ending to this sentence, and a later writer might have framed a connection by writing *subuersi* instead of *ubi eum euertit*; see next note and on Cato *Orig.* 83b.

68 *icti* See on Cato *De Agr.* 4. *euertit* varies *subuertit* 68 (cf. fr. 81 *numquam quiuerunt incendere...postquam non succendit*), but the form of connection is still unsophisticated; see on 6.

71 *sanguinulentam* This adjective is found in prose also in Varro, *Ad Herennium* and occasionally later (Lebek 238); Livy, who does not use either this word or *puluerulentus*, replaces it with *cruore respersum*, and also alters the archaic and poetical feminine gender of the noun. Since Livy makes Manlius more civilised in not cutting off the Gaul's head, the bloodstained necklet is less plausible in him.

III 41 = Gell. 3.8.8

(Litteras quas ad regem Pyrrum super ea causa (consules) miserunt Claudius Quadrigarius scripsit fuisse hoc exemplo:)

Consules Romani salutem dicunt Pyrro regi

Nos pro tuis iniuriis continuis animo tenus commoti inimiciter tecum bellare studemus. sed communis exempli et fidei ergo uisum ut te saluum uelimus, ut esset quem armis uincere possimus. ad nos uenit Nicias familiaris tuus qui sibi praemium a nobis peteret si te clam interfecisset. id nos nega<ui>mus uelle, neue ob eam rem quicquam commodi expectaret, et simul uisum est ut te certiorem faceremus, ne quid eiusmodi, si accidisset, nostro consilio ciuitates putarent factum, et quod nobis non placet pretio aut praemio aut dolis pugnare. tu, nisi caues, iacebis.

continuo animo tenui *codd.*
possemus *recc.*

tuis is placed before its noun for the same reason as in Cato Speeches 59. The placement in *nostro consilio* below also emphatically repudiates blame.

animo tenus This is the first appearance of *tenus* governing a noun; previously there had only been *quatenus*.

inimiciter This word is found in Accius *Didascalica* fr. 7, Tubero *Hist.* fr. 5. For such adverbial formations from 1st-2nd declension adjectives see Leumann 499-500, NW 2.725 sqq., and for Quadrigarius' fondness for them Wölfflin 20-21, Zimmerer 91 (refs. below).

communis...fidei Cf. Cic. *Ad Q.f.* 1.1.28 *communem fidem quae omnibus debetur* and *De Off.* 3.107.

uisum...uelimus...esset...possimus The sequence of tenses is aberrant; for such occurrences see HS 550, A. Draeger *Historische Syntax der lat. Sprache* (ed. 2, 1878) 1.323, Handford 140 n.3.

nos negauimus The pronoun is probably nominative; it would have been unstylish to repeat it as accusative. For the following *neue* see on Piso 27.

pretio aut praemio For this alliterative pair see on Gracchus 44. Here however it seems to unbalance the phrase, so that it has been proposed to delete one or the other.

nisi caues The present tense is often so used in conditions with a threatening tone (KS 1.146).

iacebis See *OLD* s.v. 6a.

The idea of incorporating letters in historiography stems from Greek historians (*RE* suppl. 5 *Epistolographie* 209); this specimen belongs to the type of 'die kurzen Brief der volkstümlicheren Literatur, die eine einfache Mitteilung...enthalten' (l.c. 48; though this one is placed in another class, 37). That these letters, like speeches, were essentially free compositions is shown by the comparison between Cic. *In Cat.* 3.12 and Sall. *Cat.* 44.5; Plutarch *Pyrrh.* 21.2-3 produces a version of this letter which is similar in purport but different in detail. Dion. Hal. *AR* 19.9-10 exhibits an earlier exchange of letters between Pyrrhus and the Romans. If Claudius himself used the phrase *hoc exemplo* with which Gellius introduces this quotation, that does not necessarily imply verbal accuracy (see my note on *ML* 5a). His composition is highly successful in conveying a sense of aloof dignity.

VI 57 = Gell. 2.2.13

Livy 24.44.9

Deinde facti consules <Ti.> Sempronius Gracchus iterum, Q. Fabius Maximus, filius eius qui priore anno erat consul. ei consuli pater proconsul obuiam in equo uehens uenit neque descendere uoluit quod pater erat, et, quod inter eos sciebant maxima concordia conuenire, lictores non ausi sunt descendere iubere. ubi iuxta uenit, tum consul ait "quid postea?". lictor ille qui apparebat cito intellexit, Maximum proconsulem descendere iussit. Fabius imperio paret et filium collaudauit, cum imperium, quod populi esset, retineret.

profecti consules Sempronius in Lucanos, in Apuliam Fabius. pater filio legatus ad Suessulam in castra uenit. cum obuiam filius progrederetur lictoresque uerecundia maiestatis eius taciti anteirent, praeter undecim fasces equo praeuectus senex, ut consul animaduertere proximum lictorem iussit et is ut descenderet ex equo inclamauit, tum demum desiliens "experiri" inquit "uolui, fili, satin scires consulem te esse".

4 *consul. ei consuli* For this type of connection see on Ennius XI. *proconsul* is wrong where Livy's *legatus* is right; see Broughton (on Piso 27) 1.265. Perhaps Quadrigarius was subconsciously attracted by the neat antithesis *consuli...proconsul*.

5 *uehens* 'riding'; see KS 1.109. Livy so uses *praeteruehens*, but not *uehens* itself (NW 3.11-12).

11 *quid postea?* is an indignant remonstrance; see *TLL* 10.2.191.25.

15 *collaudauit cum* i.e. *quod*; see KS 2.329.

The central points in Quadrigarius are emphasised by a series of repetitions, *uenit...descendere...descendere iubere...uenit...descendere iussit*; the repetition is totally eliminated by Livy. As in fr. 10, the sentences lack variety in length and construction, they show little formal connection with each other, and we encounter no subjunctive verbs until 16; contrast how Livy builds up one complex sentence covering most of the action. Again as in 10, Livy prefers direct speech (11-13) to the indirect in Quadrigarius (who admittedly does put two words into the mouth of the son).

Q. Claudius Quadrigarius, about whose life and personality nothing is known, wrote *Annales* in at least 23 books. They began with the Gallic sack of Rome, implying a belief that no reliable earlier records had survived, and fr. 82 from Book XIX refers to an event of 82 B.C., thus giving us a dating post quem for at least this book. Despite this date, he writes very much in the style of an older generation of historians (and therefore, though later than most writers covered in this book, can reasonably be included in it); on his style in general see Wölfflin, *ALL* 15 (1908), 10 and M. Zimmerer, *Der Annalist Qu. Claudius Quadrigarius* (1937) 88. Though it is praised by the archaists of the second century A.D., it is disparaged by Cicero *De Leg.* 1.6 (on the assumption that by *Clodius* he means Quadrigarius) as *nihil ad Coelium, sed potius ad antiquorum languorem et inscitiam*. The extracts analysed above are not as jejune as the narrative style of Cato or Piso, but show a very small range of stylistic effect. In general it must be said that while Roman oratory had reached considerable heights by the beginning of the first century B.C., historical style lagged far behind. It is a great pity that so little remains of Coelius Antipater, who according to Cicero did attain stylistic distinction.

APPENDIX

NARRATIVE STYLE IN PLAUTUS

It is worth while to analyse two passages of simple Plautine narrative in order to show how deeply ingrained certain stylistic habits are in archaic Latin. These passages are from expository prologues, in which Plautus has to devote special attention to lucidity; he is a writer of great stylistic virtuosity, and naturally uses the style appropriate for each context.

First from the *Menaechmi*:

57	Epidamniensis ill' quem dudum dixeram,
	geminum illum puerum qui surrupuit alterum,
	ei liberorum nisi diuitiae nihil erat:
60	adoptat illum puerum surrupticium
	sibi filium eique uxorem dotatam dedit,
	eumque heredem fecit quom ipse obiit diem.
	nam rus ut ibat forte, ut multum pluerat,
	ingressus fluuium rapidum ab urbe hau longule,
65	rapidus raptori pueri subduxit pedes
	apstraxitque hominem in maxumam malam crucem.

Here we first notice the drop-by-drop style which puts the important item first and worries about the syntax of the sentence later; the result is that the nominatives *Epidamniensis ille* (57) and *ingressus* (64) are left hanging and have to be replaced by the datives *ei* and *raptori*; cf. on Cato *Origines* 83c. *rapidus* in 65 carefully marks the change of subject by resuming *rapidum* in 64. Next we observe the insistence on clarity: *illum puerum qui surrupuit, illum puerum surrupticium, raptori pueri*. The double relative clause in 57-8, to ensure identification, is part of this insistence, and so is the presence of *eumque* 62, which classical style might have thought superfluous; cf. on Ennius III. The asyndeton between 59 and 60 is also characteristic of early Latin, and if there is connection it is of the simplest type. Where there is subordination, with the minor exception of the second *ut* in 63, it is

153

by temporal or relative clauses. The double *ut* in 63 recalls the form of expression
in Cato *De Agr.* 2.1.

A longer passage from the *Miles Gloriosus* will reinforce these points:

104   interibi hic miles forte Athenas aduenit,
        insinuat sese ad illam amicam m<ei> eri.
        occepit eius matri subpalparier
        uino, ornamentis opiparisque opsoniis,
        itaque intumum ibi se miles apud lenam facit.
        ubi primum euenit militi huic occasio,
110   sublinit os illi lenae, matri mulieris
        quam eru' meus amabat; nám is illius filiam
        conicit in nauem miles clam matrem suam
        eamque huc inuitam mulierem in Ephesum aduehit.
        ubi amicam erilem Athenis auectam scio,
115   ego quantum uiuos possum mihi nauem paro,
        inscendo, ut eam rem Naupactum ad erum nuntiem.
        ubi sumu' prouecti in altum, fit quod di uolunt,
        capiunt praedones nauem illam ubi uectus fui:
        priu' perii quam ad erum ueni quo ire occeperam.
120   ill' qui me cepit dat me huic dono militi.
        hic postquam in aedis me ad se deduxit domum
        uideo illam amicam erilem, Athenis quae fuit.
        ubi contra aspexit me, oculis mihi signum dedit
        ne se appellarem; deinde, postquam occasio est,
125   conqueritur mecum mulier fortunas suas:
        ait sese Athenas fugere cupere ex hac domu,
        sese illum amare meum erum, Athenis qui fuit,
        neque peius quemquam odisse quam istum militem.
        ego quoniam inspexi mulieris sententiam,
130   cepi tabellas, consignaui, clanculum
        dedi mercatori quoidam qui ad illum deferat
        meum erum, qui Athenis fuerat, qui hanc amauerat,
        is ut huç ueniret. is non spreuit nuntium;
        nam et uenit et is in proxumo hic deuortitur
135   apud suom paternum hospitem, lepidum senem;
        itaque illi amanti suo hospiti morem gerit   isque *Müller*
        nosque opera consilioque adhortatur, iuuat.
        itaque ego paraui hic intus magnas machinas
        qui amantis una inter se facerem conuenas.

140   nam unum conclaue, concubinae quod dedit
          miles, quo nemo nisi eapse inferret pedem,
          in eo conclaue ego perfodi parietem.

Here there is another instance of the *guttatim* style, with the same consequences as in the *Menaechmi*, in 140-2 (here there is the potential factor of reverse attraction of the antecedent of a relative pronoun to be taken into consideration; this is absent in *Men.* l.c. but possibly present in Cato there referred to). There is also the same insistence on clarity and the same repetition of demonstrative pronouns. This is so pervasive that the instances do not need to be listed, but it is worth drawing attention to 134, where it has been proposed either to delete the first *et* (so that a longer pause after *uenit* could do something to justify *is*) or to read *is et*. In either case we still have *is* in both 133 (twice) and 134, and good parallels for this can be found in Plautus; e.g. *Amph.* 107-9 *is amare occepit Alcumenam...et grauidam fecit is eam* (*istam* Lachmann), *Men.* 34-6 *pater eius...animum despondit eaque is aegritudine...emortuost* (which is similar in principle). In *MG* 134 there is the additional element of word-order, for which see Leo *AKS* 1.95. The urge for clarity also explains the pleonasm *in aedis...ad se...domum* 121; for similar pleonasm with expressions of place see on Ennius VI. Asyndeton between clauses is wide-spread, and there is an *asyndeton bimembre* in 137. Where there are connections, these are mostly either temporal (e.g. 114, 124; for *deinde postquam* 124 cf. on Ennius IV) or by demonstratives (e.g. 121, 133); apart from this there are five occurrences of the simple logical connectives *itaque* and *nam*. There is little subordination, and where it occurs it is mainly with relative or temporal clauses; the most syntactically complex sentence is in 129-133.

INDEX OF GRAMMAR AND STYLE

Adjunct extraction: 8, 54, 82, 147

Ad sensum construction: see Number

Adverbs: in *-ter* 150; as predicate of *esse* 59, 125; function as adjectives 34, 83

Adjectives: double superlative 125; degrees of comparison from *-ius, -uus* 52; verbal in *-bundus* 148-9; accumulated 58; possessive preceding noun 31, 53, 82, 88-9, 102, 127, 130, 137, 148, 150; other adjectives placed before noun for contrast or emphasis 35, 55, 61, 80, 149 (see also Word Order); become substantives 71, 91, 137

Alliteration: 3, 63, 80-1, 85-6, 109, 116, 121; alliterative pairs 3, 52, 63-6, 77-8, 80-1, 86-7, 111, 127, 137, 151

Ambiguous word-formation clarified by context: 65, 109-10

Anacoluthon: 4, 25, 33, 77, 143, 153

Analogical formation: 65, 96

Antiphrasis: 71

Apposition: partitive, 117, 148; see also Parataxis

Archaism in morphology: 91, 95, 100-1, 123; false 95, 97, 147

Argumentation: *a fortiori* 86-7; *ex contrario* 83-4

Assonance and Homoeoteleuton: 35, 77, 81, 87, 121, 125; in religious formulae 63, 66, 118

Asymmetry: 31, 76

Asyndeton: 6; bimembre 6, 35, 55, 65, 90, 116-7, 155; between clauses 58, 82, 153, 155

Bicolon, expanding: 118

Calque: 8, 24-5, 70, 138

Chiasmus: 6-7, 33, 58, 63, 69, 83, 86, 111, 123, 127

Clarity, insistence on: 8, 53, 153, 155; see also Word Repitition and Relative Pronoun, antecedent repeated

Conditional clauses: in Twelve Tables 18; unreal and potential 51; paratactic 60, 74; 'if...(and) if...then' 17, 22, 26, 58, (55, 59); *ast* = 'and if' 26; *si non* 73

Conjunctions, copulative: 3, 33, 42, 52, 59, 64, 75, 80, 98, 111, 113, 123, 127, 136, 143, 146; *-que...et* 131; connecting dissimilars 68; *et ne = neue* 53; *et* ending enumeration 58; see also Index of Words, *-que*

Connection: 6; temporal 7, 39, 73, 146-7, 155; by demonstrative 7, 31, 39, 76, 102, 130, 142, 146, 150, 155; by repitition of noun 7, 36, 54, 72, 123, 152, of verb 7, 73, (150), by participle 76; logical connectives largely absent from Cato 51, 59, 72, 81 and Ennius 39; connection by *et hoc* and *hoc amplius* 7, 67, 73

Pronouns cluster 78; ablative in *posthac* etc. 96-8; *is* and *se* interchanged 25, 36, 68, 87; *ille* = 'the relevant' 110, = 'such and such' 83, *ille Iuppiter* 139; *is* repeated and redundant 9, 31, 36, 76, 142, 155; resumptive 4, 31, 53, 60, (67, 71), 105, 110, 126, 153; replacing second relative 25

Pun: 120

Purpose clause: introduced by *quo* without comparative 24, 91

Relative pronouns and clauses: antecedent repeated 8, 116-7, 142, attracted into rel. cl. 34, 52, 137, leaves pronoun behind 137, leaves adjective behind 34, reverse attraction of 31, 77, 155, pronominal in oblique case absent 52, 57, 95; enclitic position of rel. pron. 57, 72; rel. cl. loosely attached 8, 25, 70; consecutive rel. 83; second rel. replaced by demonstrative 25

Retrograde formation: 100

Sententia: 54, 57, 77, 80

Specification after generality: 4-5, 33, 35, 128

Subject unexpressed: 2, 16, 21, 54, 66-7, 70, 76, 142; in indirect speech 55, 84, 110; unexpressed changes 2, 16, 55, 60, 86, 142

Synonym and near-synonym coupling: 8, 30, 32, 42, 52, 64, 76, 80-1, 97, 121, 137

'Tmesis': 2, 22, 73-4; see also Enclitic Position

Tricolon: 35, 63; deliberately introduced 63, 111; rising 9, 88, 109, 121; falling 9, 42, 86, 88, 90, 123; negative 88; assonant 118.

Variation: avoided 42, 51, 54-5, 62, 76-7, 80, 101; sought 8-9, 81-2, 84, 126, 150

Verbs: frequentative 72, 85, 91, 147; compound followed by uncompounded 2, 22, 89, 126, uncompounded followed by compounded 2, 70; initial placement of 5, 66, 86, 89; exceptions to usual final position 96, 99, 146, 149.

   forms: periphrastic present 52, 99; position of auxiliary verb in compound tenses 111, 147; *-assim* etc. 65, *faxit, occisit* 22, *-a(ue)ro* etc. 51, *-ere* and *-erunt* in perf. ind. 31, 75-6, 84, 95, future in *-ibo* in 4th conjug. 62, passive infin. in *-ier* 123, deponent imper. in *-mino* 17, 63, in *-tor* 24.

   tense: historic present 31, 90, 130, 149; present in future conditions 151; sequence aberrant 150-1.

   mood: imperative, present and future 56, 125, negative future 23; infinitive, imperatival (51), 56-7, final 143; supine 62; participles, not much used 76, 148, 150, future final 127, present governing direct object 85, 143, in passive sense 152; indicative, in indirect questions 11, 82, in subord. cl. in indirect speech 54, 67, 82, 87, with causal *quom* (*cum*) 81, 128, 137; subjunctive, iterative 121, jussive 10, 53, 58, jussive with *ut(i)* 10, 53, 64, 98, 110, 115, by attraction 56, 58, depending on infinitive 91, 3rd person perf. in prohibition 61, subordinate without *ut*, see Parataxis

   verbal adjs. in *-bundus* 148-9

Word order: ἀπὸ κοινοῦ 73, 112, 155; important words and phrases put first 4-5, 51, 53-5, 60, 62, 67-8, 77, 96, 110, 131, 148, 153, put last 60-1, 70-1; adjectives (q.v.) and nouns 5, 51, 55, 147-8; verbs (q.v.) in final position and subject - object - verb order 5, 75, 96, 143, 146; postponement of words for special effect 54, 130, 146

Word repetition: 8-9 and passim; in different senses 50-1, 76, 119; for clarity (q.v.) 5, 31, 56, 60, 62, 70, 81, 130, 137; expansion on second occurrence 9, 52, 81, 137; see also Variation.

INDEX OF LATIN WORDS
AND PHRASES

INDEX OF SUBJECTS

CPSIA information can be obtained
at www.ICGtesting.com
Printed in the USA
BVHW041128170722
642342BV00001B/9

9 780788 505454